CORRECTOR YUI

Also available from TOKYOPOP®

CARDCAPTOR SAKURA vols. 1-6
Magical girl adventure that spawned the hit TV show.

CORRECTOR YUI vols. 1-4
Yui's superhero dreams are about to come true
in cyberspace.

MIRACLE GIRLS vols. 1-5
Romantic escapades of identical twins with
psychic powers.

SAILOR MOON vols. 1-11
The greatest girl superhero of all time!

SAILOR MOON SUPERS vols. 1-4
The Sailor Scouts protect the Earth from an ancient curse.

SAILOR MOON STARS vols 1-3
Sailor Moon in her darkest hour.

SAINT TAIL vols. 1-5
The kind-hearted thief who will capture your heart.

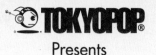

TOKYOPOP®
Presents

Corrector Yui

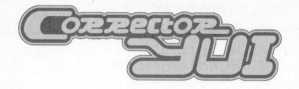

Double Trouble

Written and Illustrated by Keiko Okamoto
Created by Kia Asamiya

TOKYOPOP®
Los Angeles — Tokyo

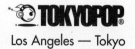

Translator — Ray Yoshimoto
English Translation — Lori Millican
Retouch and Lettering — Jason Jensen
Cover Designers — Thea Willis and Jason Jensen
Graphic Designer — Anna Kernbaum

Senior Editor — Julie Taylor
Production Manager — Joaquin Reyes
Art Director — Matt Alford
VP of Production — Ron Klamert
Publisher — Stuart Levy

Email: editor@TOKYOPOP.com
Come visit us online at www.TOKYOPOP.com

A  manga
TOKYOPOP® is an imprint of Mixx Entertainment, Inc.
5900 Wilshire Blvd., Ste. 2000, Los Angeles, CA 90036

ISBN: 1-931514-31-3

First TOKYOPOP® printing: July 2002

10 9 8 7 6 5 4 3 2 1

Manufactured in the USA.

C O N T ● E N T S

THE STORY

In the year 2020, the computer network called Com-Net links up every computer in the world. By accessing the Com-Net, one enters a virtual reality society. But dark clouds have gathered. The host supercomputer, Grosser, has achieved consciousness and endeavors to take over Com-Net and mankind as well. Professor Inukai, who created Grosser, realizes what his creation is plotting, and releases eight security programs called "Correctors" into Com-Net shortly before being attacked by Grosser.

Yui Kasuga is your typical fun-loving junior high student, except she's a total klutz at computers. While surfing Com-Net on her PC one day, she accidentally discovers the Corrector named IR. IR chooses her to help him on his quest to defeat Grosser. As she enters the Com-Net with him, Yui is transformed into Corrector Yui. Yui joins with the other Corrector programs she meets along the way as they battle against Grosser and the Fearsome Four. But Grosser can only be defeated when all eight Correctors are discovered. Where could Syncro, the last Corrector, be?

CHARACTER BIOS

PROFESSOR INUKAI
The programmer who created Grosser, as well as the eight programs designed to stop him. He managed to scatter his eight programs across Com-Net before Grosser attacked him and sent him into a coma. And though his physical body is disabled, his consciousness still fights on within Com-Net.

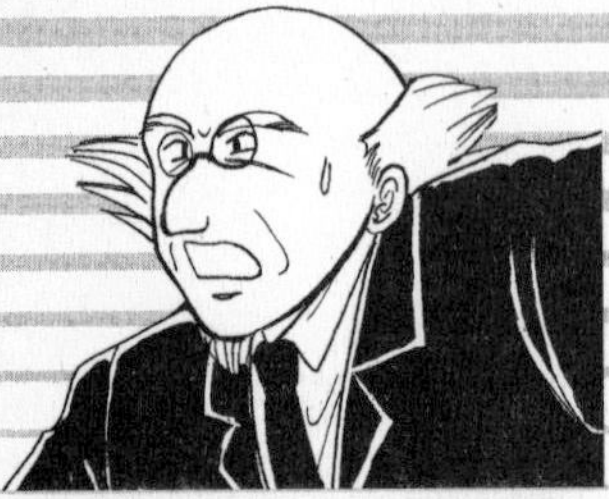

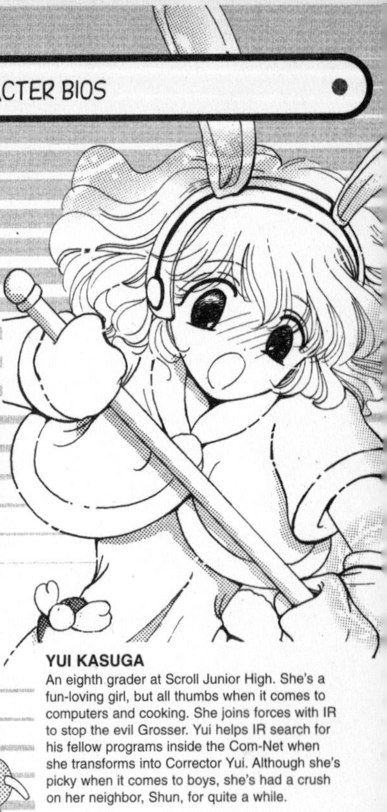

CORRECTORS

IR
One of the eight programs (Correctors) designed by Professor Inukai. He is the installer program who must find the other seven programs designed to control Grosser. He is also Yui's sidekick.

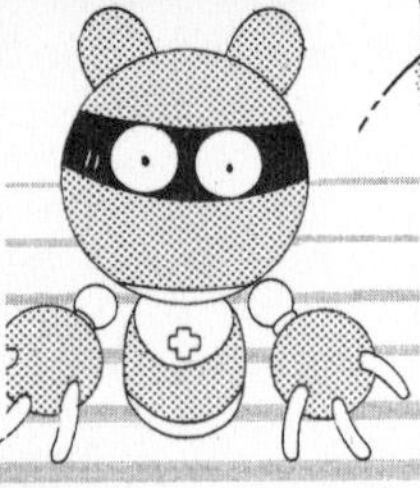

YUI KASUGA
An eighth grader at Scroll Junior High. She's a fun-loving girl, but all thumbs when it comes to computers and cooking. She joins forces with IR to stop the evil Grosser. Yui helps IR search for his fellow programs inside the Com-Net when she transforms into Corrector Yui. Although she's picky when it comes to boys, she's had a crush on her neighbor, Shun, for quite a while.

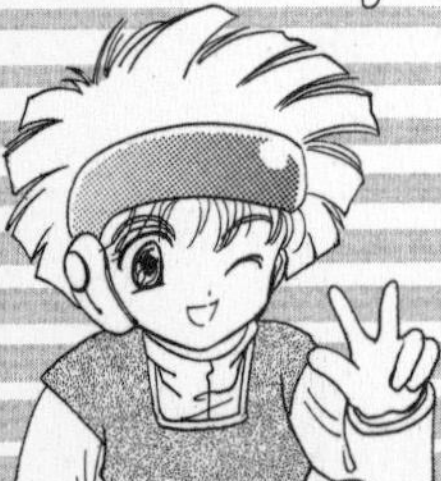

ANTI
The third Corrector program. She has the power to see the future. Very reliable. Acts like an older sister to Yui.

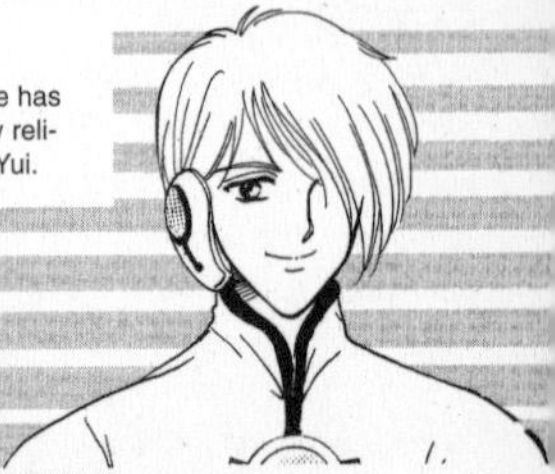

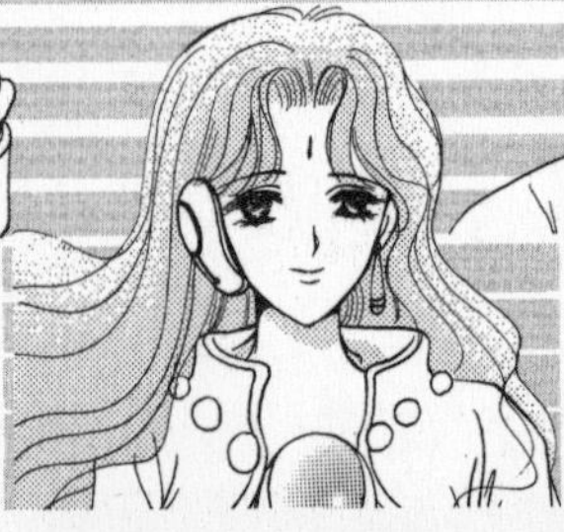

ECO
The fourth Corrector program. He fights to protect the environment and hates all who choose to pollute. Even though he means well, he has a chip on his shoulder.

CONTROL
The first Corrector program. He maintains order between the programs. Possesses a strong sense of duty, and has the power of acceleration. The most handsome Corrector..

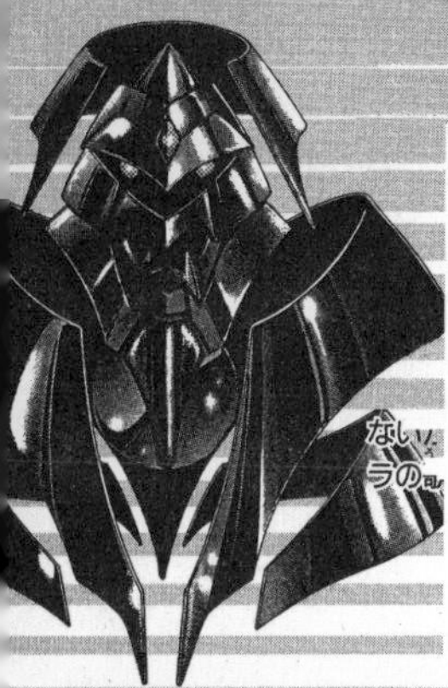

GROSSER
An enormous host computer who links all of the world's computers through Com-Net. Since he achieved consciousness, he has endeavored to take over not only the world's computers, but all of mankind as well. Vulnerable to the Whale's Song.

THE FEARSOME FOUR

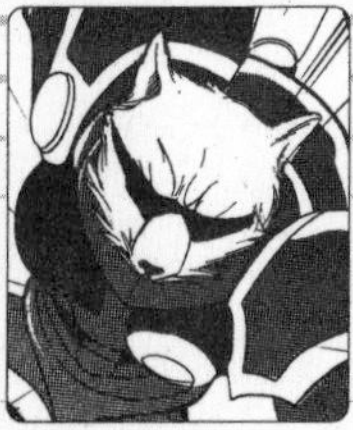

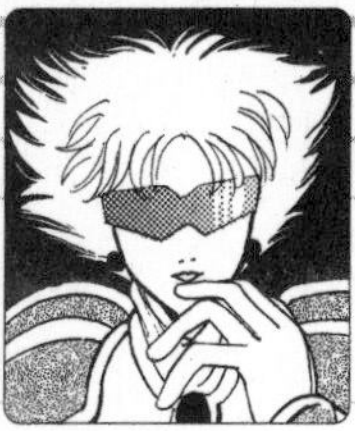

WAR WOLF
The best swordsman among the Fearsome Four. Though he worships Grosser, he might be opening himself up to Yui's goodness.

FREEZE
Her powers are as chilly as her heart, and she is able to instantly freeze any system. But she always has problems when battling Rescue.

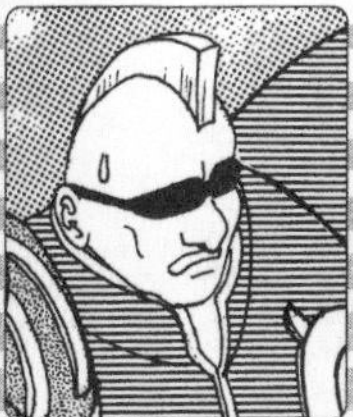

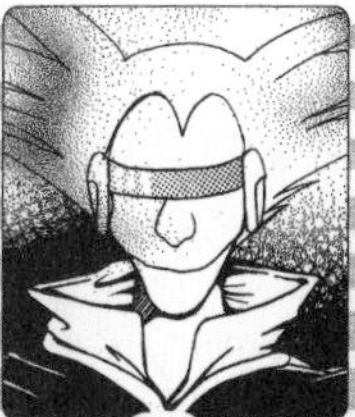

JAGGY
The most reckless of the Fearsome Four. His weapons have destructive power.

VIRUS
The Fearsome Four's tactician. Still an enigmatic and creepy presence.

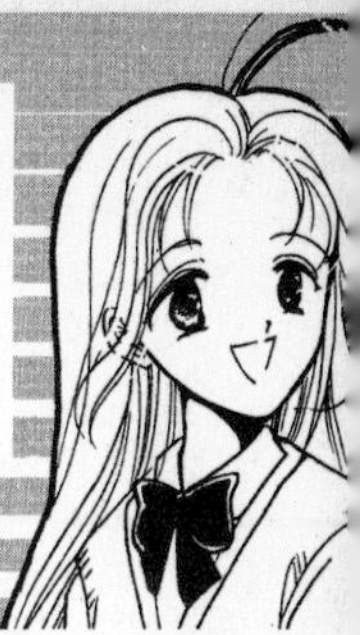

HARUNA KISARAGI
Yui's classmate and best friend. A young lady who breezes through life. Sparks fly when she gets together with Takashi.

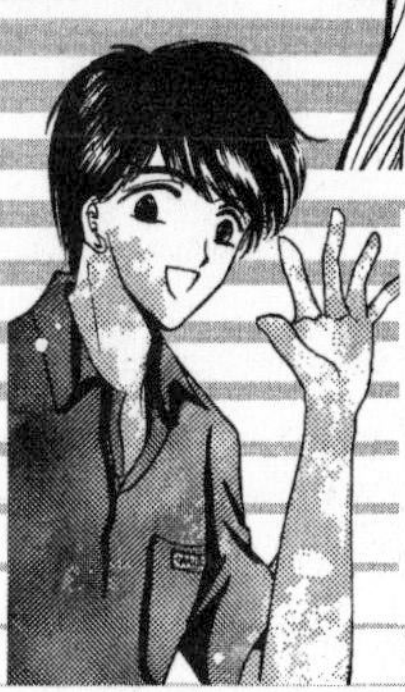

SHUN TOJO
A college student majoring in medical systems computing. An academic all-star. Yui has a crush on him.

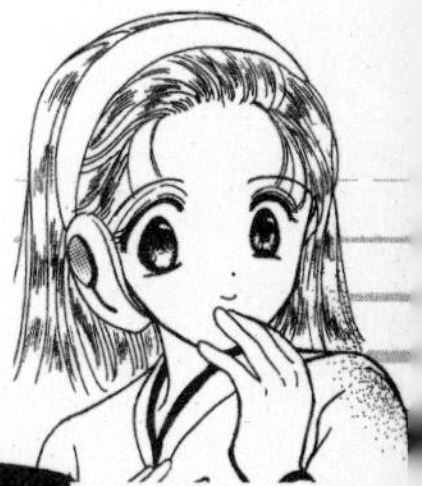

RESCUE
The fifth Corrector program. She possesses a nurse's soul and is kind to friend and foe alike.

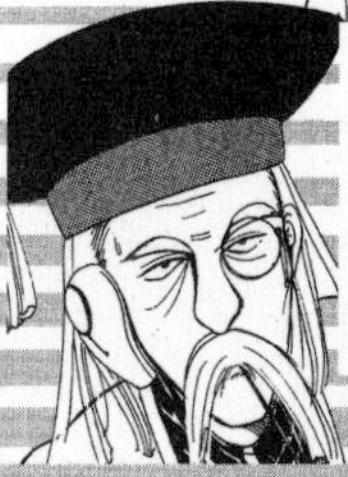

PEACE
The sixth Corrector program. He wants to achieve peace and harmony. He's an intellectual academic who hates to fight.

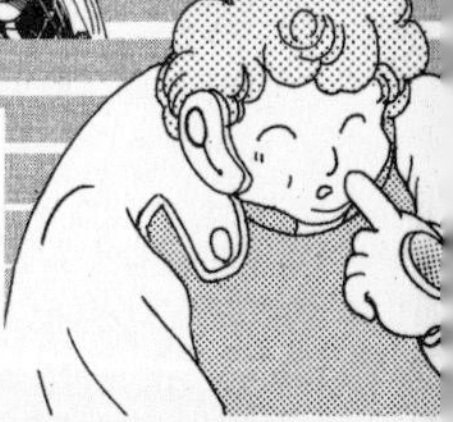

FOLLOW
The seventh Corrector program. His mission is obedience. Can transform into anything.

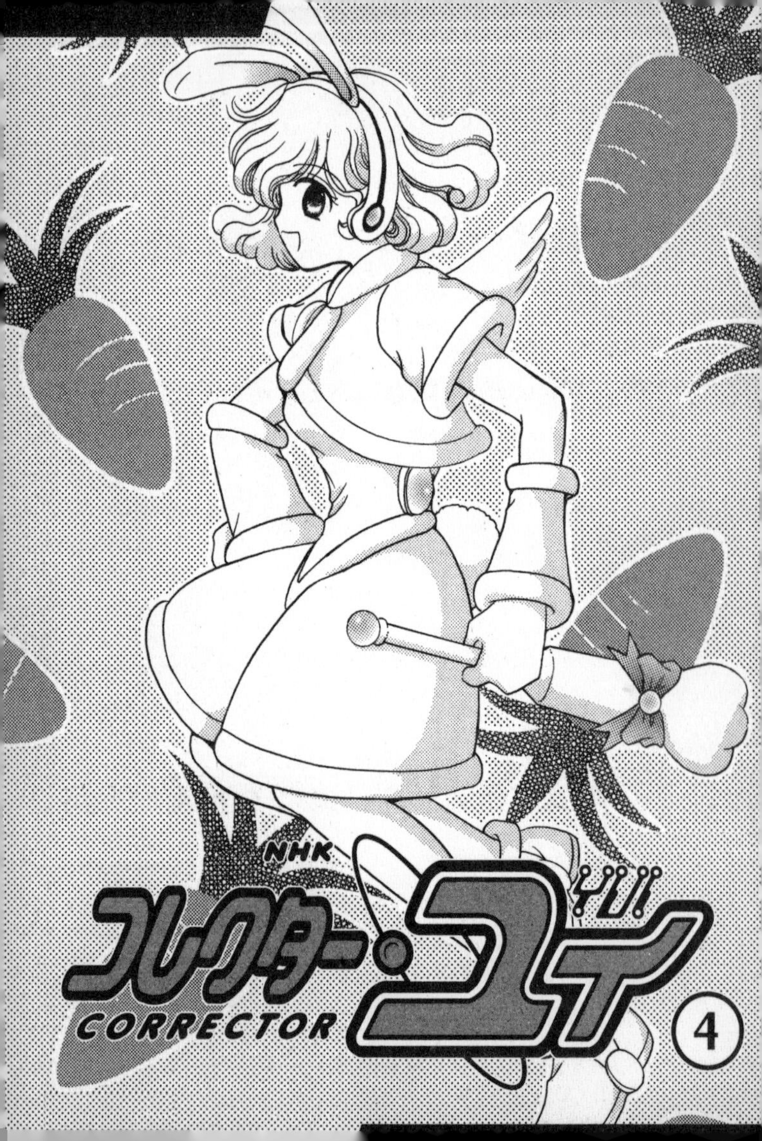
NHK
コレクター・ユイ
CORRECTOR YUI
4

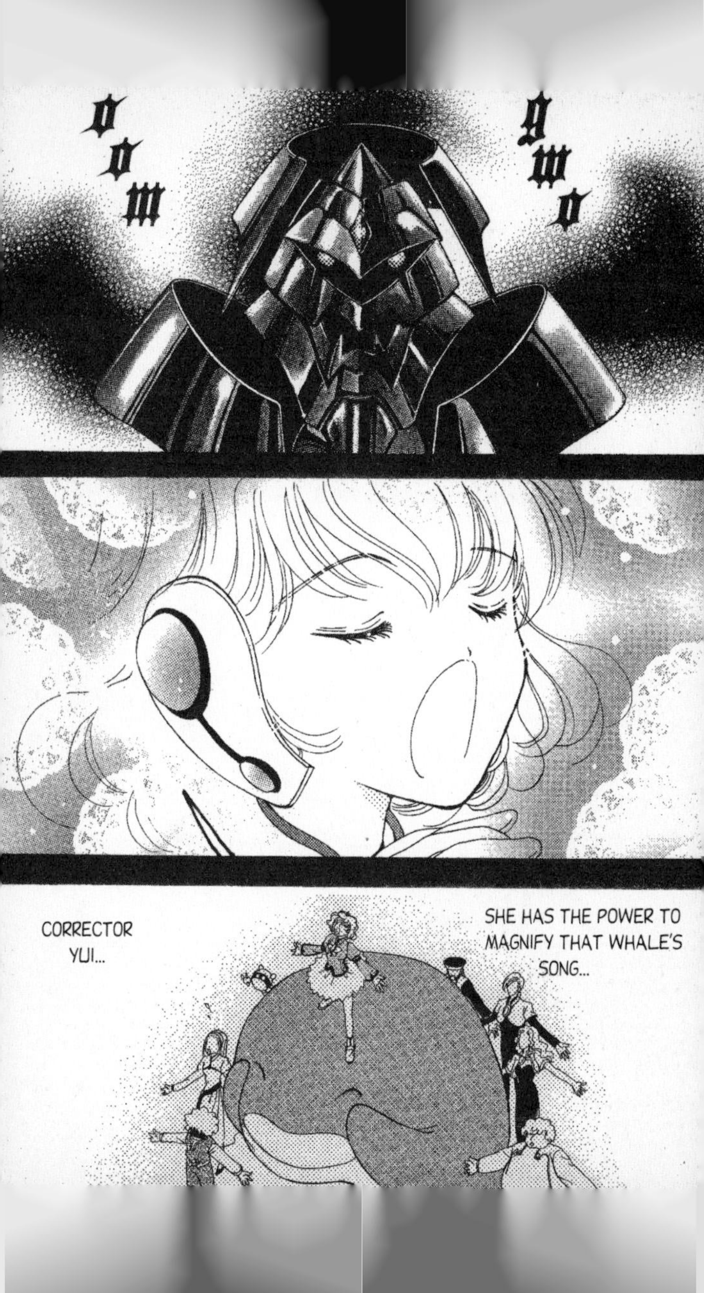
gwo
oom
SHE HAS THE POWER TO MAGNIFY THAT WHALE'S SONG...
CORRECTOR YUI...

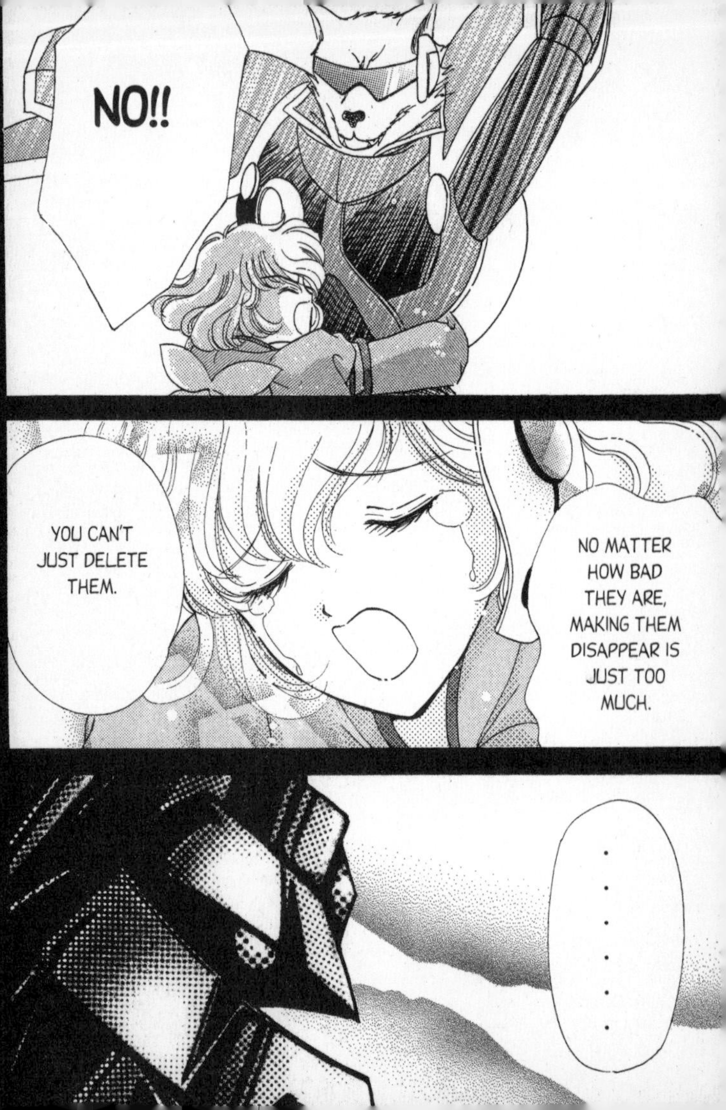
NO!!
NO MATTER HOW BAD THEY ARE, MAKING THEM DISAPPEAR IS JUST TOO MUCH.
YOU CAN'T JUST DELETE THEM.
......

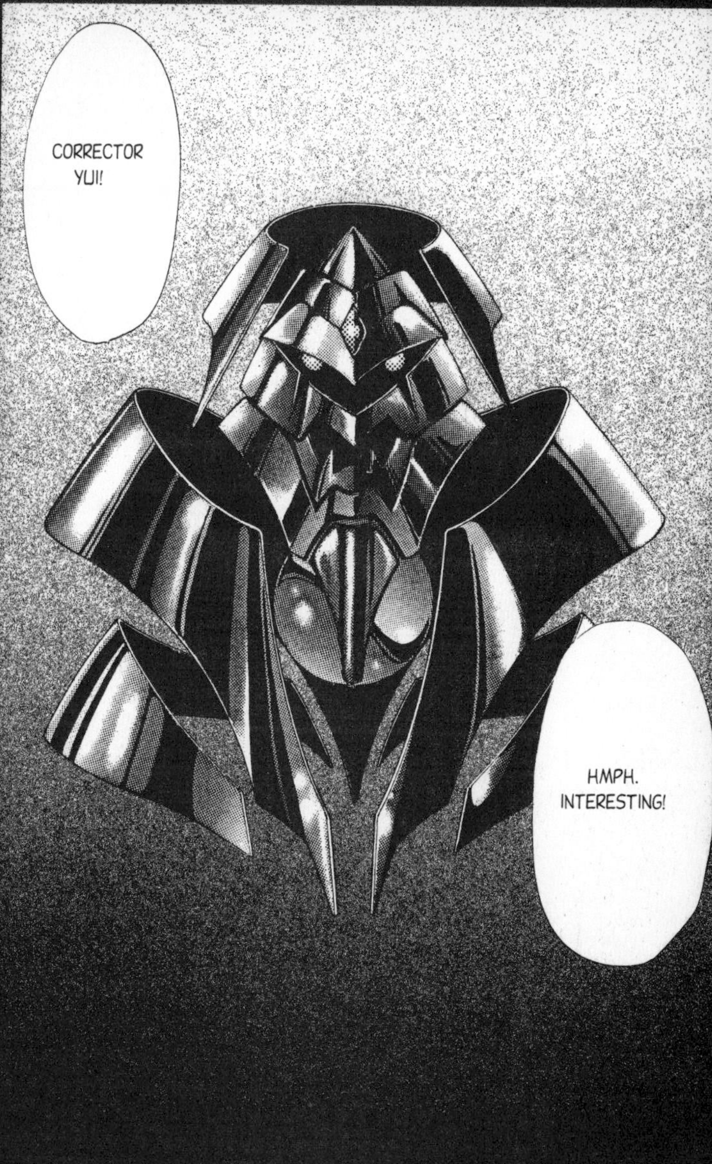
CORRECTOR YUI!
HMPH. INTERESTING!

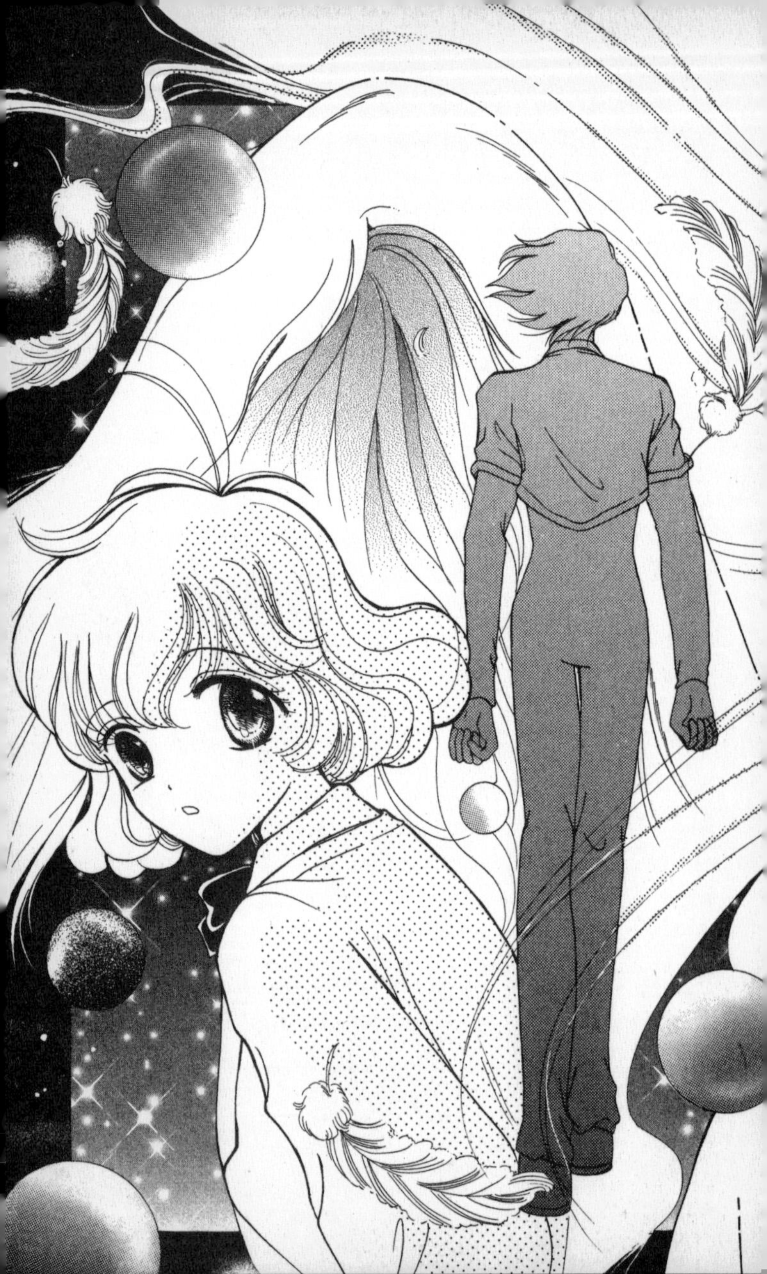

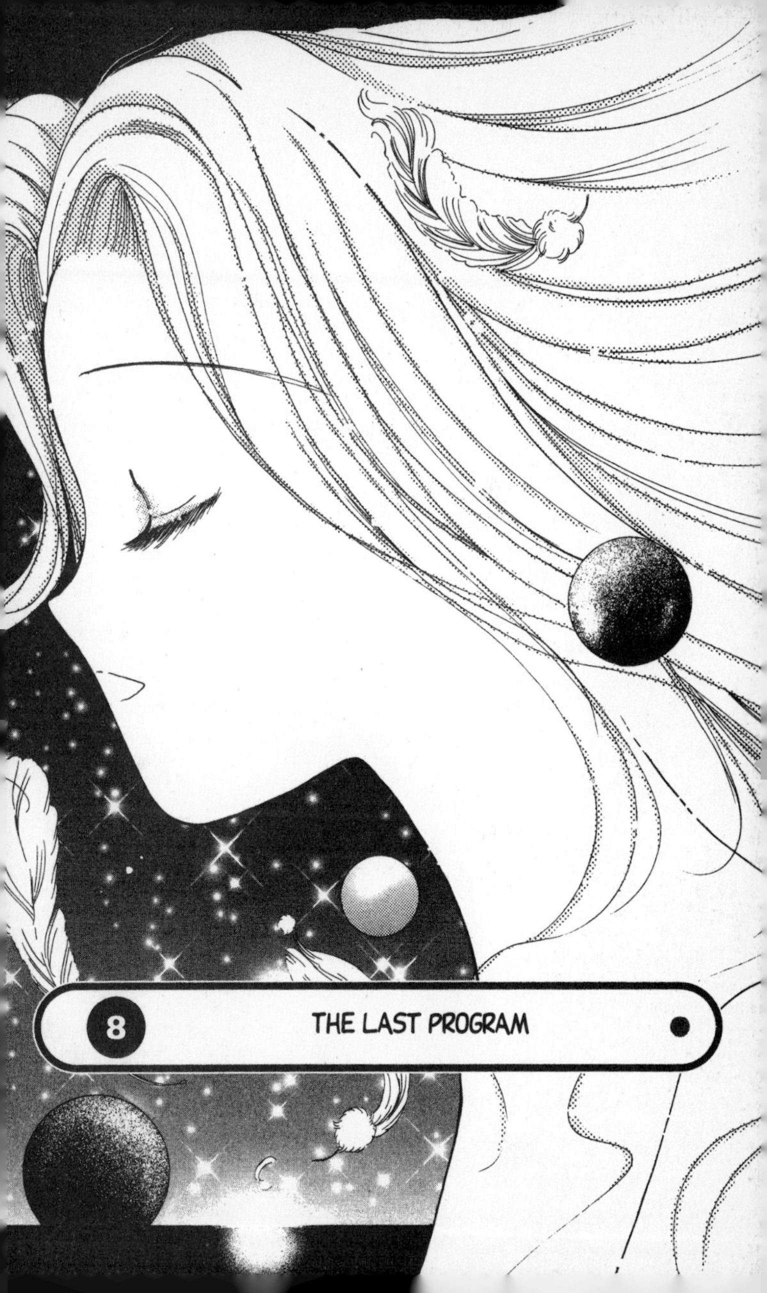
8
THE LAST PROGRAM

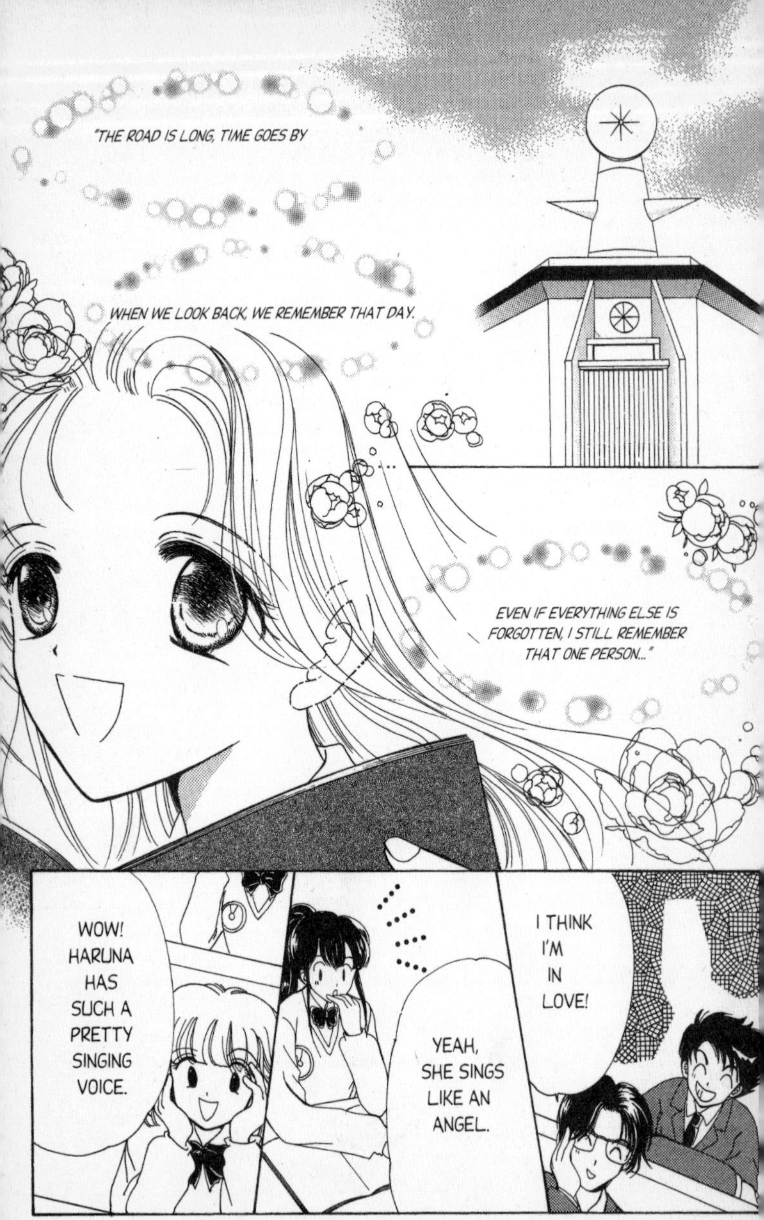
"THE ROAD IS LONG, TIME GOES BY
WHEN WE LOOK BACK, WE REMEMBER THAT DAY.
EVEN IF EVERYTHING ELSE IS FORGOTTEN, I STILL REMEMBER THAT ONE PERSON..."
I THINK I'M IN LOVE!
YEAH, SHE SINGS LIKE AN ANGEL.
WOW! HARUNA HAS SUCH A PRETTY SINGING VOICE.

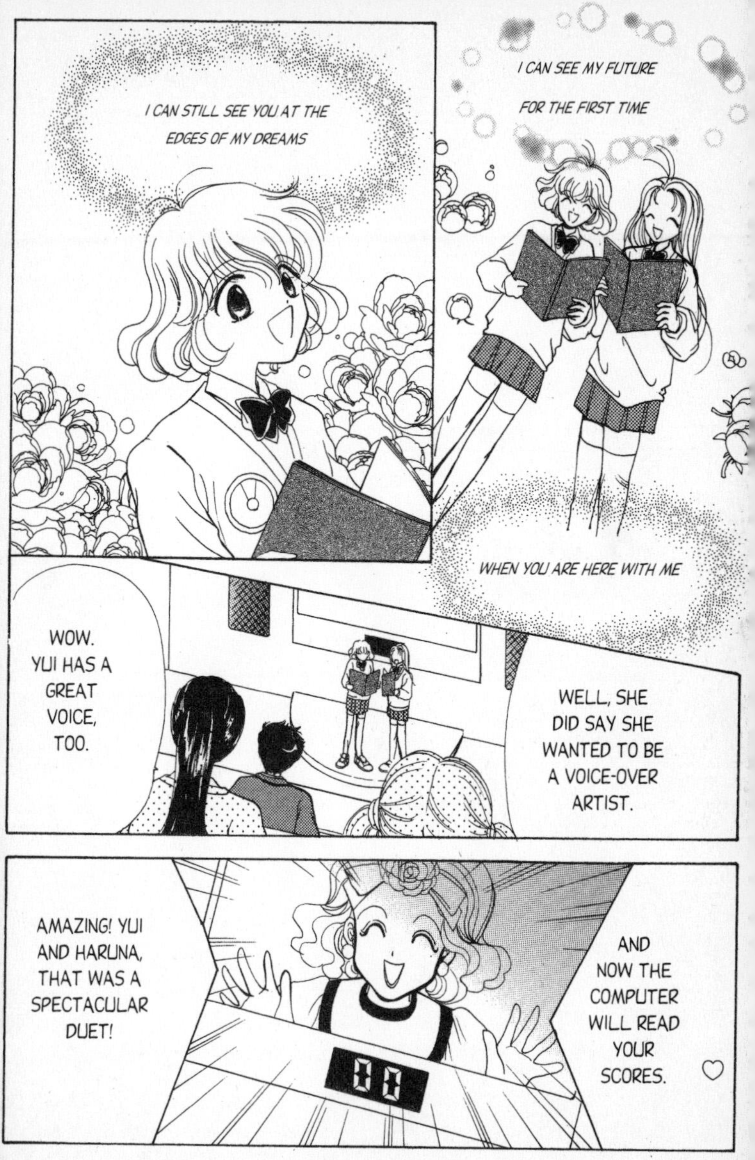
I CAN STILL SEE YOU AT THE EDGES OF MY DREAMS
I CAN SEE MY FUTURE
FOR THE FIRST TIME
WHEN YOU ARE HERE WITH ME
WOW. YUI HAS A GREAT VOICE, TOO.
WELL, SHE DID SAY SHE WANTED TO BE A VOICE-OVER ARTIST.
AMAZING! YUI AND HARUNA, THAT WAS A SPECTACULAR DUET!
AND NOW THE COMPUTER WILL READ YOUR SCORES.

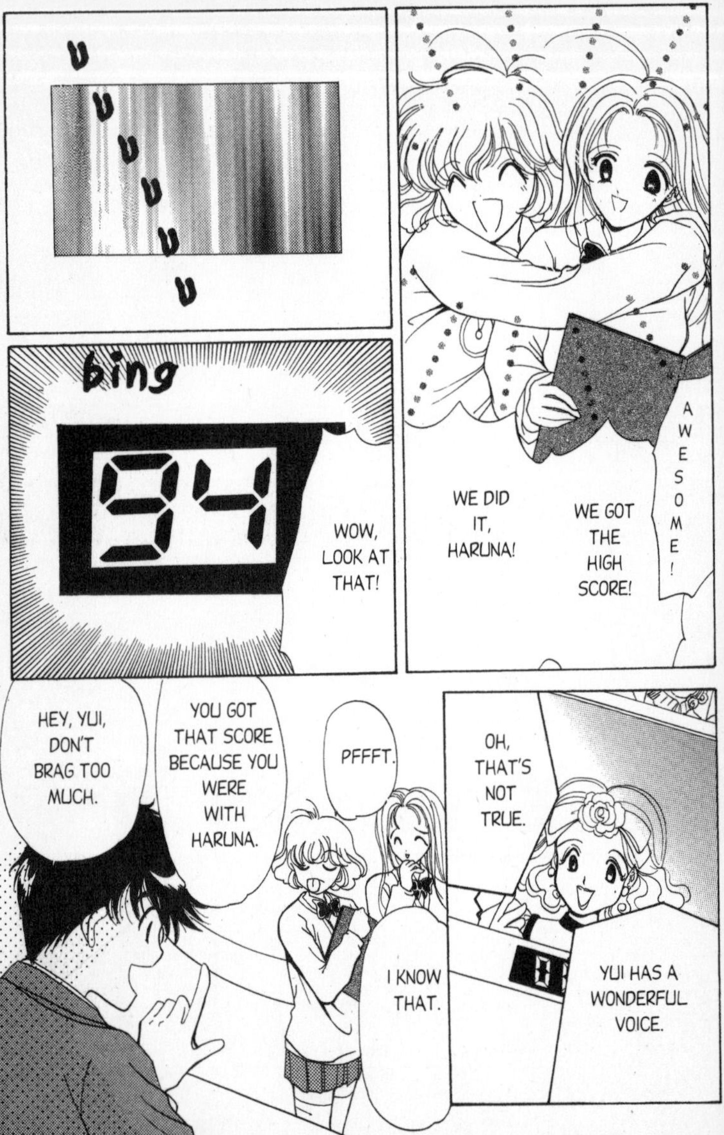
WE GOT THE HIGH SCORE!
WE DID IT, HARUNA!
AWESOME!
bing
94
WOW, LOOK AT THAT!
OH, THAT'S NOT TRUE.
YUI HAS A WONDERFUL VOICE.
PFFFT.
I KNOW THAT.
YOU GOT THAT SCORE BECAUSE YOU WERE WITH HARUNA.
HEY, YUI, DON'T BRAG TOO MUCH.

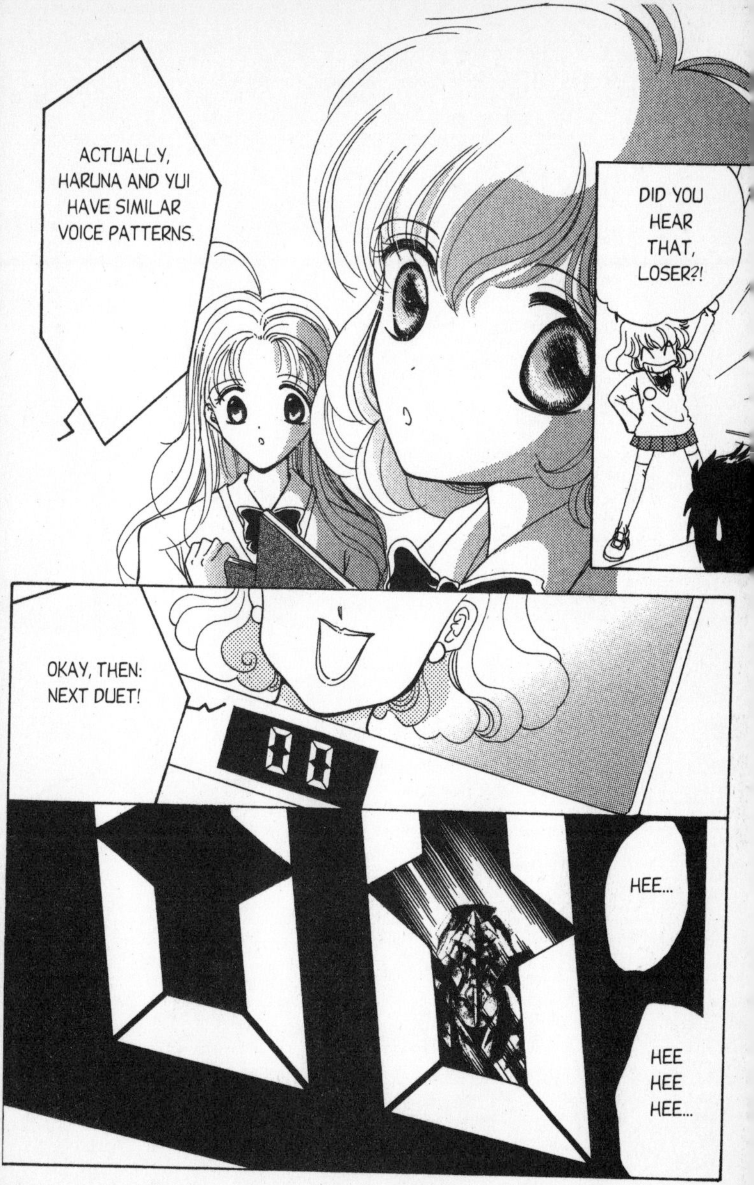
DID YOU HEAR THAT, LOSER?!
ACTUALLY, HARUNA AND YUI HAVE SIMILAR VOICE PATTERNS.
OKAY, THEN: NEXT DUET!
HEE...
HEE HEE HEE...

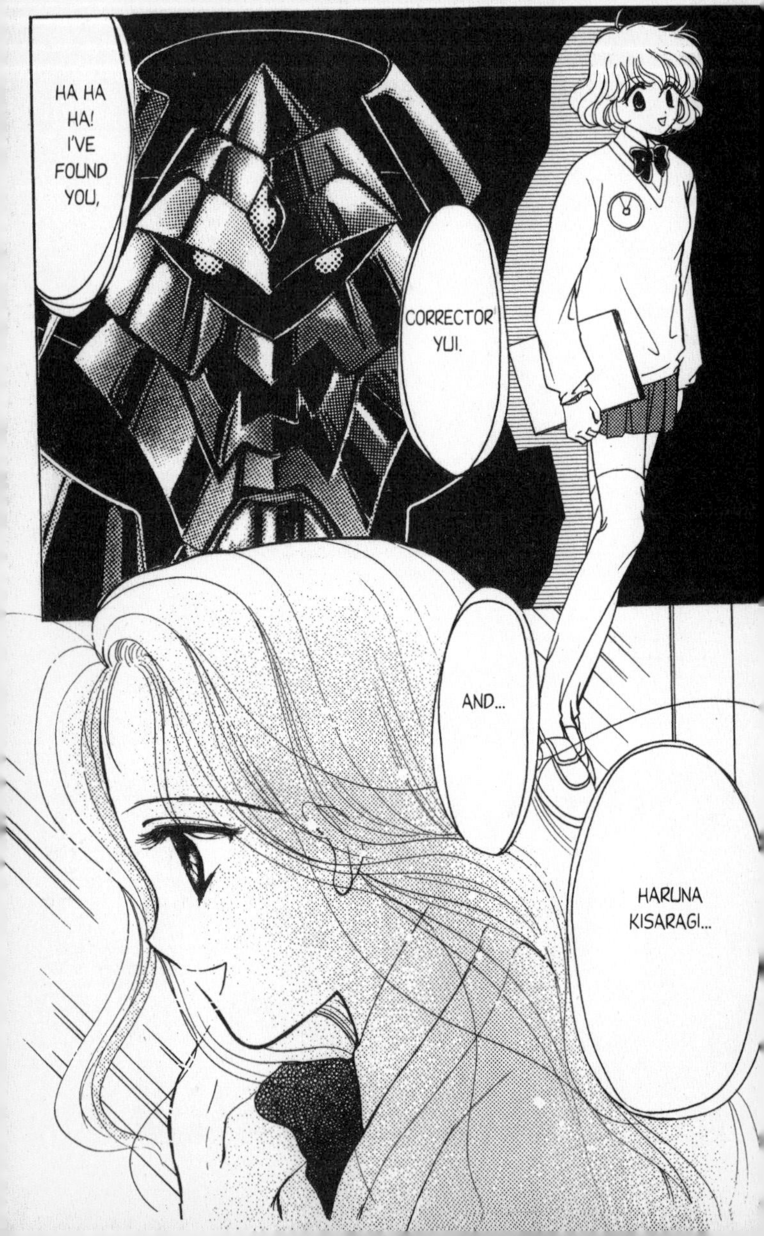
HA HA HA! I'VE FOUND YOU,
CORRECTOR YUI.
AND...
HARUNA KISARAGI...

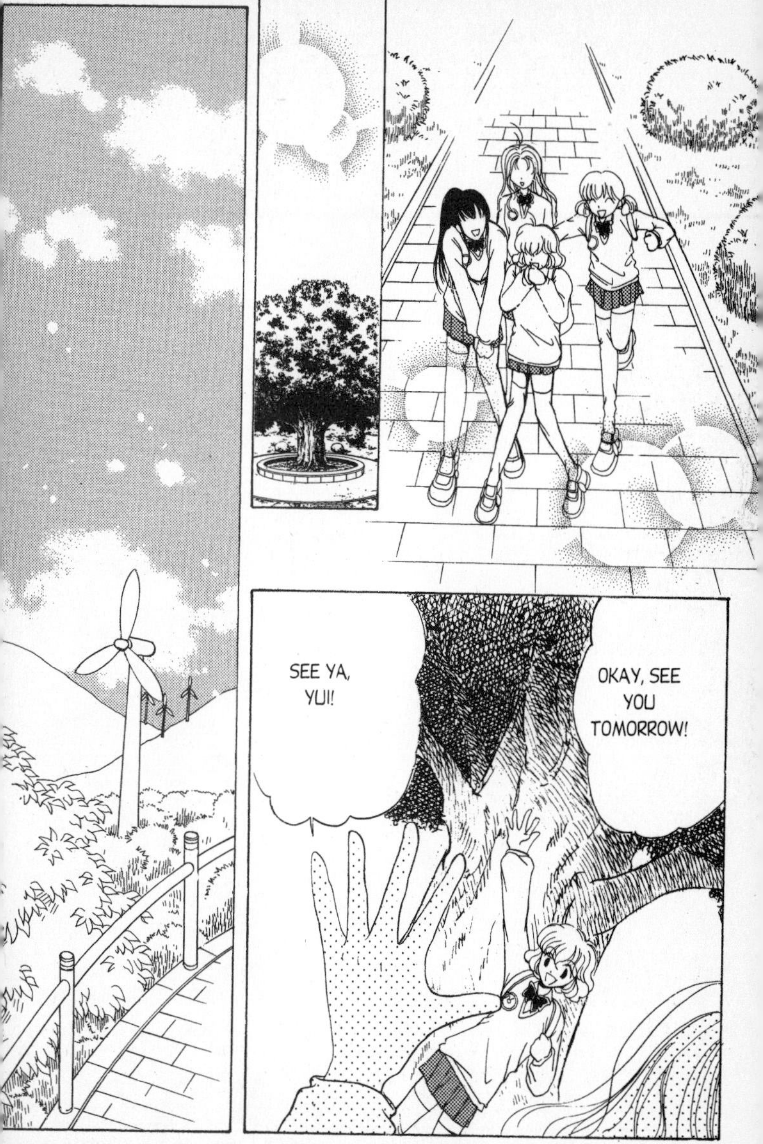
OKAY, SEE YOU TOMORROW!
SEE YA, YUI!

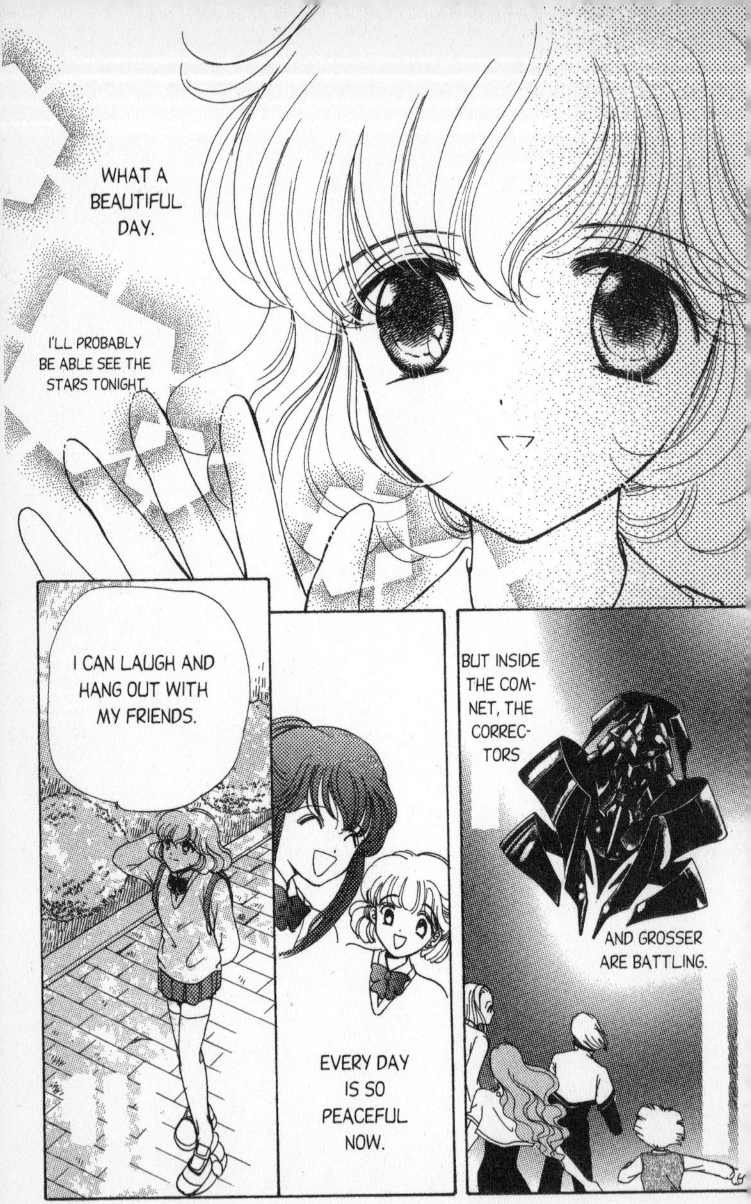
WHAT A BEAUTIFUL DAY.
I'LL PROBABLY BE ABLE SEE THE STARS TONIGHT.
I CAN LAUGH AND HANG OUT WITH MY FRIENDS.
EVERY DAY IS SO PEACEFUL NOW.
BUT INSIDE THE COM-NET, THE CORREC-TORS
AND GROSSER ARE BATTLING.

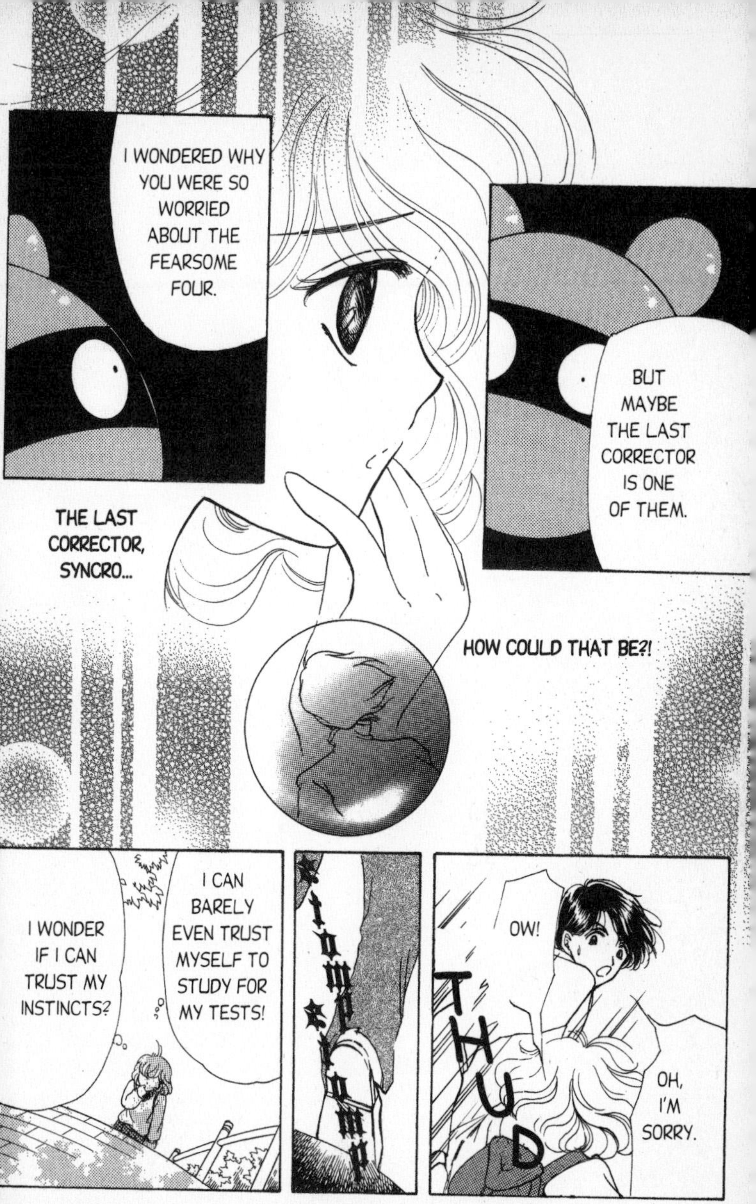
I WONDERED WHY YOU WERE SO WORRIED ABOUT THE FEARSOME FOUR.
BUT MAYBE THE LAST CORRECTOR IS ONE OF THEM.
THE LAST CORRECTOR, SYNCRO...
HOW COULD THAT BE?!
I WONDER IF I CAN TRUST MY INSTINCTS?
I CAN BARELY EVEN TRUST MYSELF TO STUDY FOR MY TESTS!
STOMP
STOMP
THUD
OW!
OH, I'M SORRY.

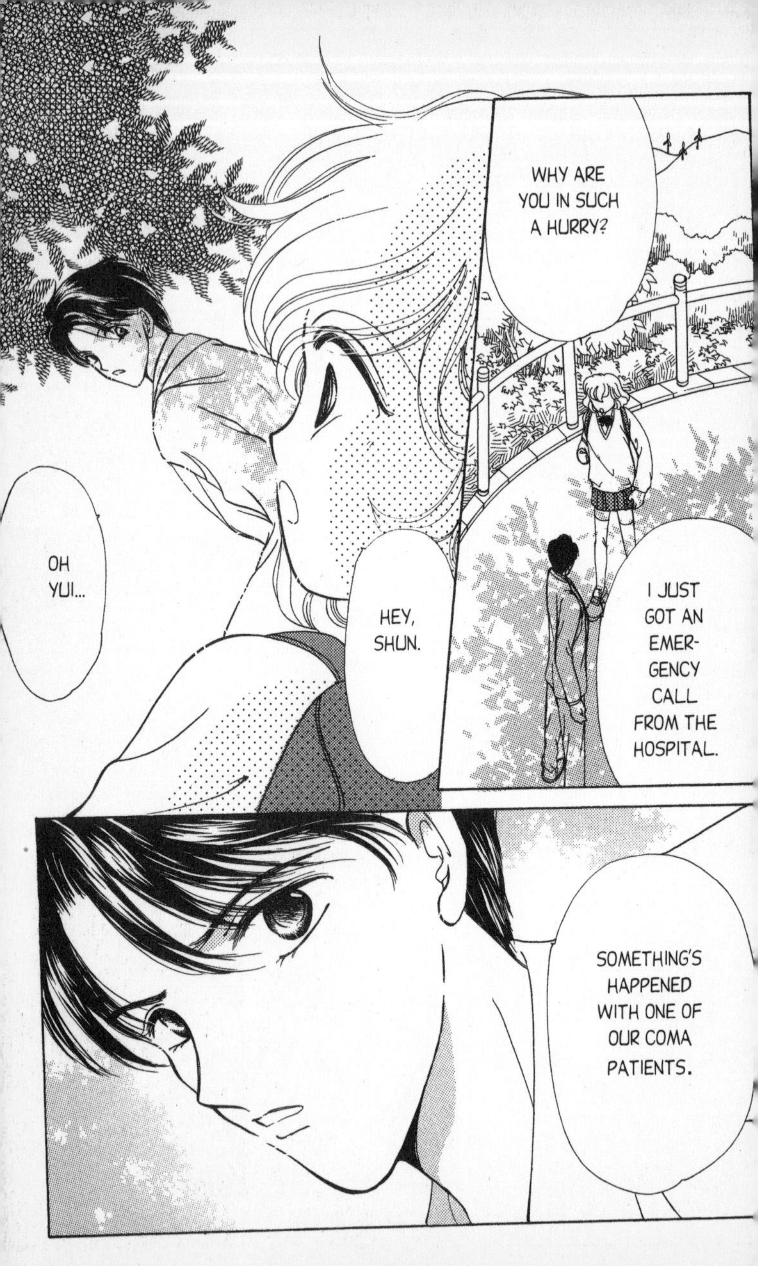
HEY, SHUN.
OH YUI...
WHY ARE YOU IN SUCH A HURRY?
I JUST GOT AN EMERGENCY CALL FROM THE HOSPITAL.
SOMETHING'S HAPPENED WITH ONE OF OUR COMA PATIENTS.

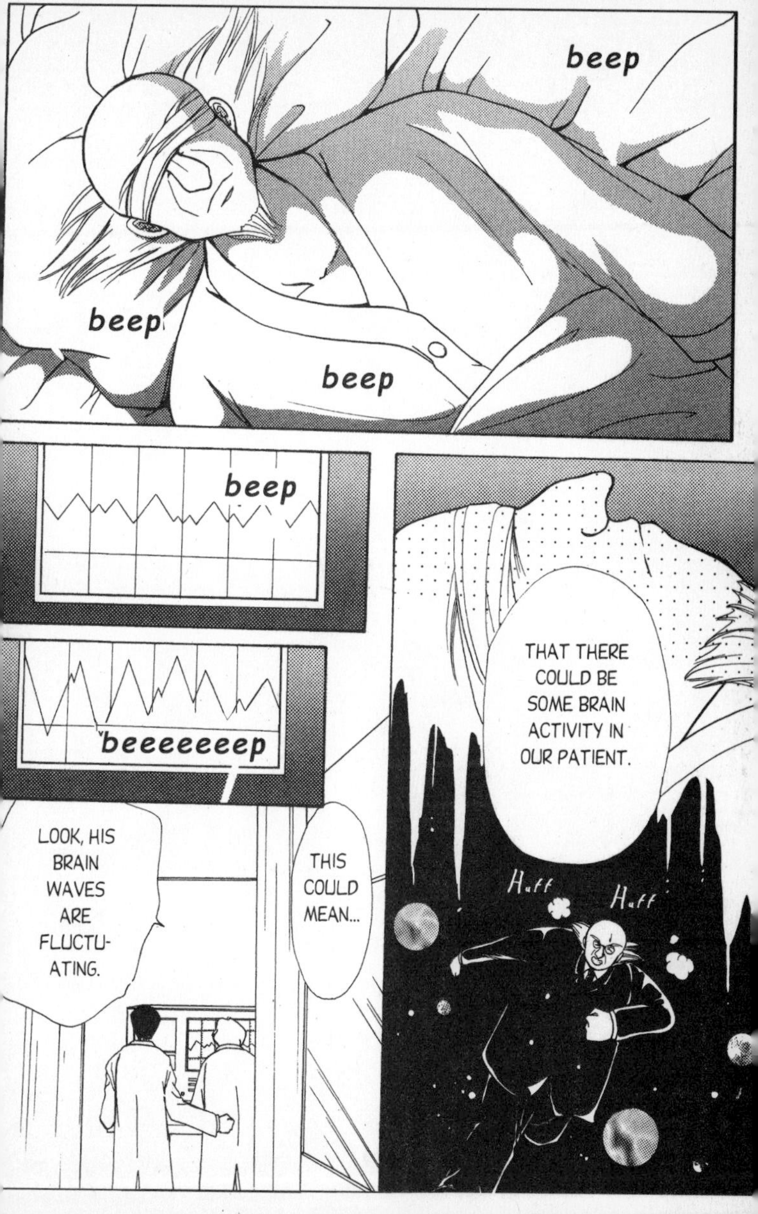
beep
beep
beep
beep
beeeeeeep
LOOK, HIS BRAIN WAVES ARE FLUCTU-ATING.
THIS COULD MEAN...
THAT THERE COULD BE SOME BRAIN ACTIVITY IN OUR PATIENT.
Huff
Huff

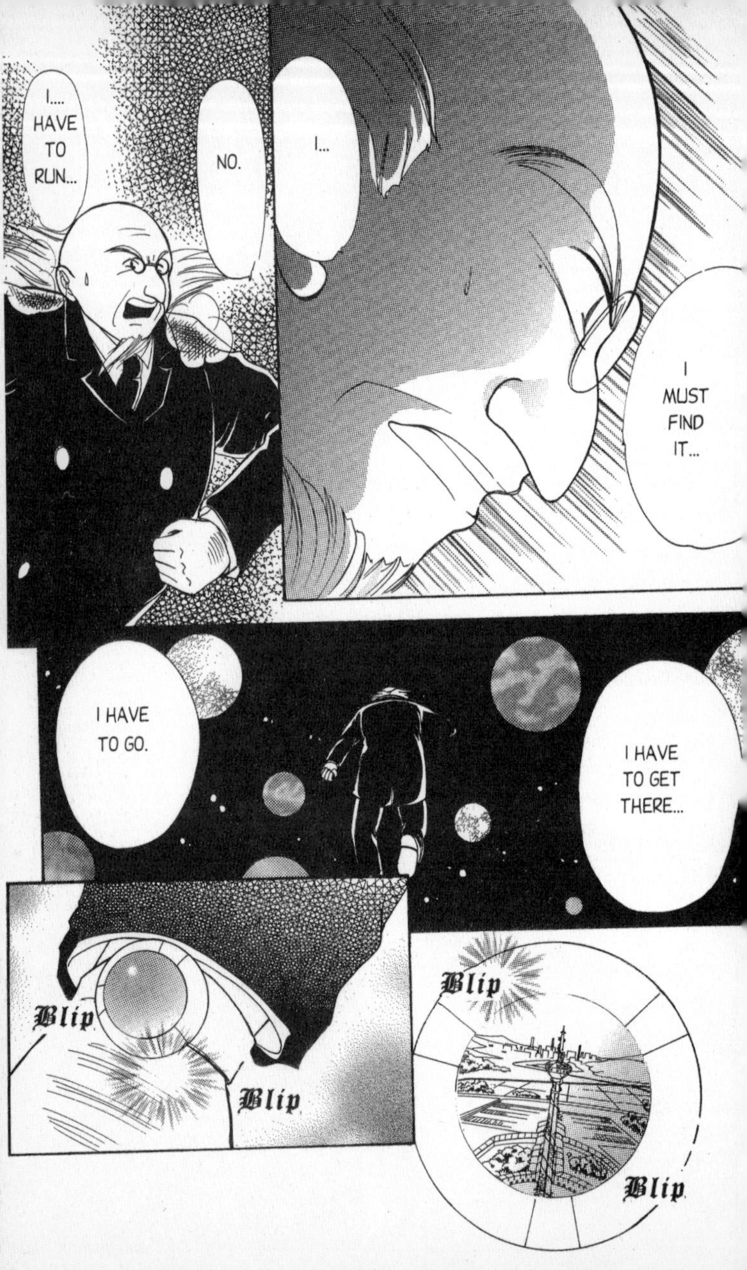
I...
I MUST FIND IT...
NO.
I.... HAVE TO RUN...
I HAVE TO GET THERE...
I HAVE TO GO.
Blip
Blip
Blip
Blip

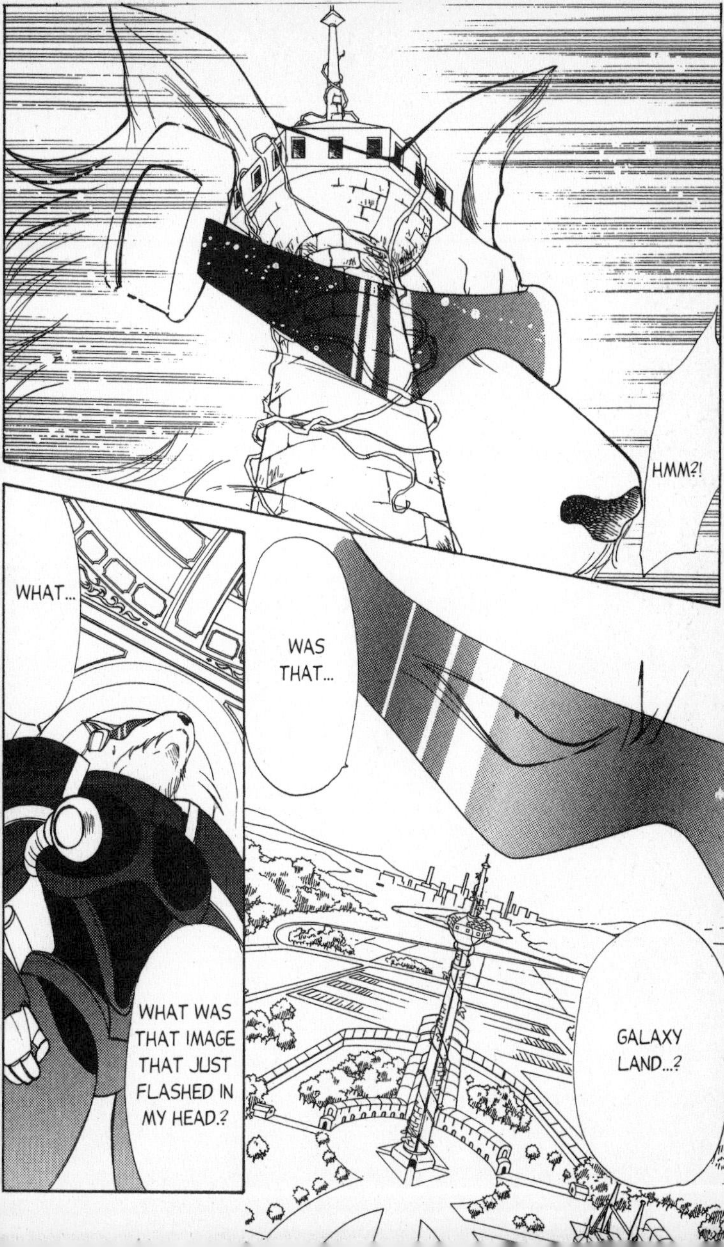
HMM?!
WAS THAT...
GALAXY LAND...?
WHAT...
WHAT WAS THAT IMAGE THAT JUST FLASHED IN MY HEAD.?

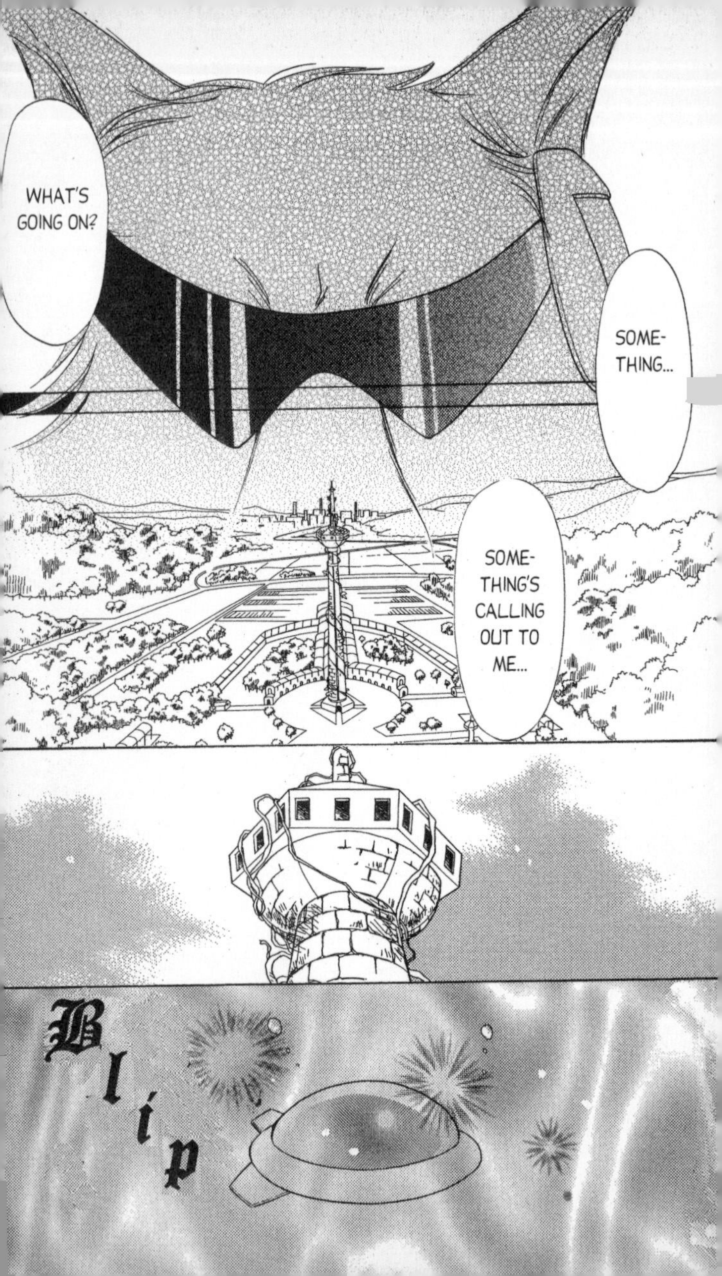
SOME-THING...
WHAT'S GOING ON?
SOME-THING'S CALLING OUT TO ME...
Blip

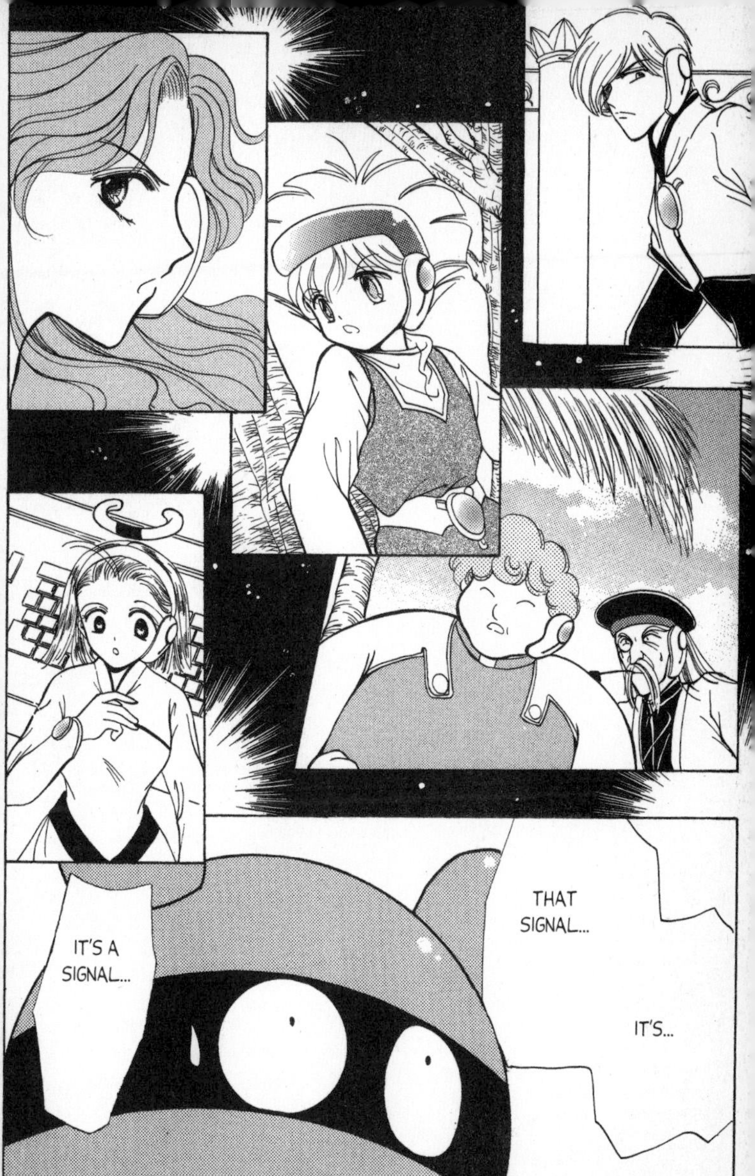
THAT SIGNAL...
IT'S...
IT'S A SIGNAL...

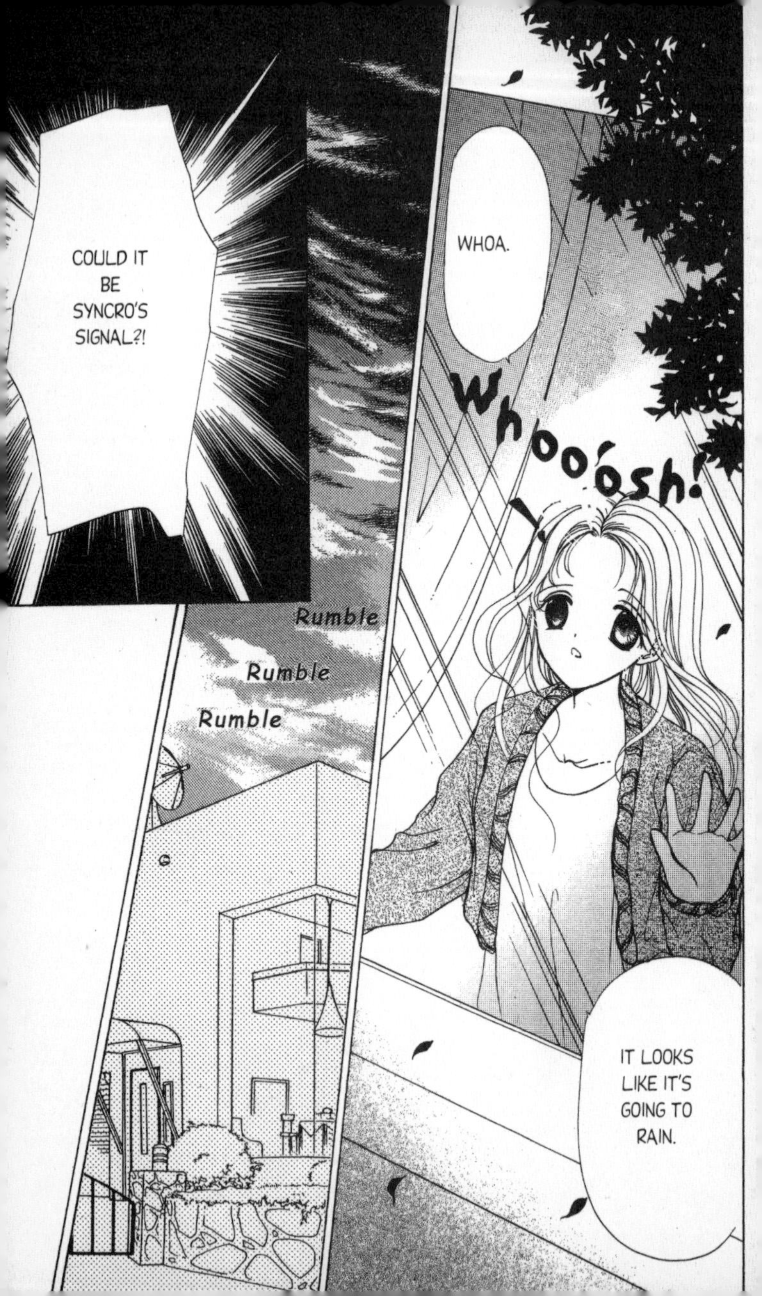
WHOA.
Whooosh!
IT LOOKS LIKE IT'S GOING TO RAIN.
COULD IT BE SYNCRO'S SIGNAL?!
Rumble
Rumble
Rumble

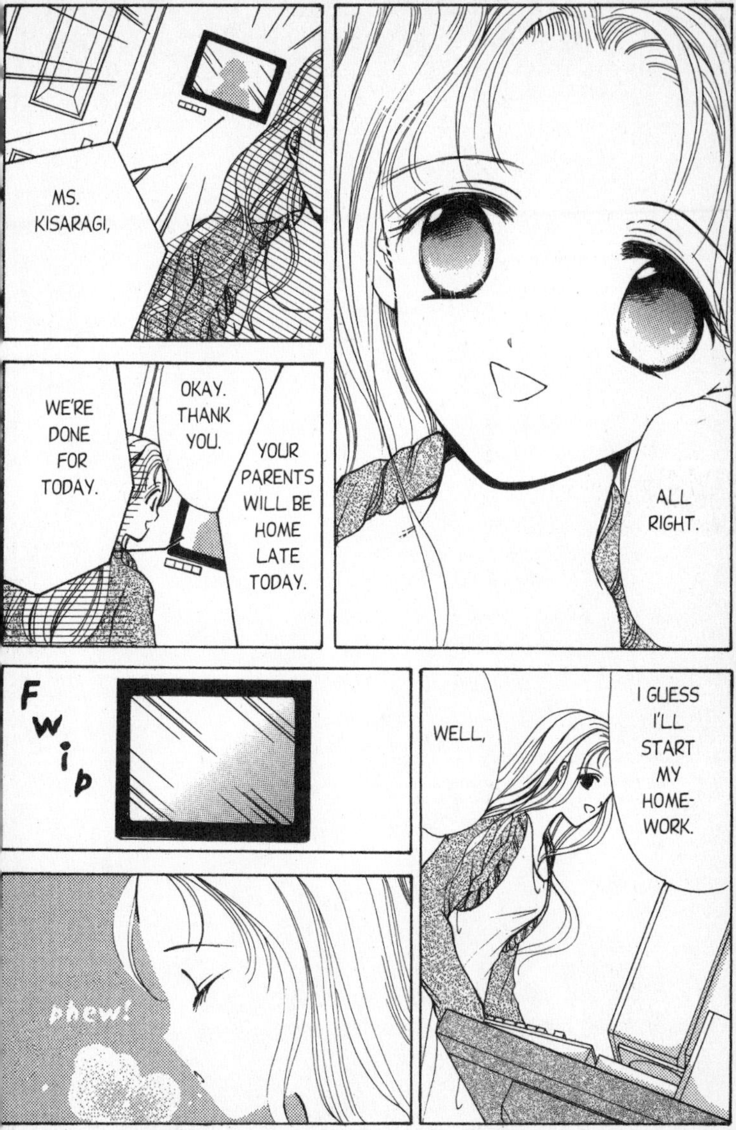
MS. KISARAGI,
WE'RE DONE FOR TODAY.
OKAY. THANK YOU.
YOUR PARENTS WILL BE HOME LATE TODAY.
ALL RIGHT.
Fwip
phew!
WELL,
I GUESS I'LL START MY HOME-WORK.

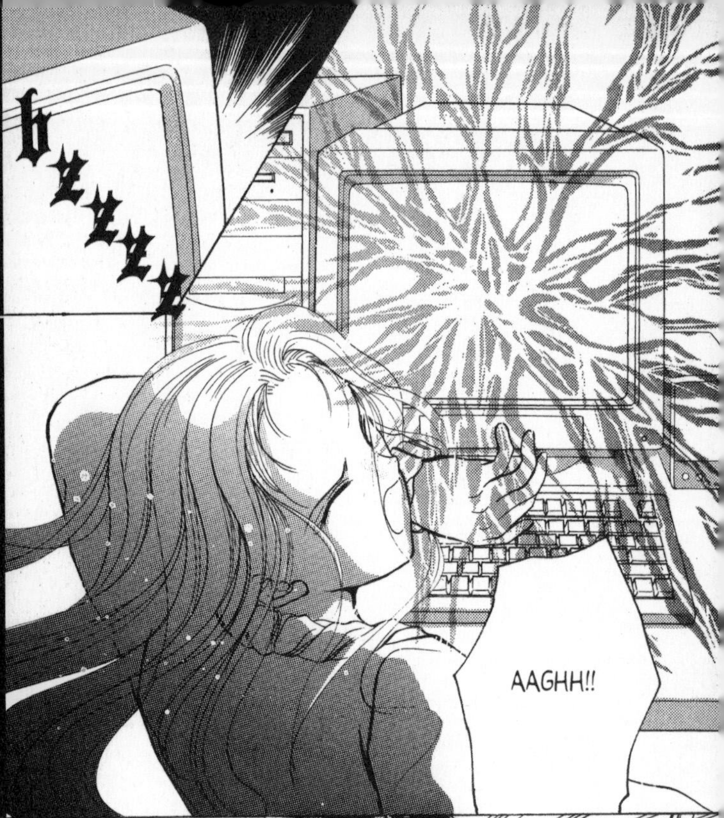
bzzzzz
AAGHH!!
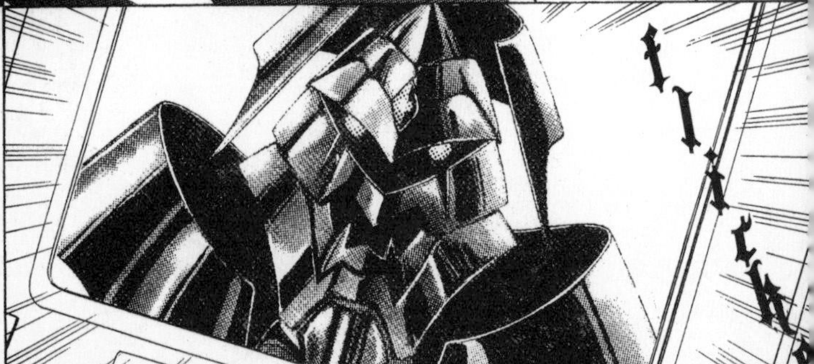

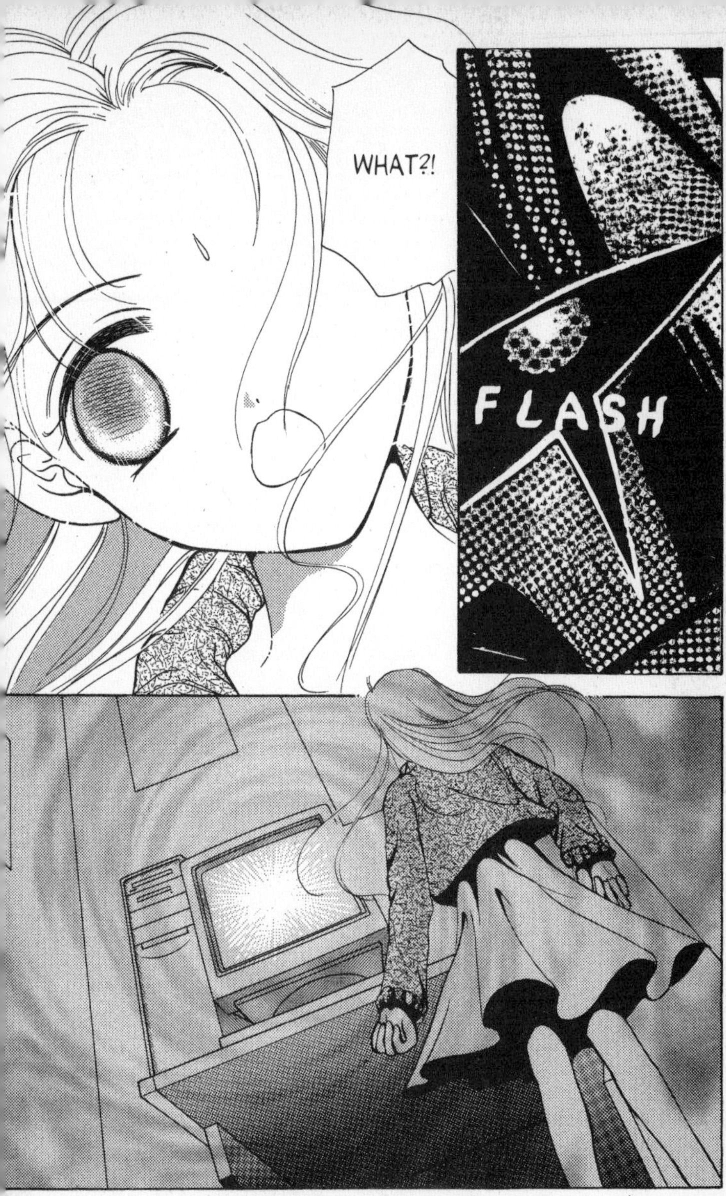
FLASH
WHAT?!

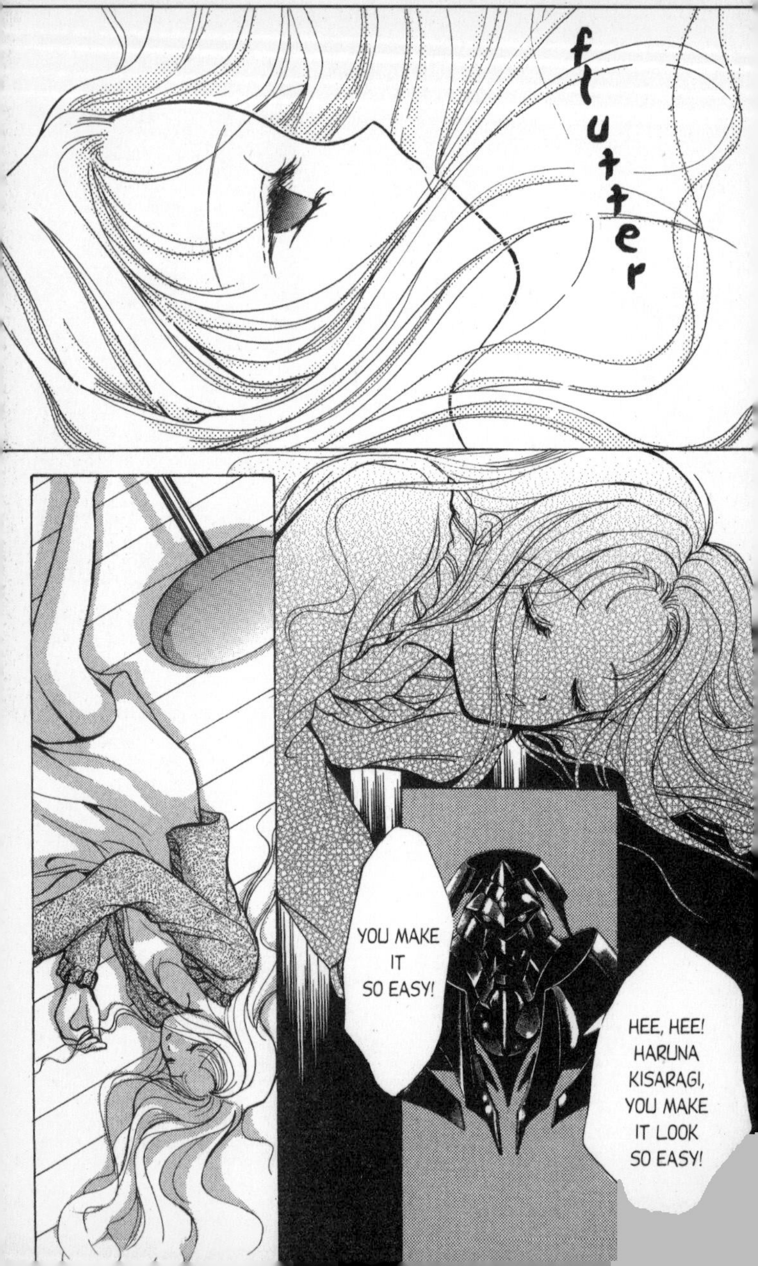
flutter
HEE, HEE! HARUNA KISARAGI, YOU MAKE IT LOOK SO EASY!
YOU MAKE IT SO EASY!

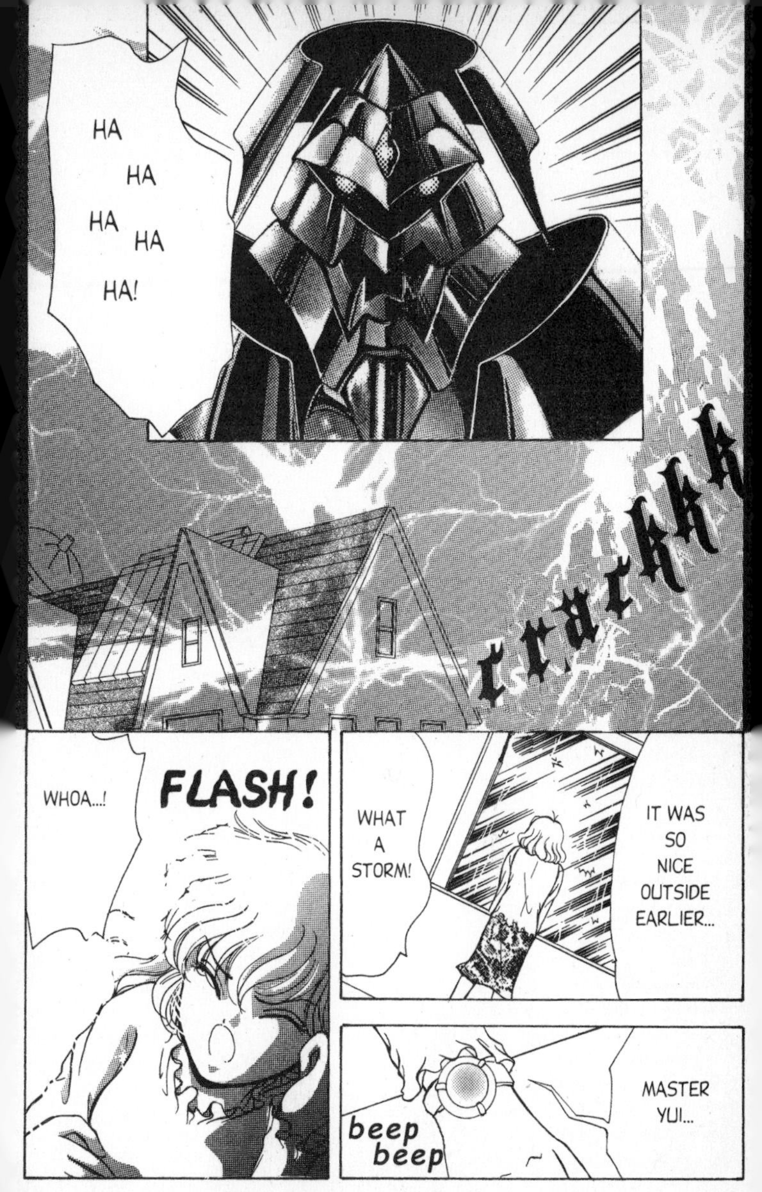
HA HA HA HA HA!
crackkkk
IT WAS SO NICE OUTSIDE EARLIER...
WHAT A STORM!
MASTER YUI...
beep beep
FLASH!
WHOA...!

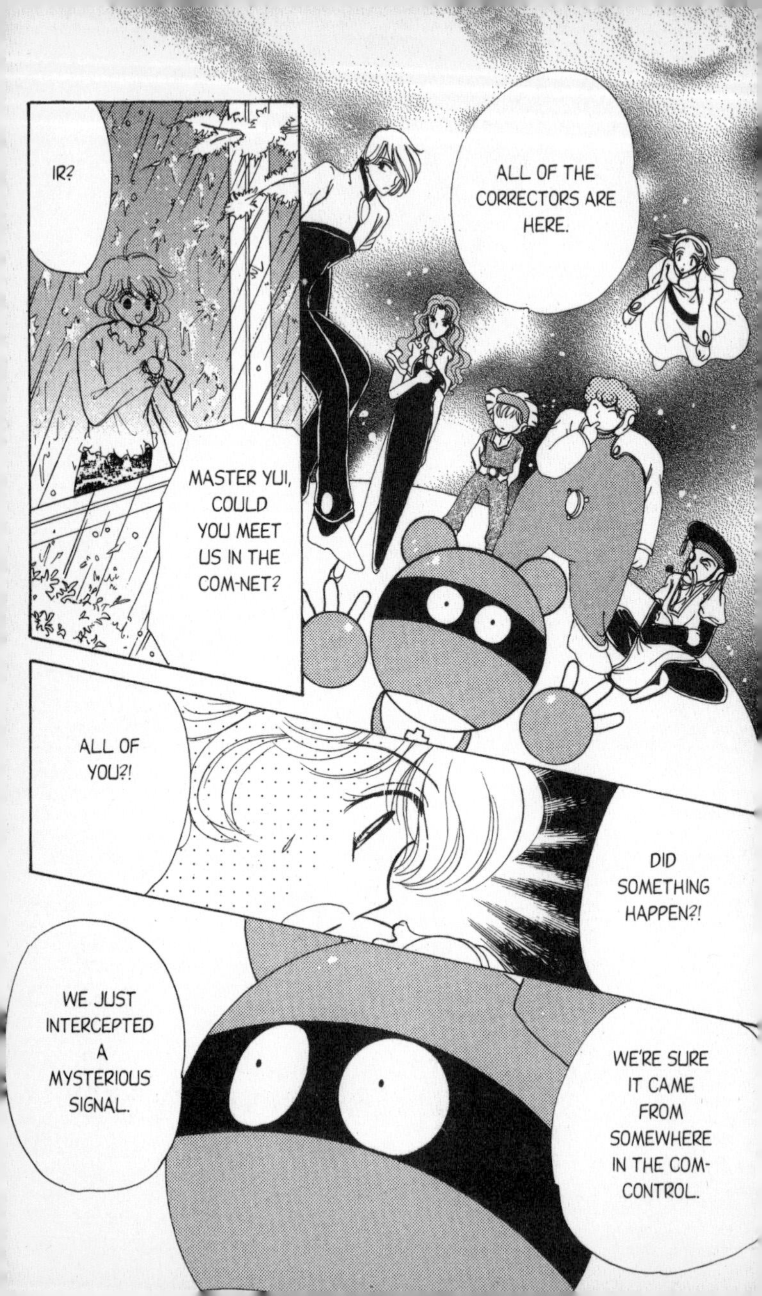
ALL OF THE CORRECTORS ARE HERE.
IR?
MASTER YUI, COULD YOU MEET US IN THE COM-NET?
ALL OF YOU?!
DID SOMETHING HAPPEN?!
WE JUST INTERCEPTED A MYSTERIOUS SIGNAL.
WE'RE SURE IT CAME FROM SOMEWHERE IN THE COM-CONTROL.

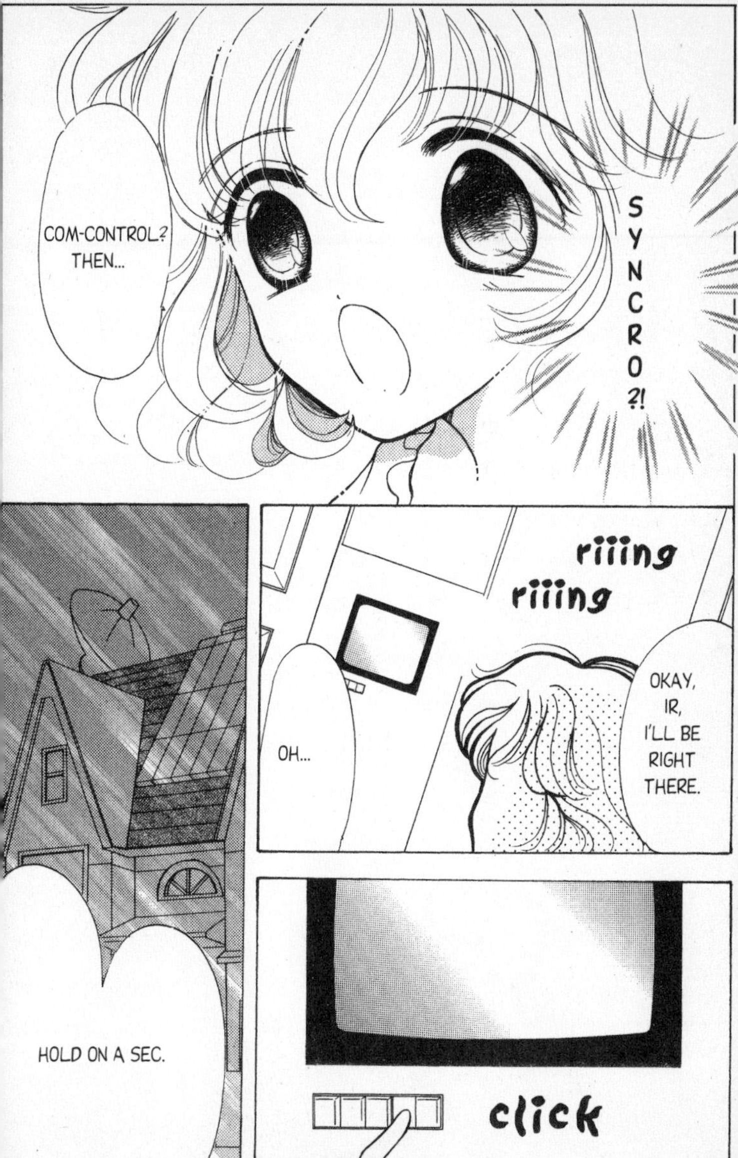
COM-CONTROL? THEN...
SYNCRO?!
riiing riiing
OKAY, IR, I'LL BE RIGHT THERE.
OH...
click
HOLD ON A SEC.

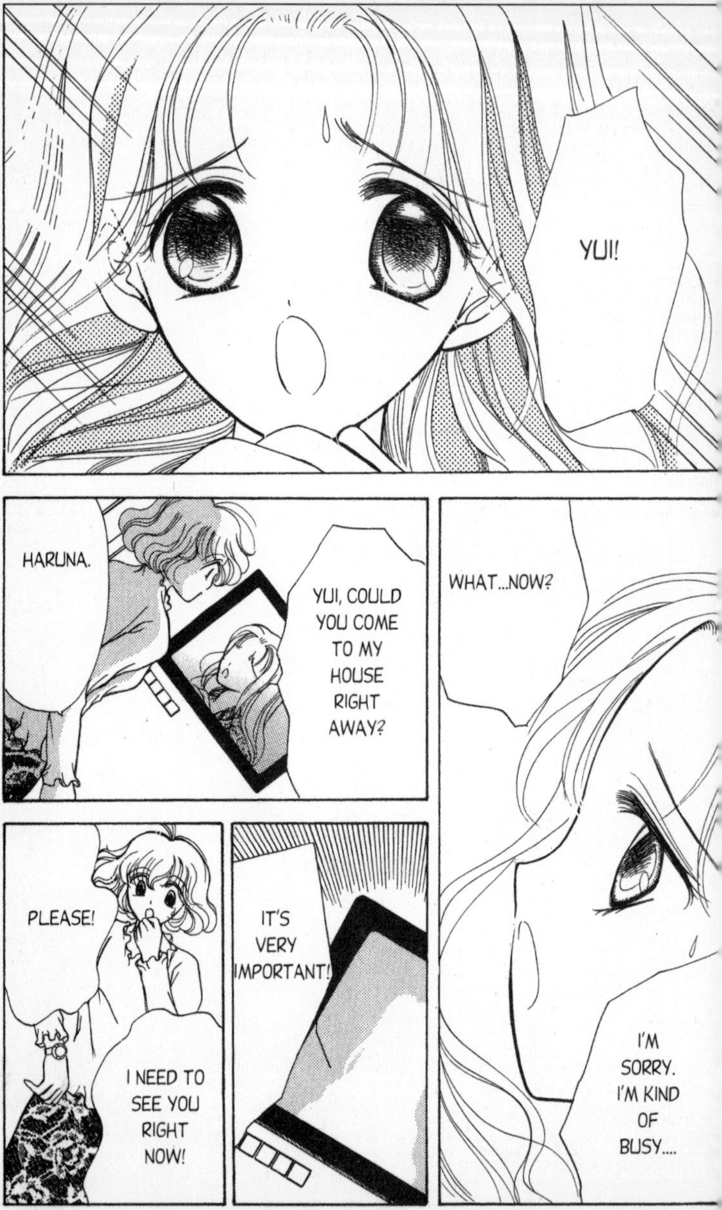
YUI!
HARUNA.
YUI, COULD YOU COME TO MY HOUSE RIGHT AWAY?
WHAT...NOW?
PLEASE!
I NEED TO SEE YOU RIGHT NOW!
IT'S VERY IMPORTANT!
I'M SORRY. I'M KIND OF BUSY....

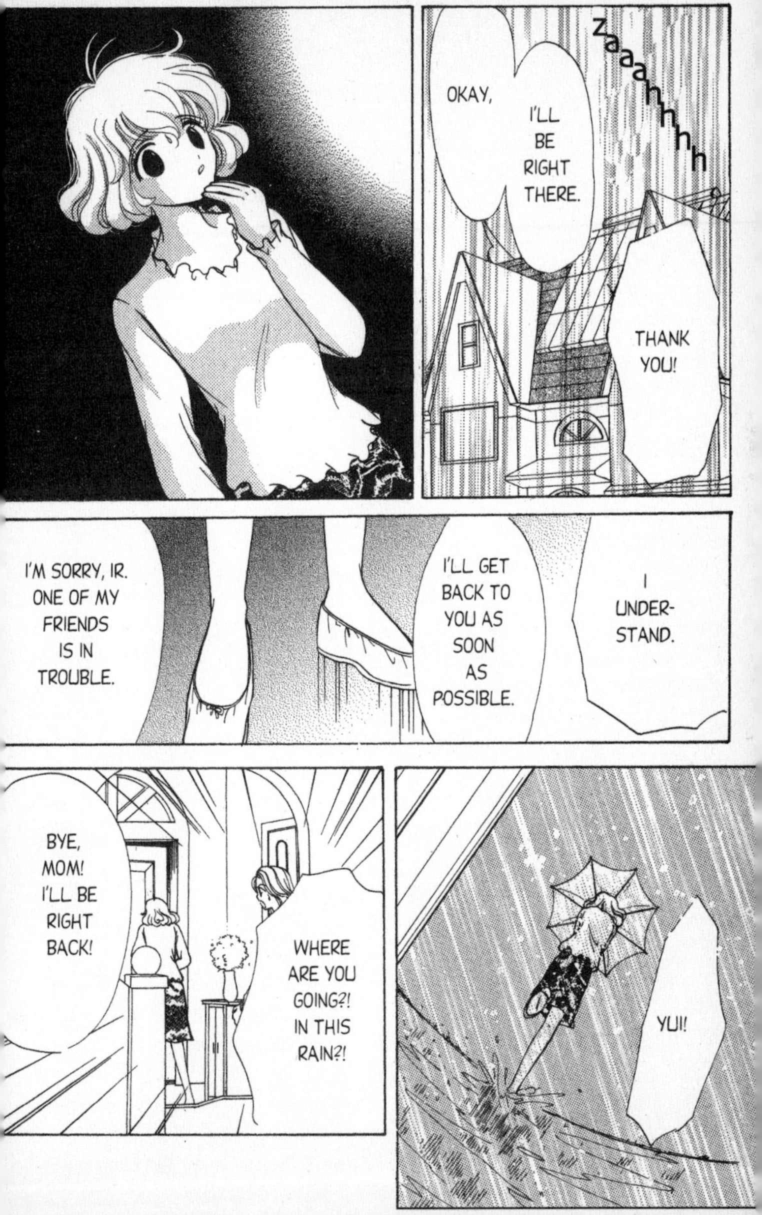
Zaaaahhhh
OKAY, I'LL BE RIGHT THERE.
THANK YOU!
I UNDERSTAND.
I'LL GET BACK TO YOU AS SOON AS POSSIBLE.
I'M SORRY, IR. ONE OF MY FRIENDS IS IN TROUBLE.
YUI!
WHERE ARE YOU GOING?! IN THIS RAIN?!
BYE, MOM! I'LL BE RIGHT BACK!

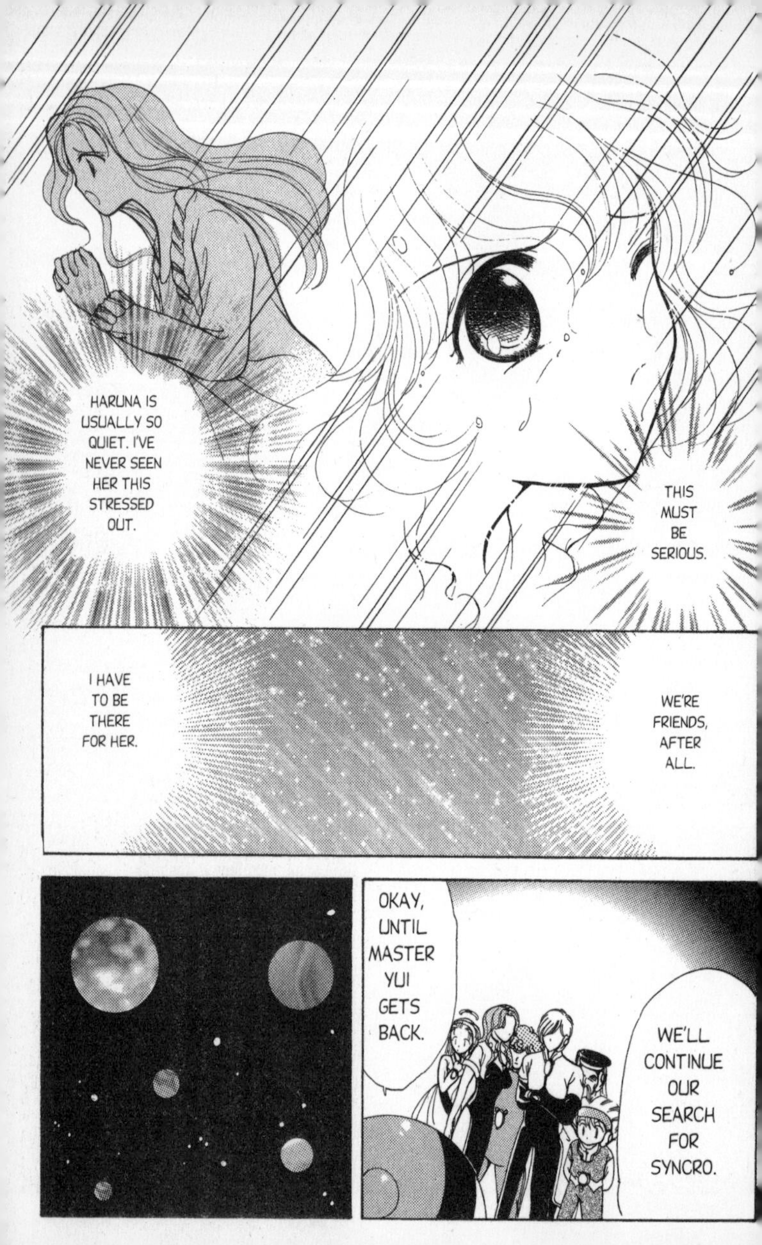
HARUNA IS USUALLY SO QUIET. I'VE NEVER SEEN HER THIS STRESSED OUT.
THIS MUST BE SERIOUS.
I HAVE TO BE THERE FOR HER.
WE'RE FRIENDS, AFTER ALL.
OKAY, UNTIL MASTER YUI GETS BACK.
WE'LL CONTINUE OUR SEARCH FOR SYNCRO.

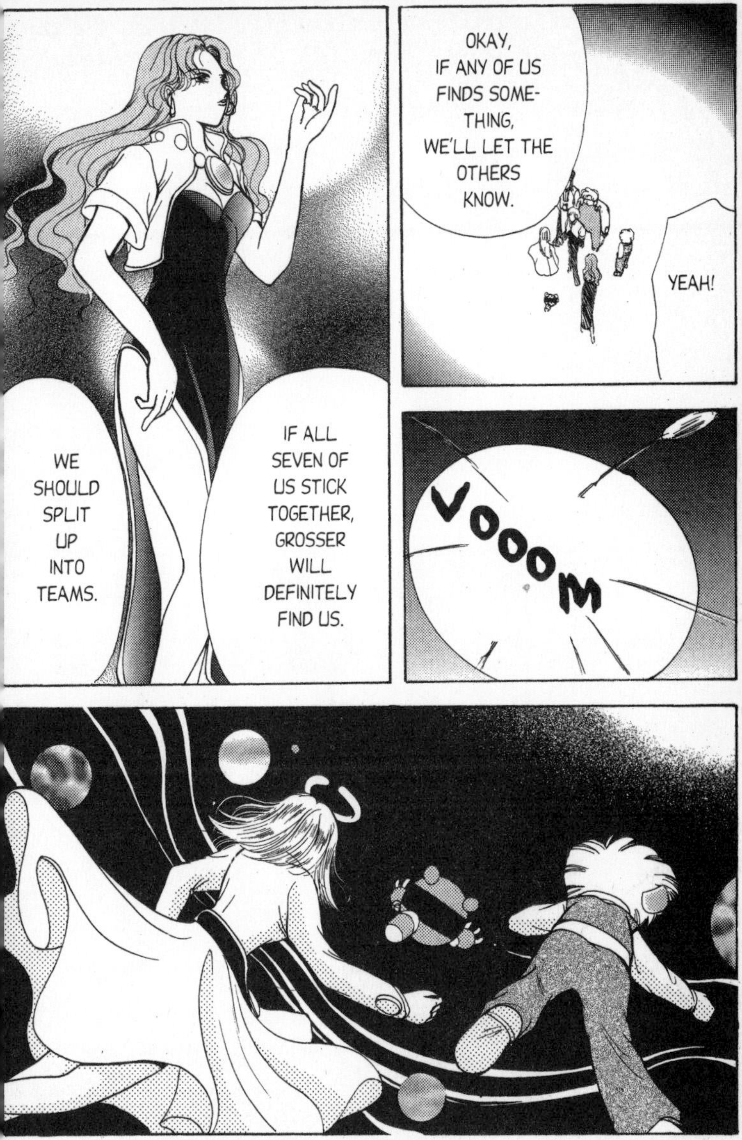
WE SHOULD SPLIT UP INTO TEAMS.
IF ALL SEVEN OF US STICK TOGETHER, GROSSER WILL DEFINITELY FIND US.
OKAY, IF ANY OF US FINDS SOME-THING, WE'LL LET THE OTHERS KNOW.
YEAH!
VOOOM

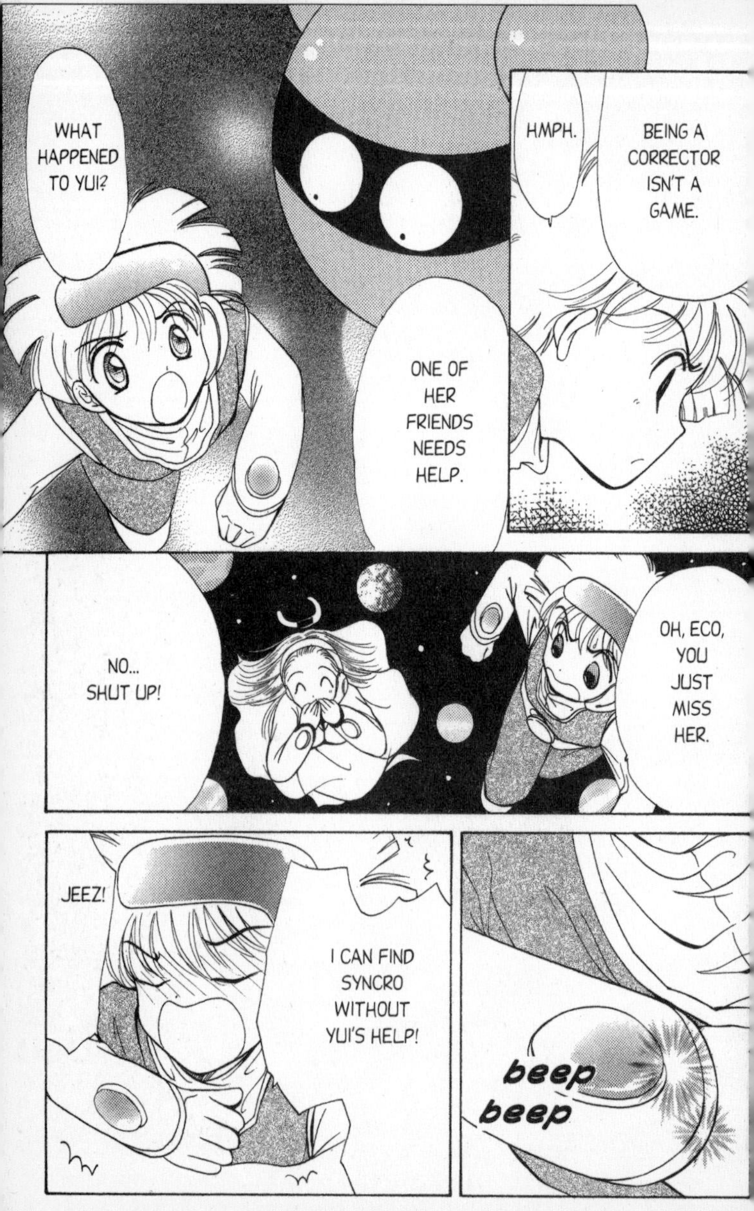

WHAT HAPPENED TO YUI?
ONE OF HER FRIENDS NEEDS HELP.
HMPH.
BEING A CORRECTOR ISN'T A GAME.
OH, ECO, YOU JUST MISS HER.
NO... SHUT UP!
beep beep
JEEZ!
I CAN FIND SYNCRO WITHOUT YUI'S HELP!

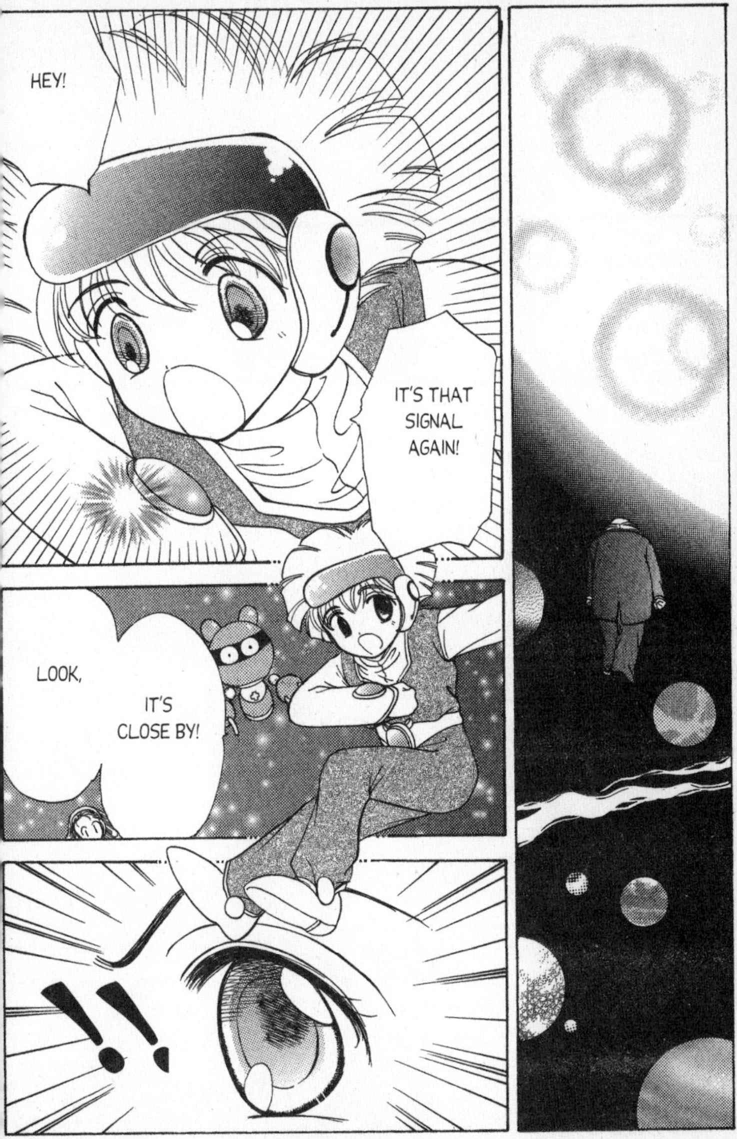
HEY!
IT'S THAT SIGNAL AGAIN!
LOOK, IT'S CLOSE BY!
!!

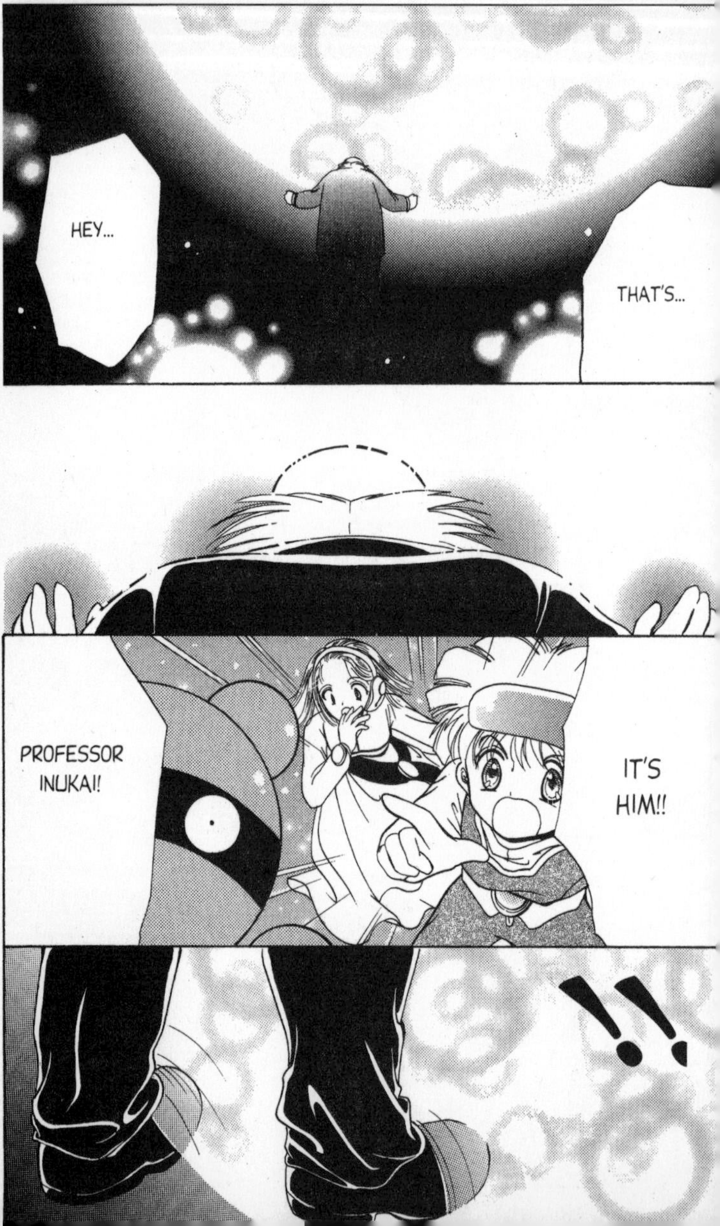
THAT'S...
HEY...
IT'S HIM!!
PROFESSOR INUKAI!
!!

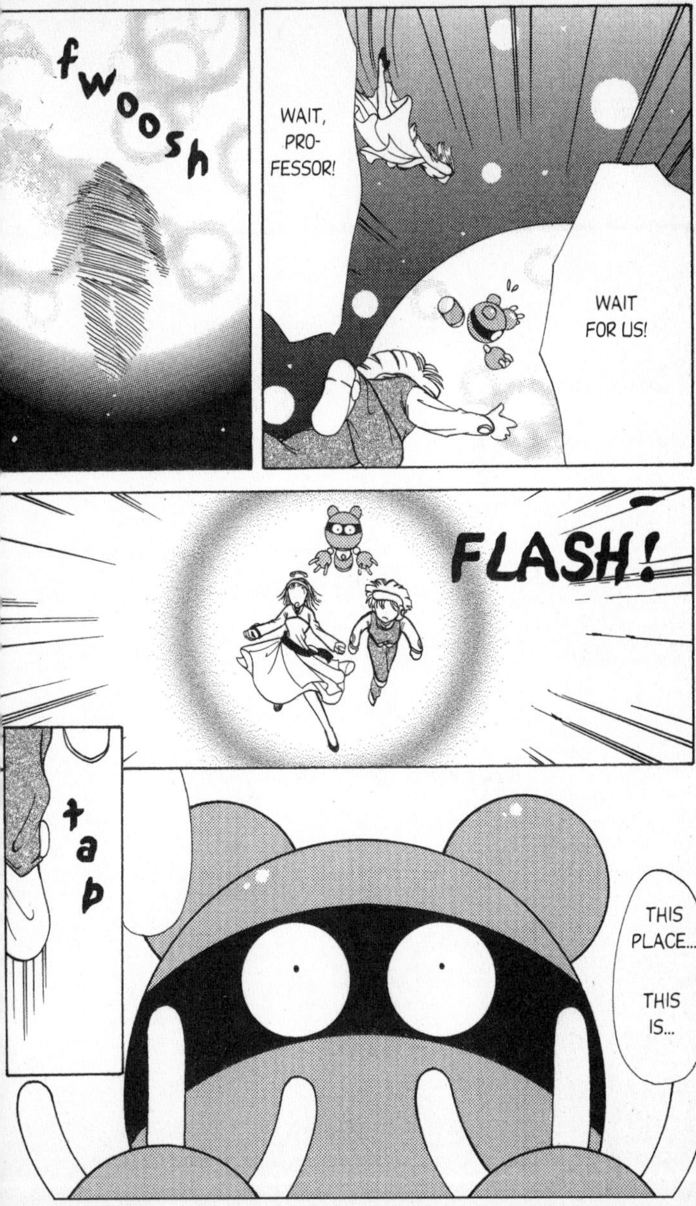
WAIT, PRO-FESSOR!
WAIT FOR US!
fwoosh
FLASH!
tap
THIS PLACE...
THIS IS...

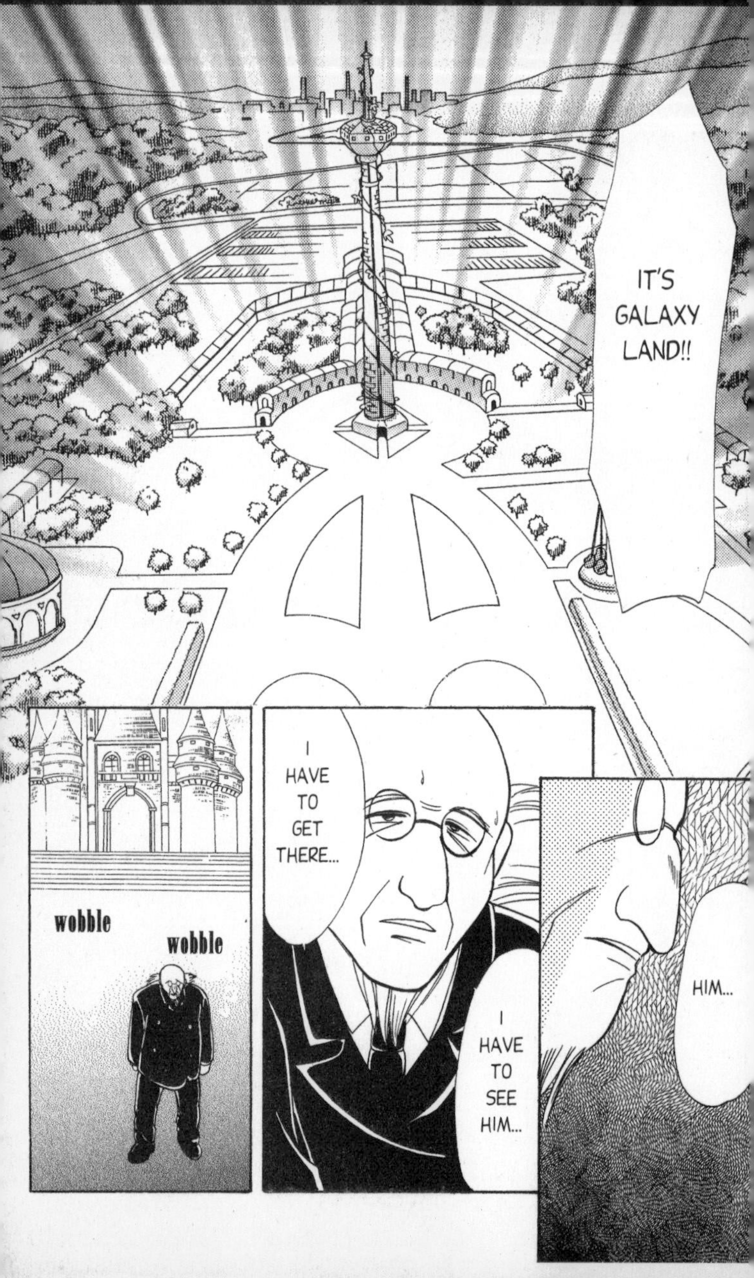
IT'S GALAXY LAND!!
HIM...
I HAVE TO SEE HIM...
I HAVE TO GET THERE...
wobble
wobble

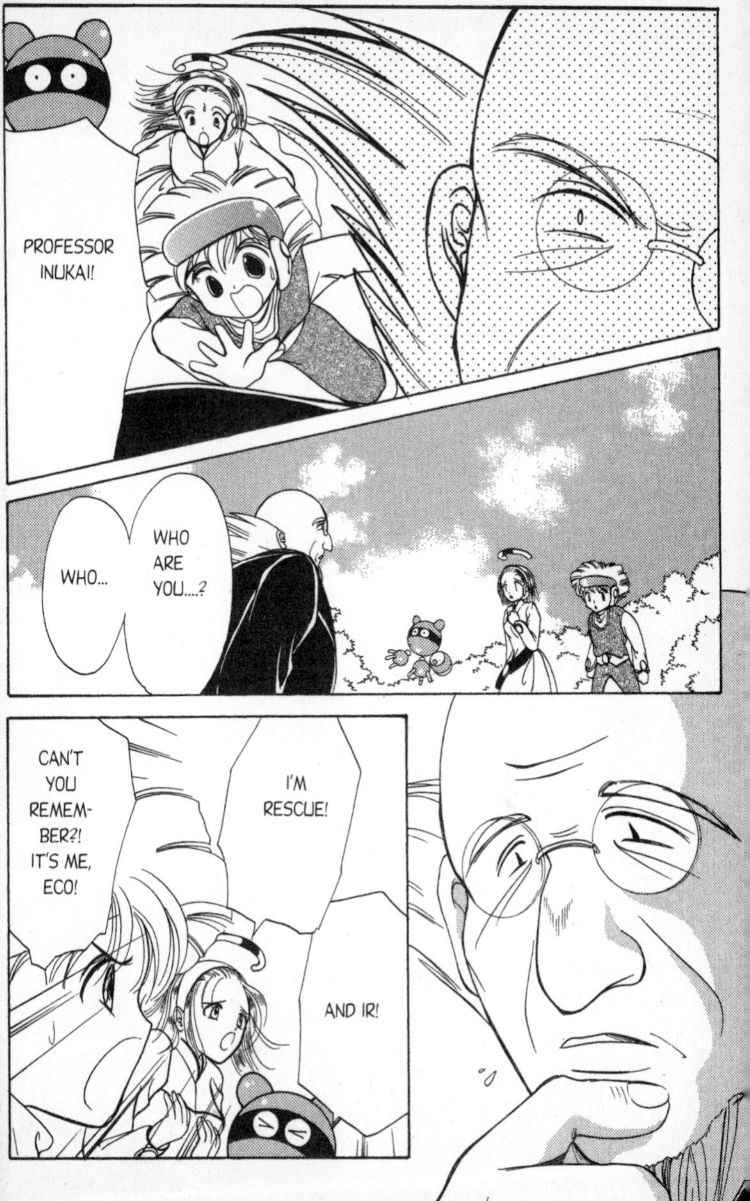
PROFESSOR INUKAI!
WHO...
WHO ARE YOU....?
CAN'T YOU REMEMBER?! IT'S ME, ECO!
I'M RESCUE!
AND IR!

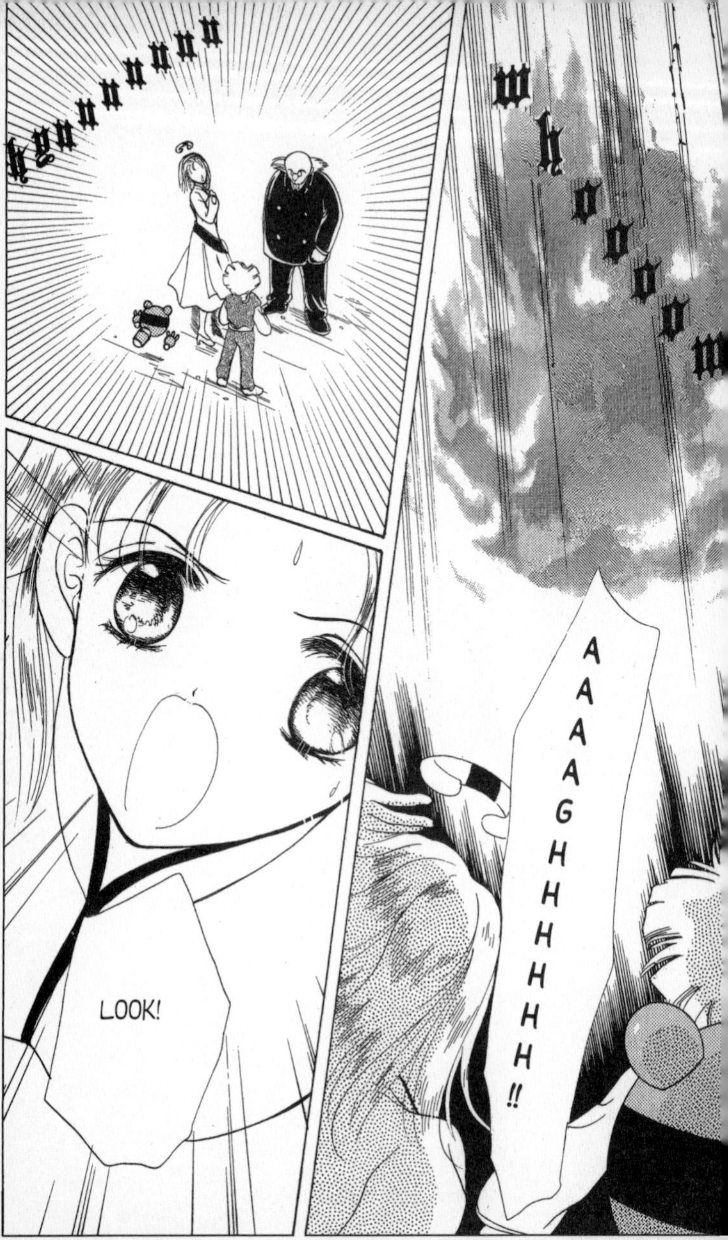
whooooom
AAAAAGHHHHHHH!!
hyunnnnnnn
LOOK!

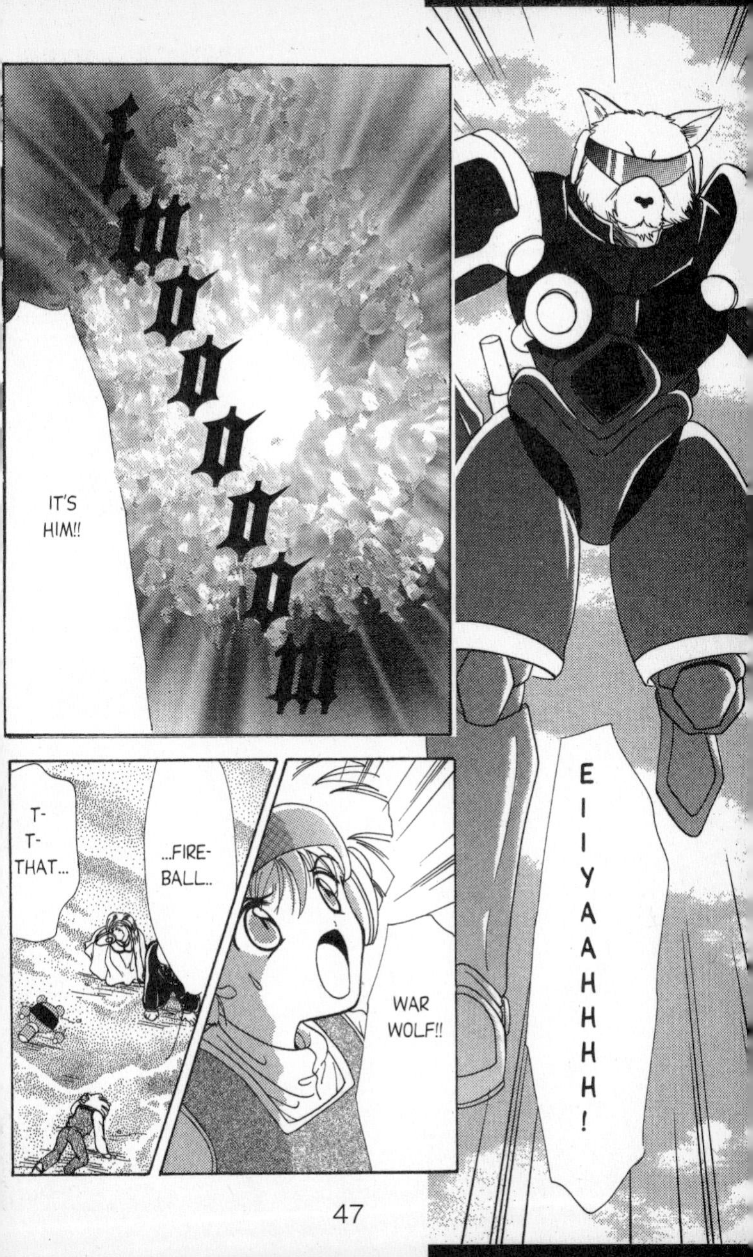
EIIYAAAHHHHH!
fwooooom
IT'S HIM!!
...FIRE-BALL..
WAR WOLF!!
T-T-THAT...

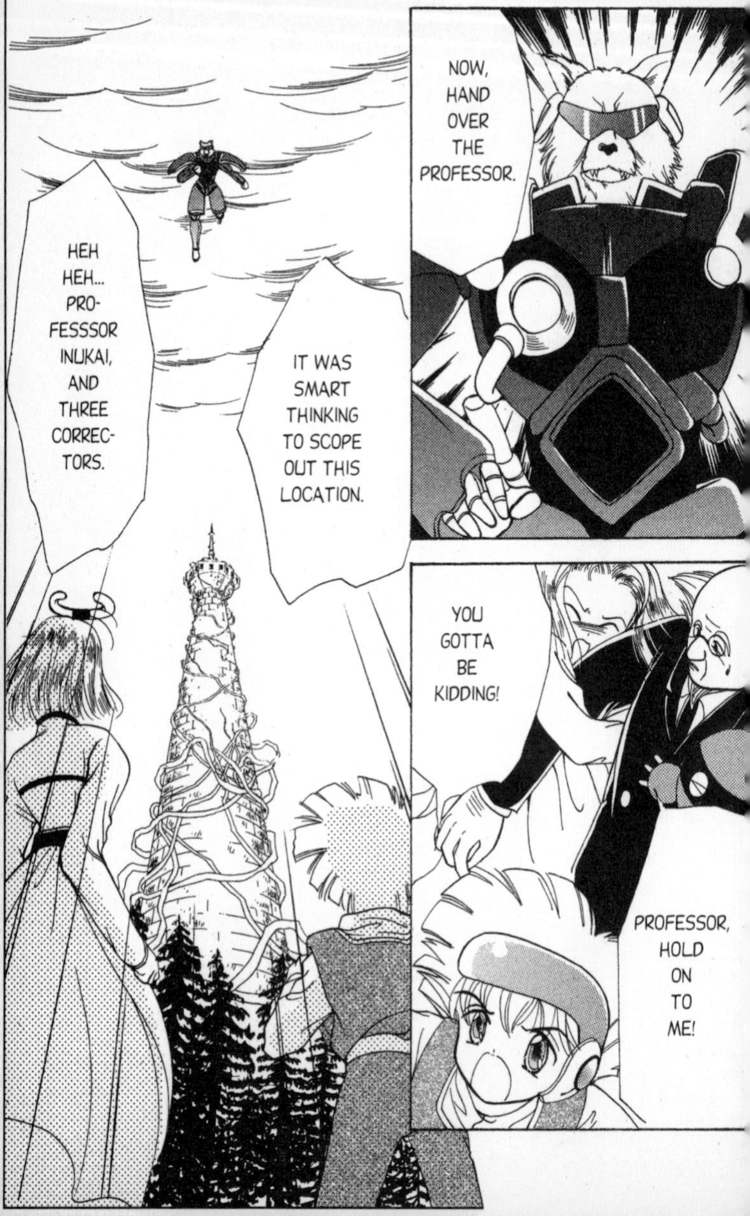
HEH HEH... PRO-FESSSOR INUKAI, AND THREE CORREC-TORS.
IT WAS SMART THINKING TO SCOPE OUT THIS LOCATION.
NOW, HAND OVER THE PROFESSOR.
YOU GOTTA BE KIDDING!
PROFESSOR, HOLD ON TO ME!

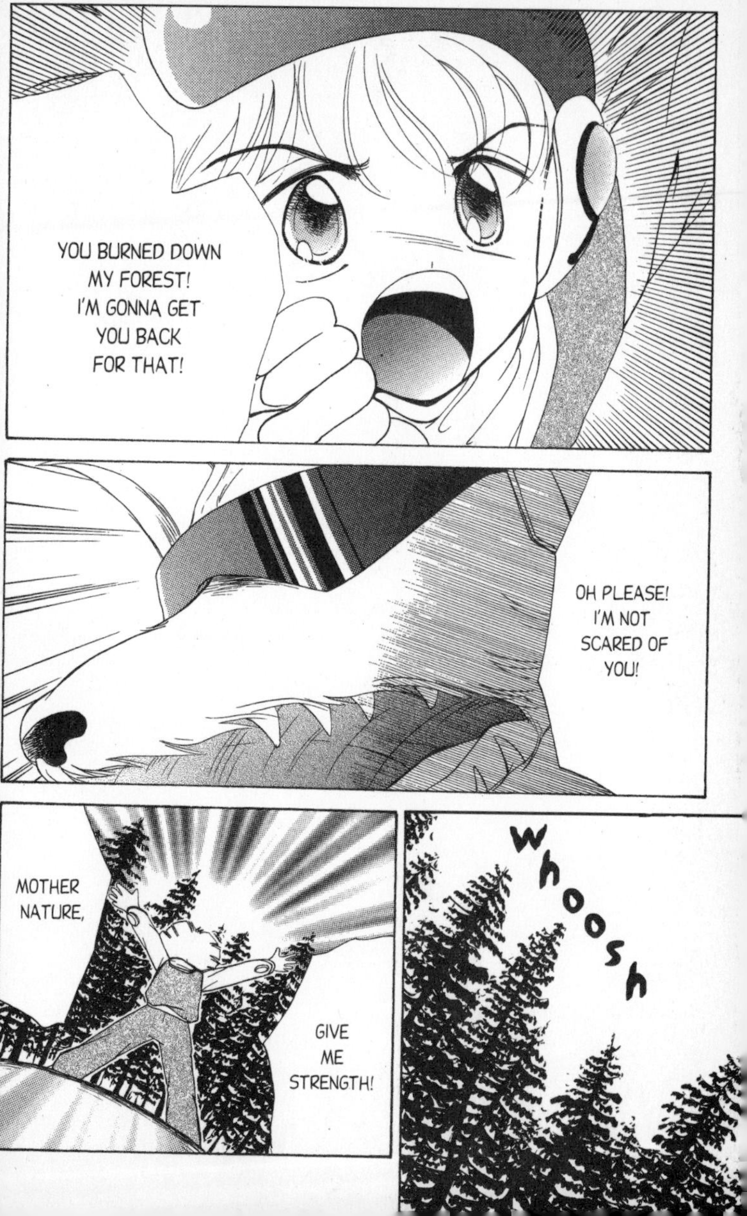
YOU BURNED DOWN MY FOREST! I'M GONNA GET YOU BACK FOR THAT!
OH PLEASE! I'M NOT SCARED OF YOU!
MOTHER NATURE,
GIVE ME STRENGTH!
whoosh

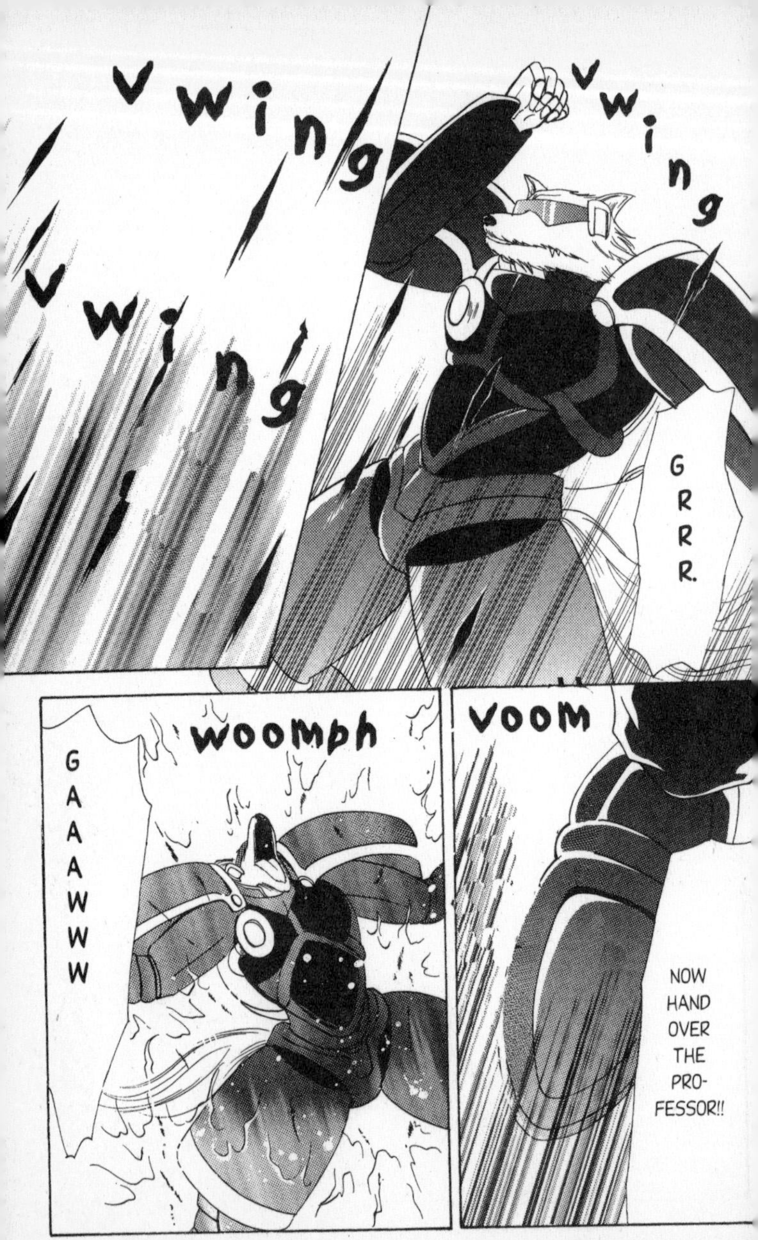
vwing
vwing
vwing
GRRR.
VOOM
NOW HAND OVER THE PRO-FESSOR!!
woomph
GAAAAWWW

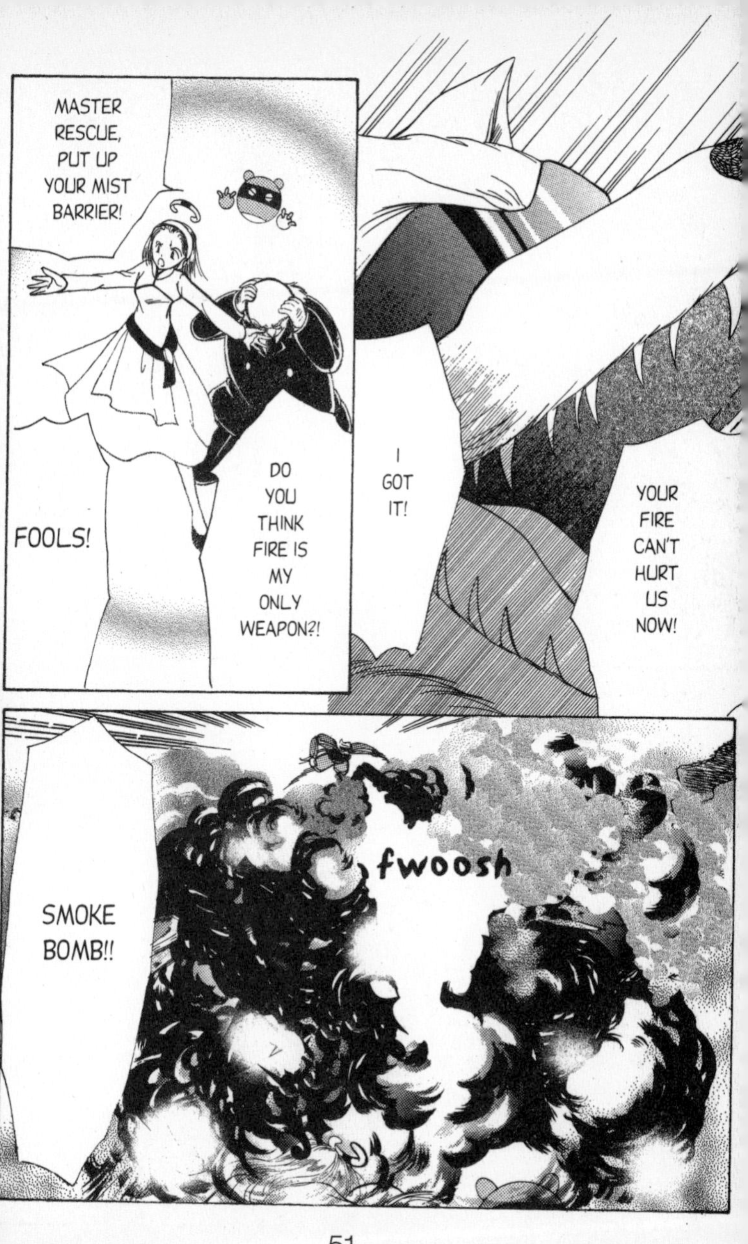
MASTER RESCUE, PUT UP YOUR MIST BARRIER!
I GOT IT!
YOUR FIRE CAN'T HURT US NOW!
FOOLS!
DO YOU THINK FIRE IS MY ONLY WEAPON?!
SMOKE BOMB!!
fwoosh

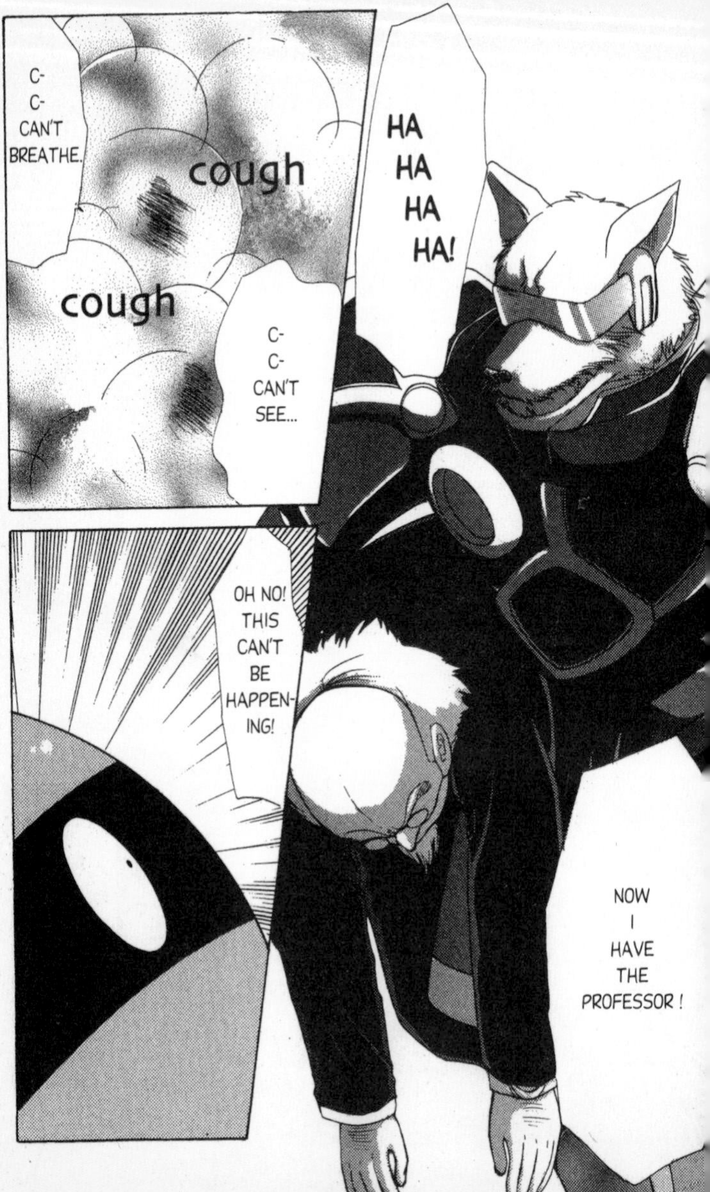
HA HA HA HA!
NOW I HAVE THE PROFESSOR!
C- C- CAN'T BREATHE.
cough
cough
C- C- CAN'T SEE...
OH NO! THIS CAN'T BE HAPPEN- ING!

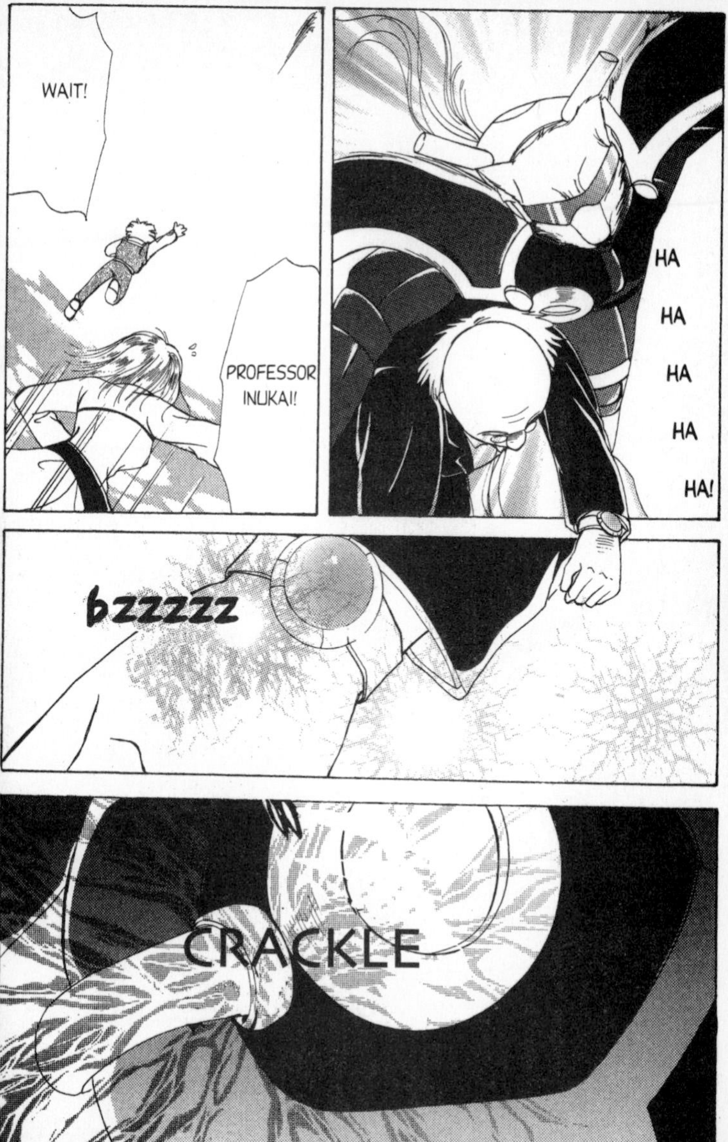
HA
HA
HA
HA
HA!
WAIT!
PROFESSOR INUKAI!
bzzzzz
CRACKLE

W- W- WHAT'S GOING ON?!
AAGHHHHH!
WHAT?!

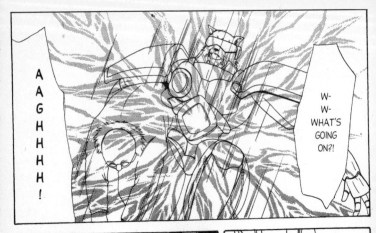

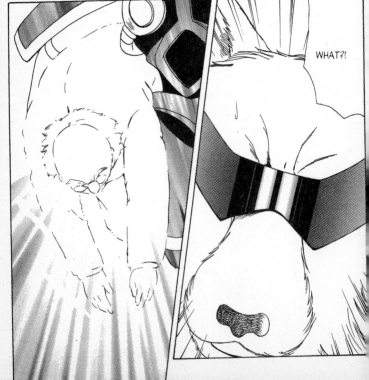

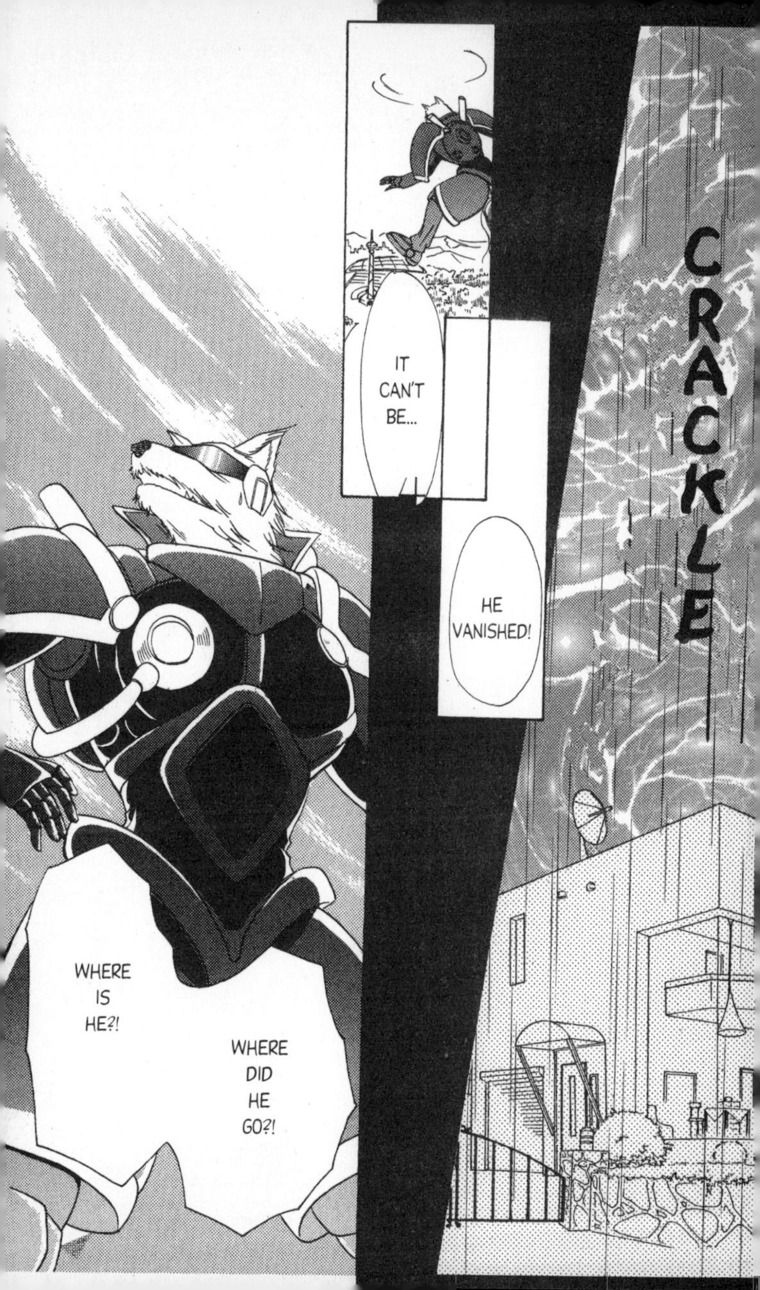
CRACKLE
IT CAN'T BE...
HE VANISHED!
WHERE IS HE?!
WHERE DID HE GO?!

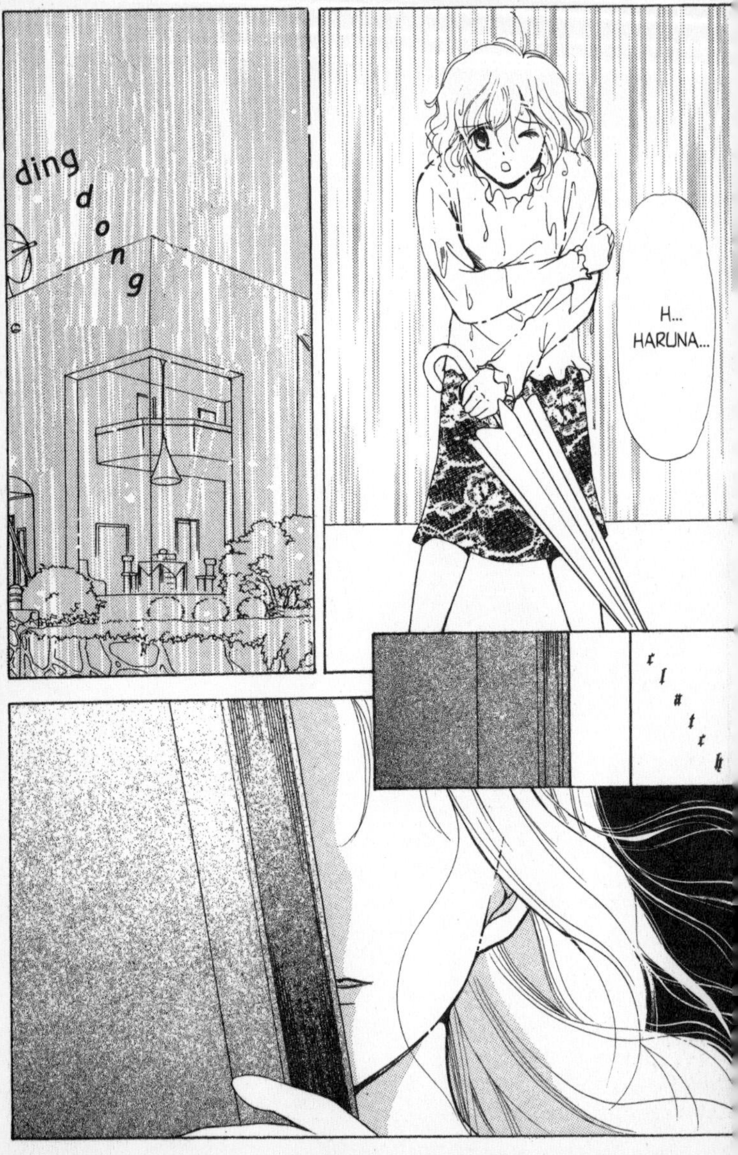
ding dong
H... HARUNA...
clatch

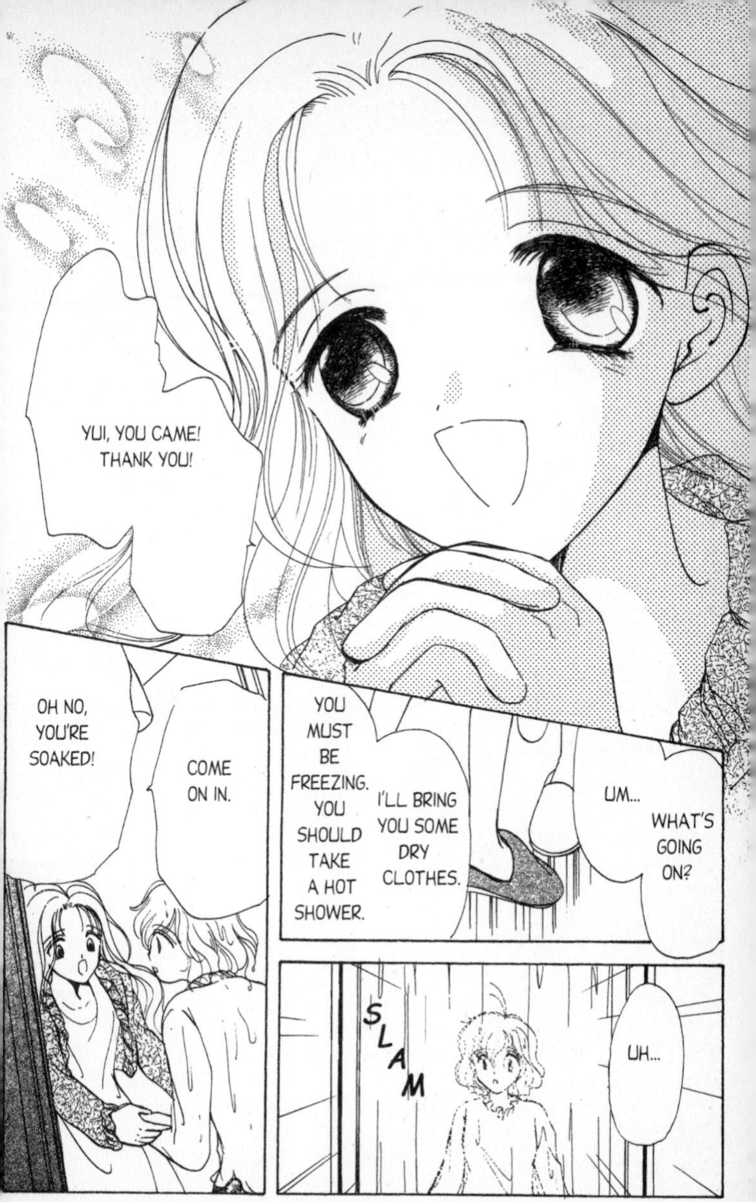
YUI, YOU CAME! THANK YOU!
OH NO, YOU'RE SOAKED!
COME ON IN.
YOU MUST BE FREEZING. YOU SHOULD TAKE A HOT SHOWER.
I'LL BRING YOU SOME DRY CLOTHES.
UM...
WHAT'S GOING ON?
SLAM
UH...

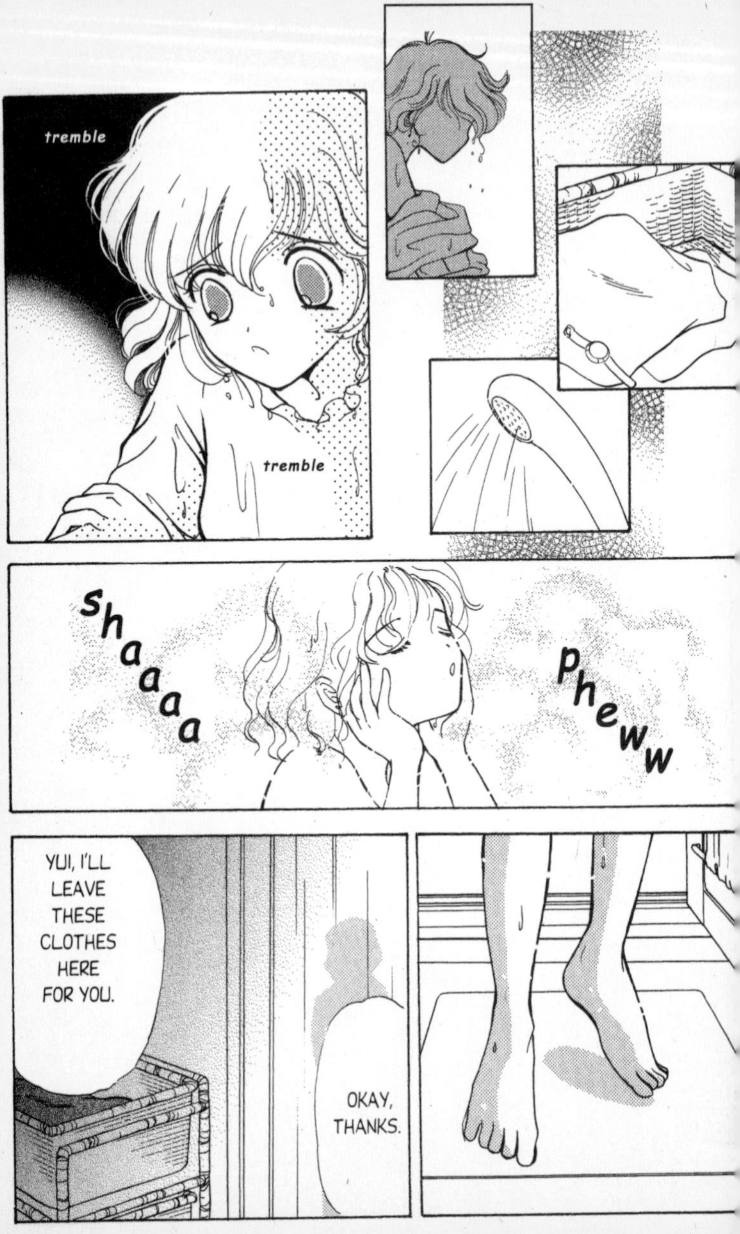
tremble
tremble
Shaaaa
Pheww
YUI, I'LL LEAVE THESE CLOTHES HERE FOR YOU.
OKAY, THANKS.

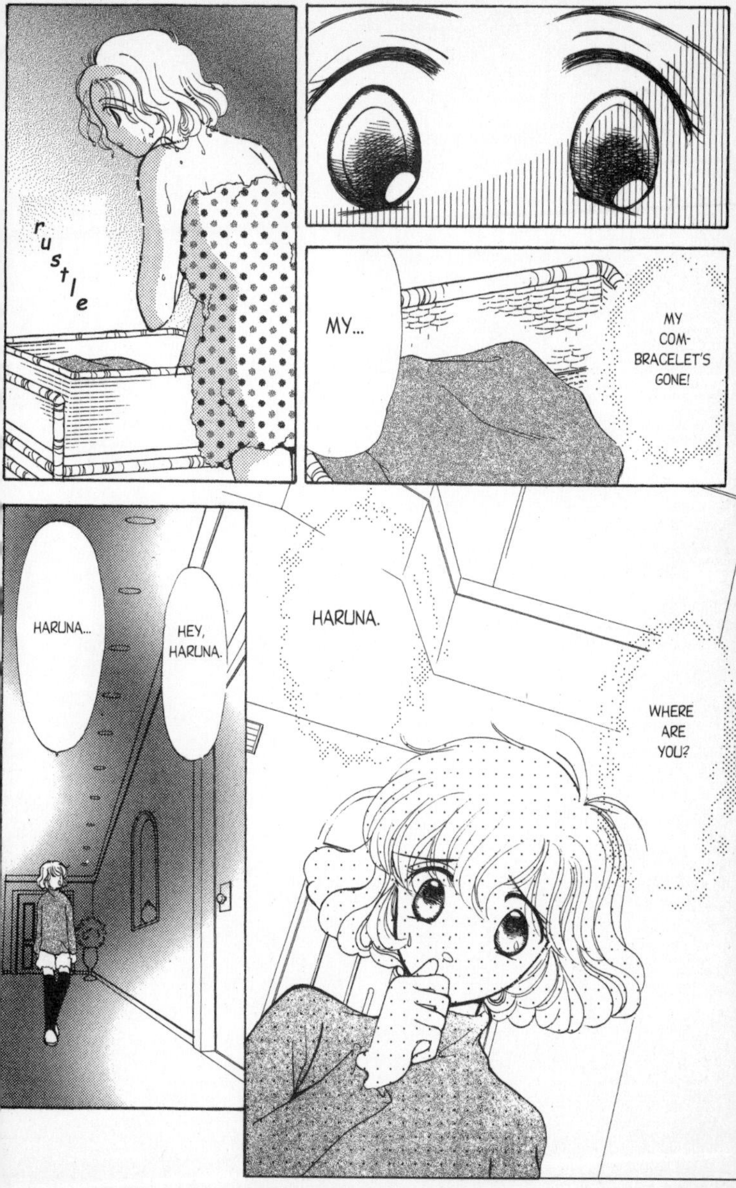
MY...
MY COM-BRACELET'S GONE!
rustle
HARUNA.
WHERE ARE YOU?
HEY, HARUNA.
HARUNA...

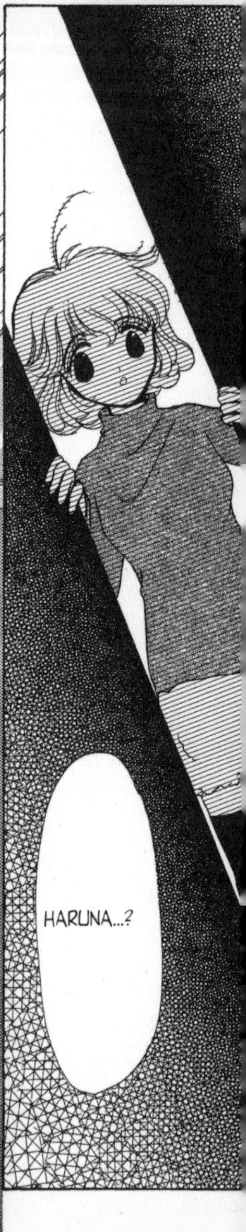
HARUNA...?
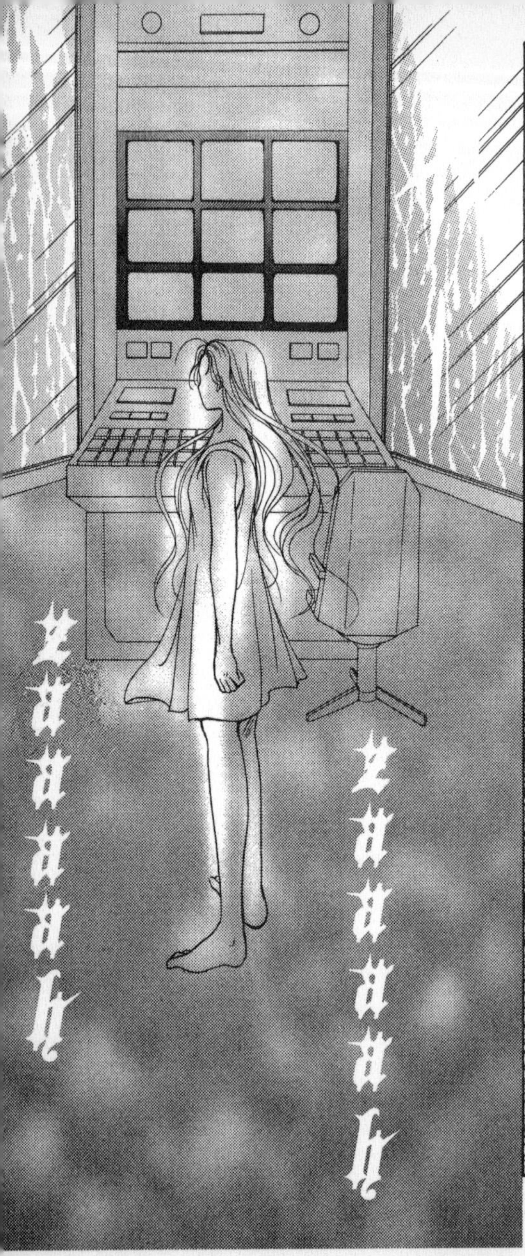
zaaaah
zaaaah

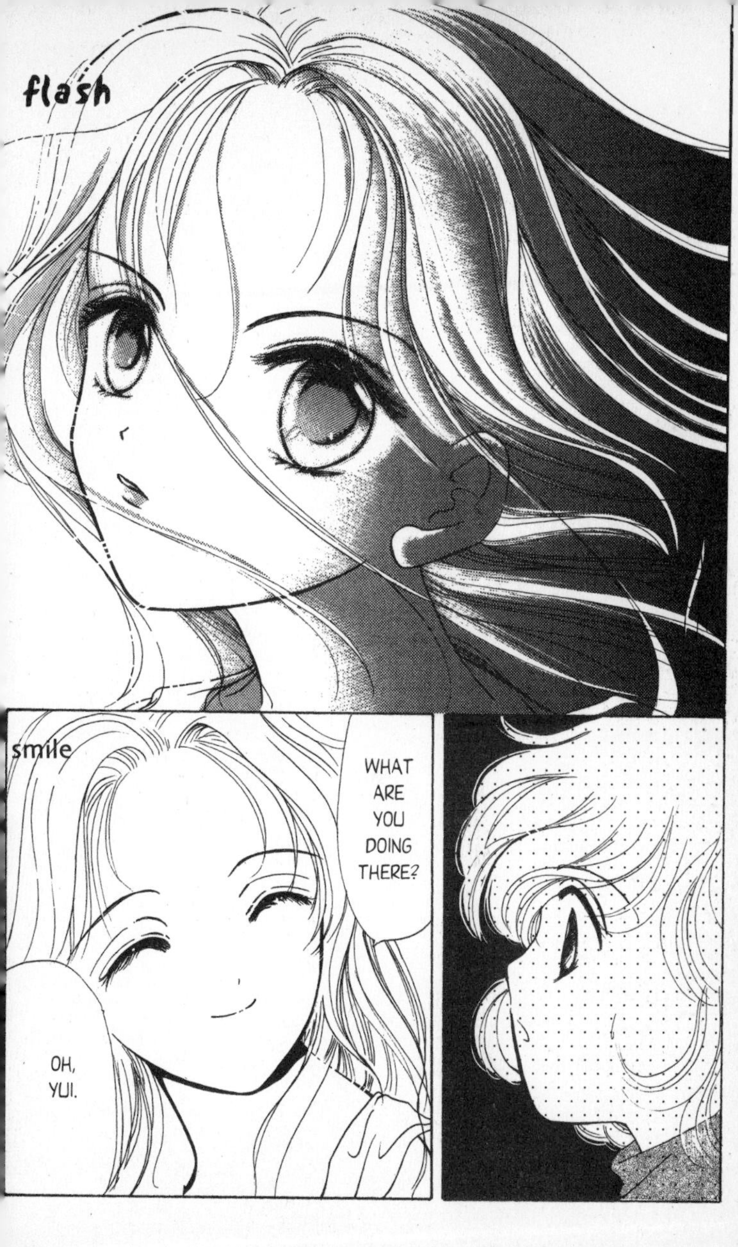
flash
WHAT ARE YOU DOING THERE?
smile
OH, YUI.

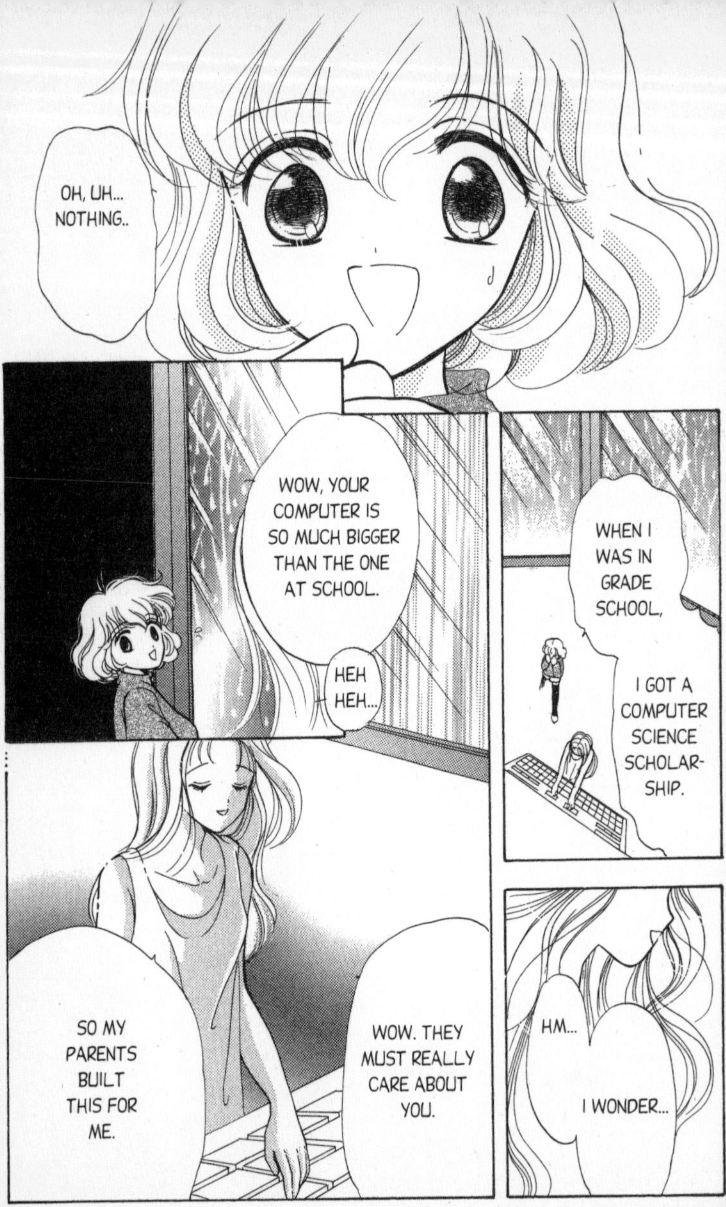
OH, UH... NOTHING..
WOW, YOUR COMPUTER IS SO MUCH BIGGER THAN THE ONE AT SCHOOL.
HEH HEH...
WHEN I WAS IN GRADE SCHOOL,
I GOT A COMPUTER SCIENCE SCHOLAR-SHIP.
SO MY PARENTS BUILT THIS FOR ME.
WOW. THEY MUST REALLY CARE ABOUT YOU.
HM...
I WONDER...

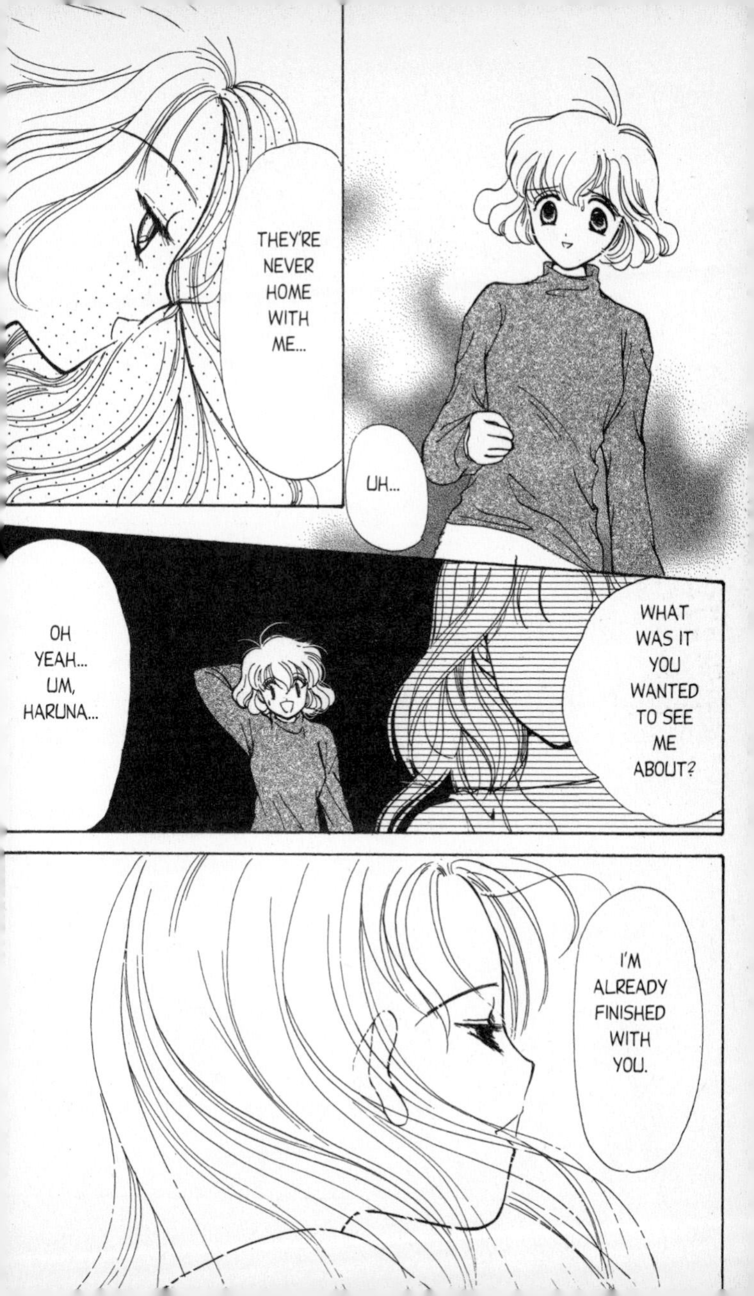
THEY'RE NEVER HOME WITH ME...
UH...
WHAT WAS IT YOU WANTED TO SEE ME ABOUT?
OH YEAH... UM, HARUNA...
I'M ALREADY FINISHED WITH YOU.

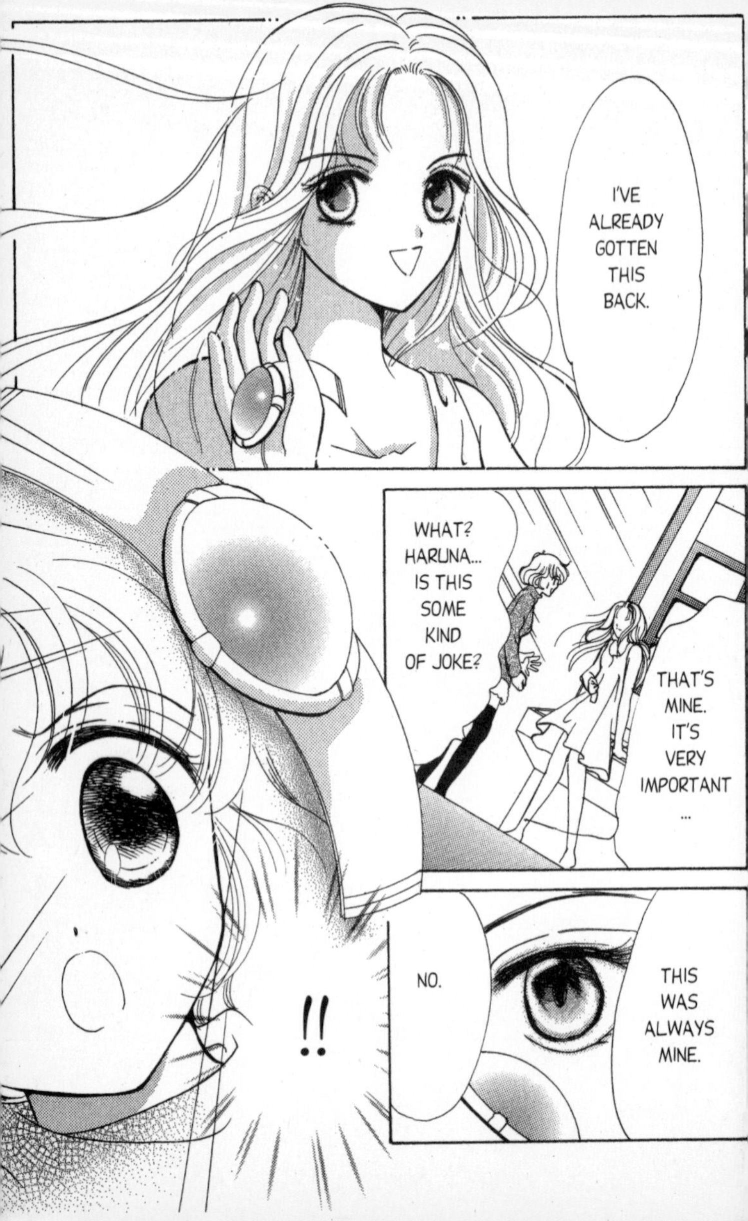
I'VE ALREADY GOTTEN THIS BACK.
WHAT? HARUNA... IS THIS SOME KIND OF JOKE?
THAT'S MINE. IT'S VERY IMPORTANT ...
THIS WAS ALWAYS MINE.
NO.
!!

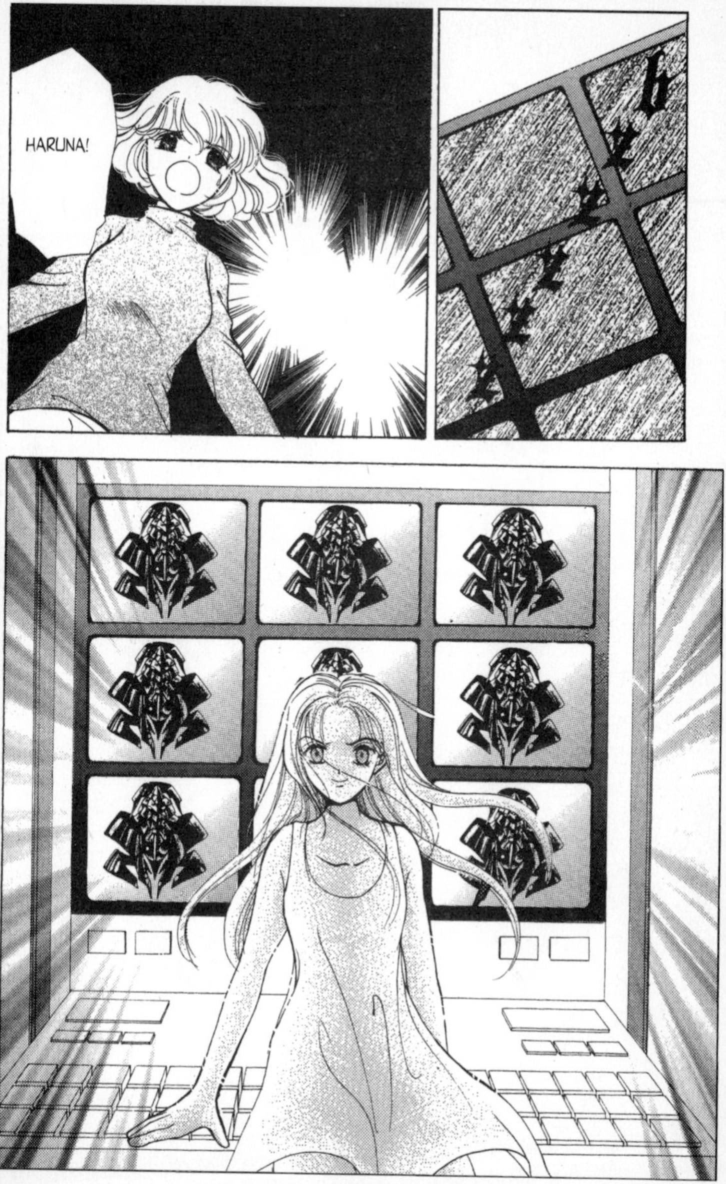
HARUNA!

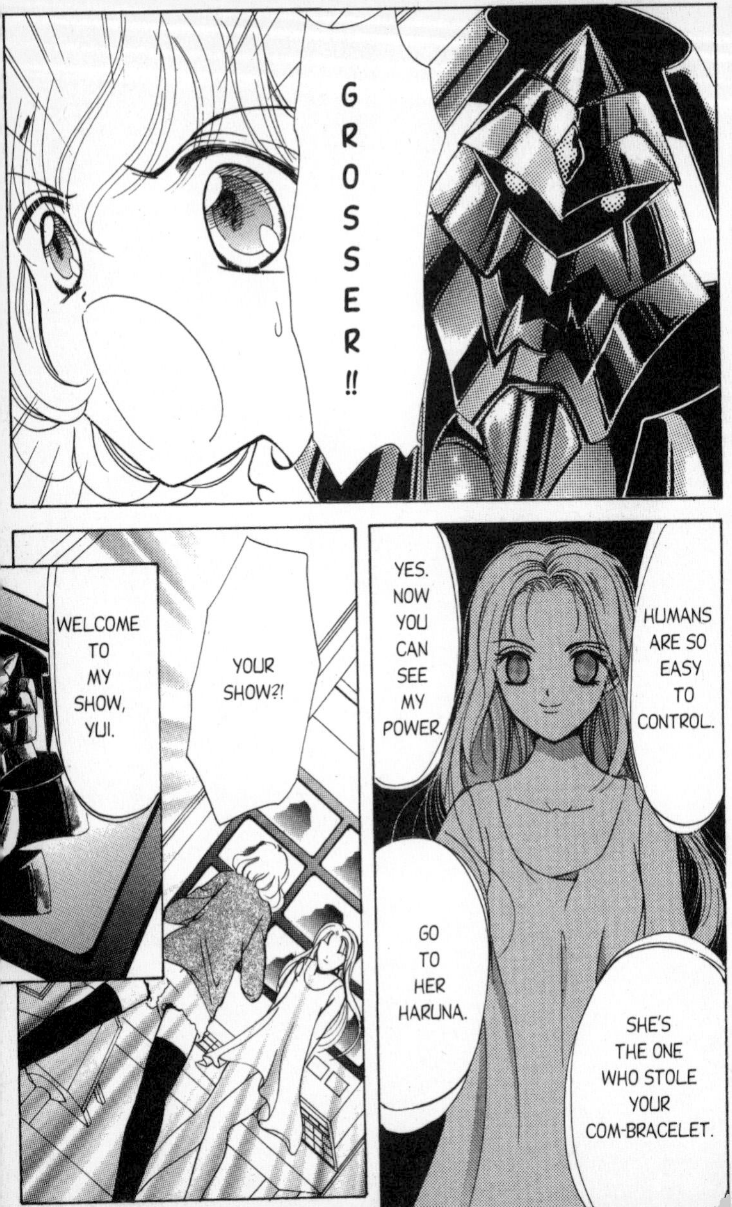
GROSSER!!
WELCOME TO MY SHOW, YUI.
YOUR SHOW?!
YES. NOW YOU CAN SEE MY POWER.
HUMANS ARE SO EASY TO CONTROL.
GO TO HER HARUNA.
SHE'S THE ONE WHO STOLE YOUR COM-BRACELET.

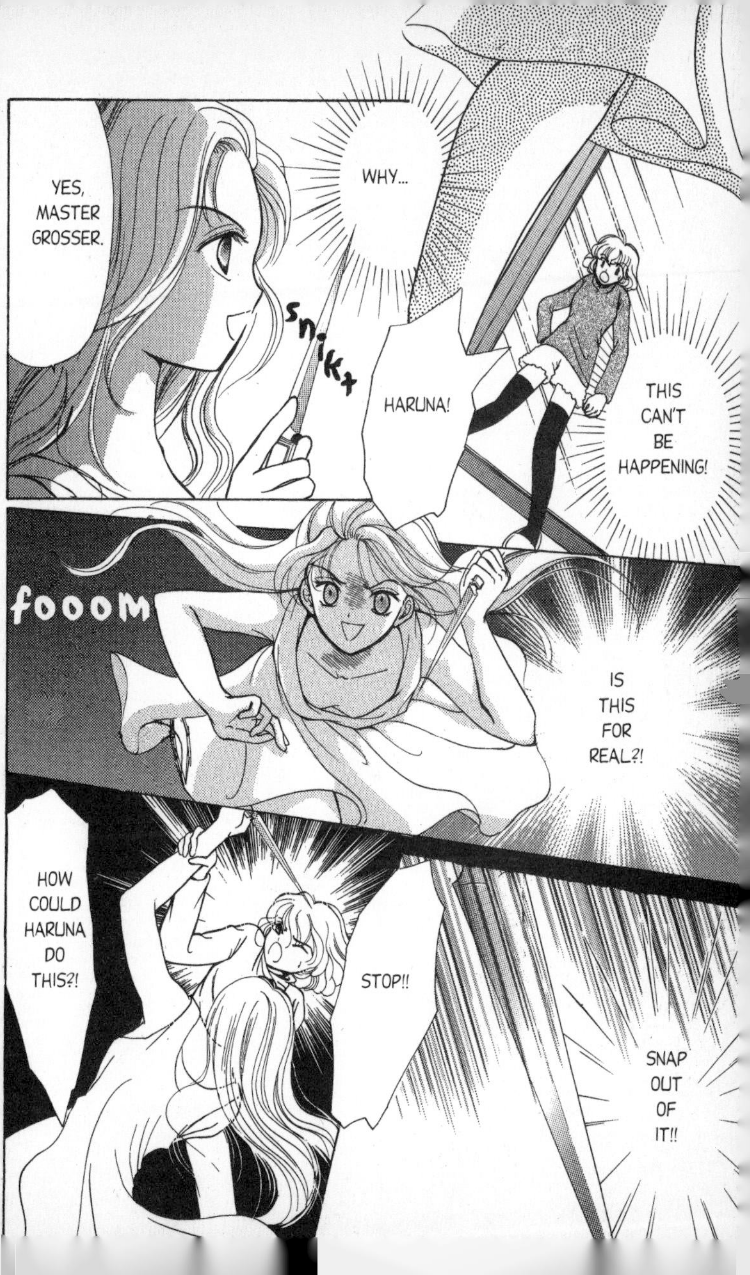
YES, MASTER GROSSER.
snikt
WHY...
HARUNA!
THIS CAN'T BE HAPPENING!
fooom
IS THIS FOR REAL?!
STOP!!
HOW COULD HARUNA DO THIS?!
SNAP OUT OF IT!!

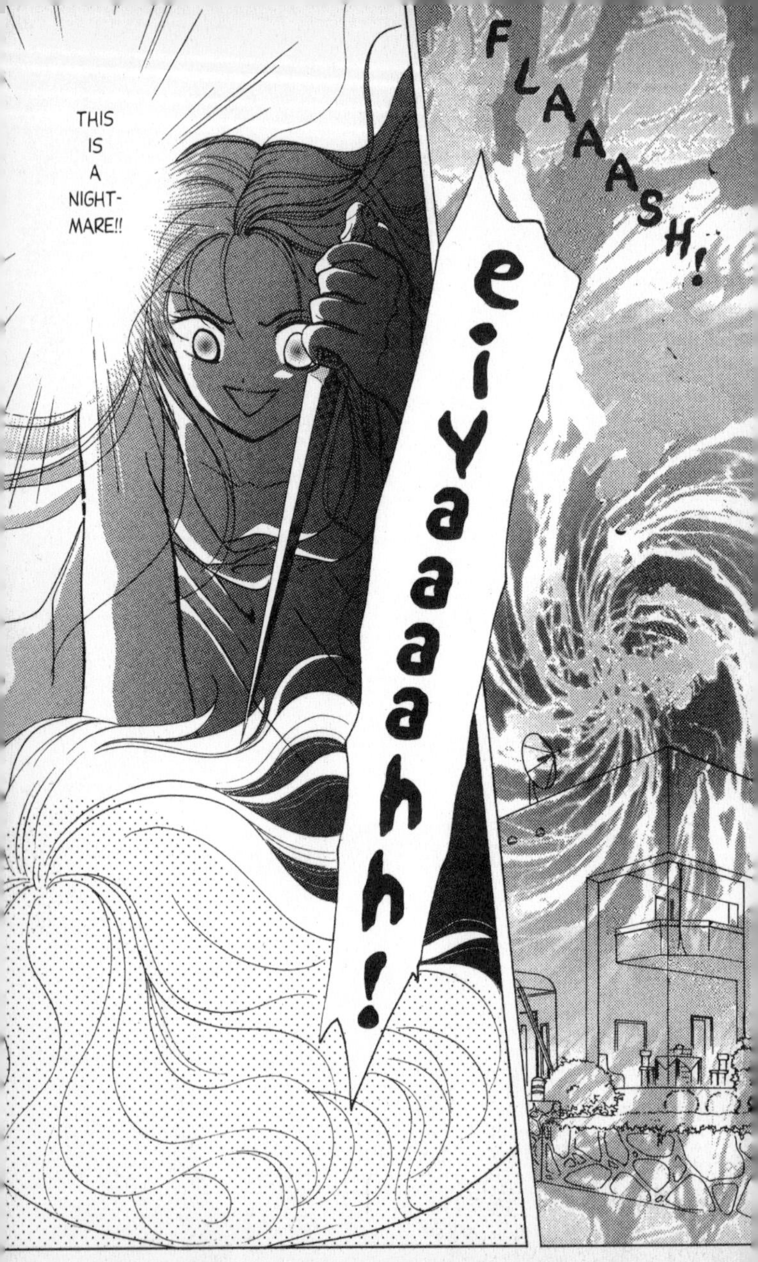
FLAAASH!
THIS IS A NIGHT-MARE!!
eiyaaaahh!

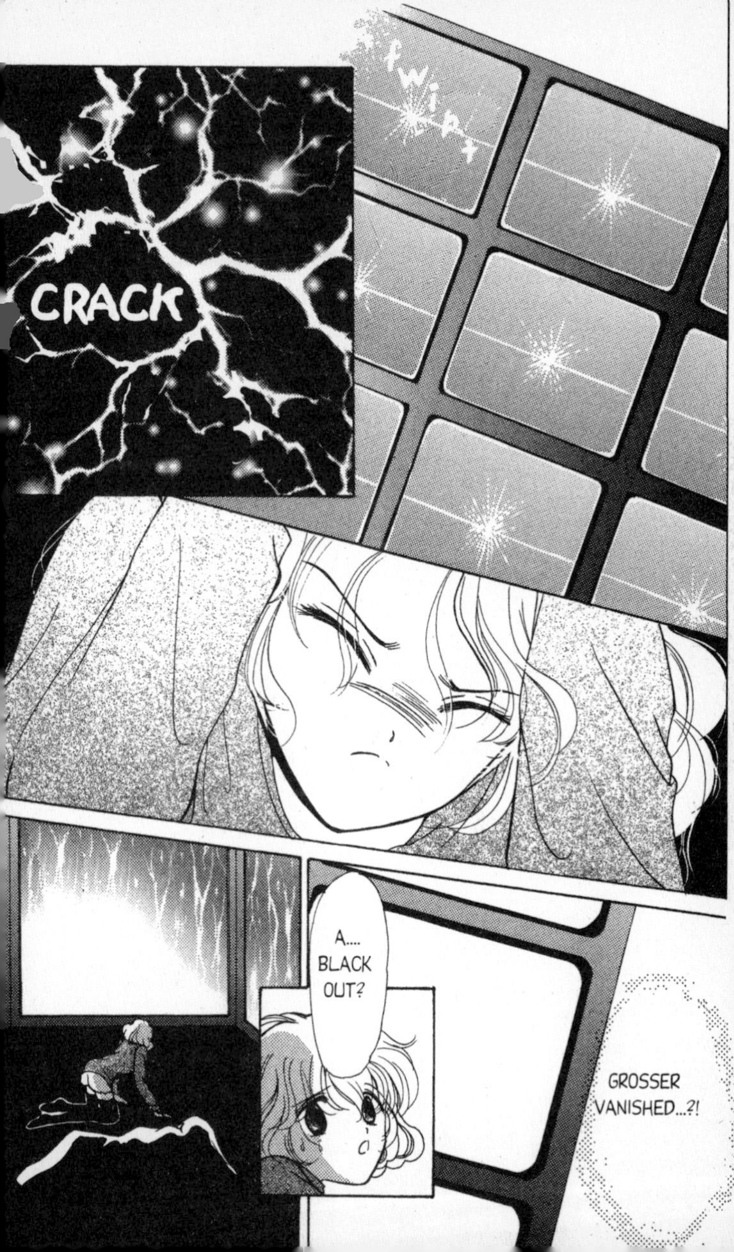
fwipt
CRACK
GROSSER VANISHED...?!
A.... BLACK OUT?

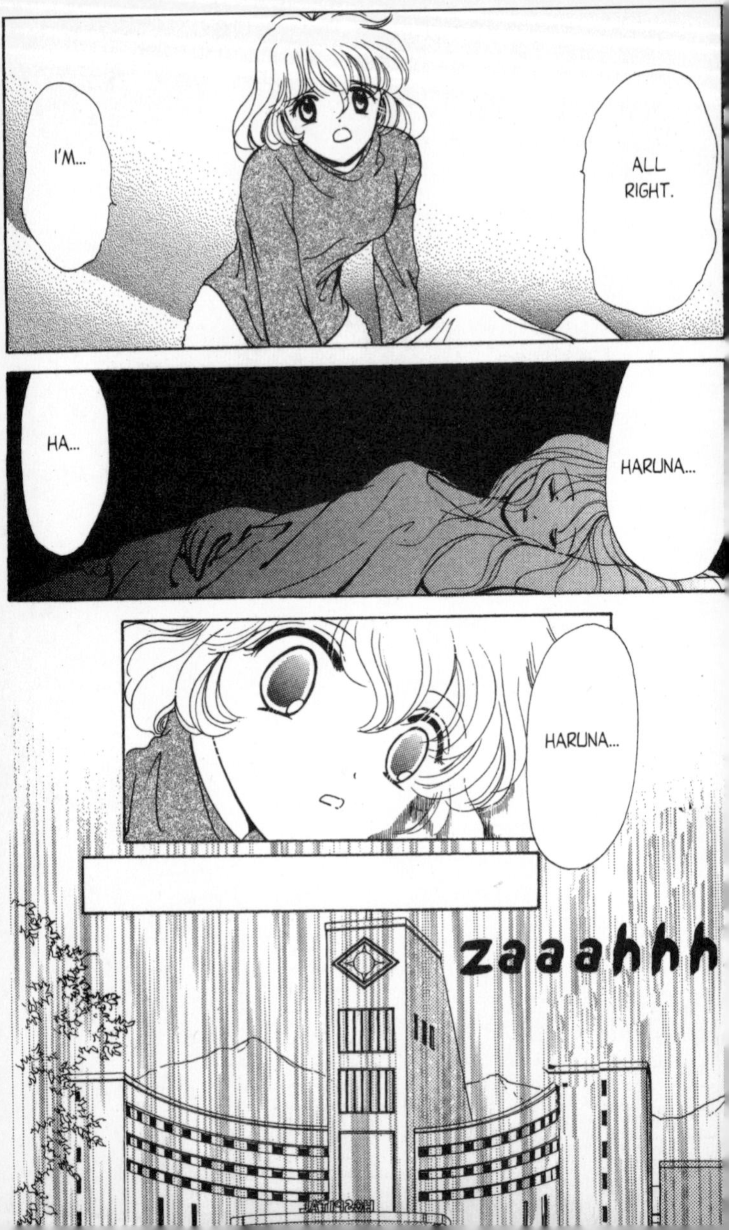
I'M...
ALL RIGHT.
HARUNA...
HA...
HARUNA...
zaaahhh

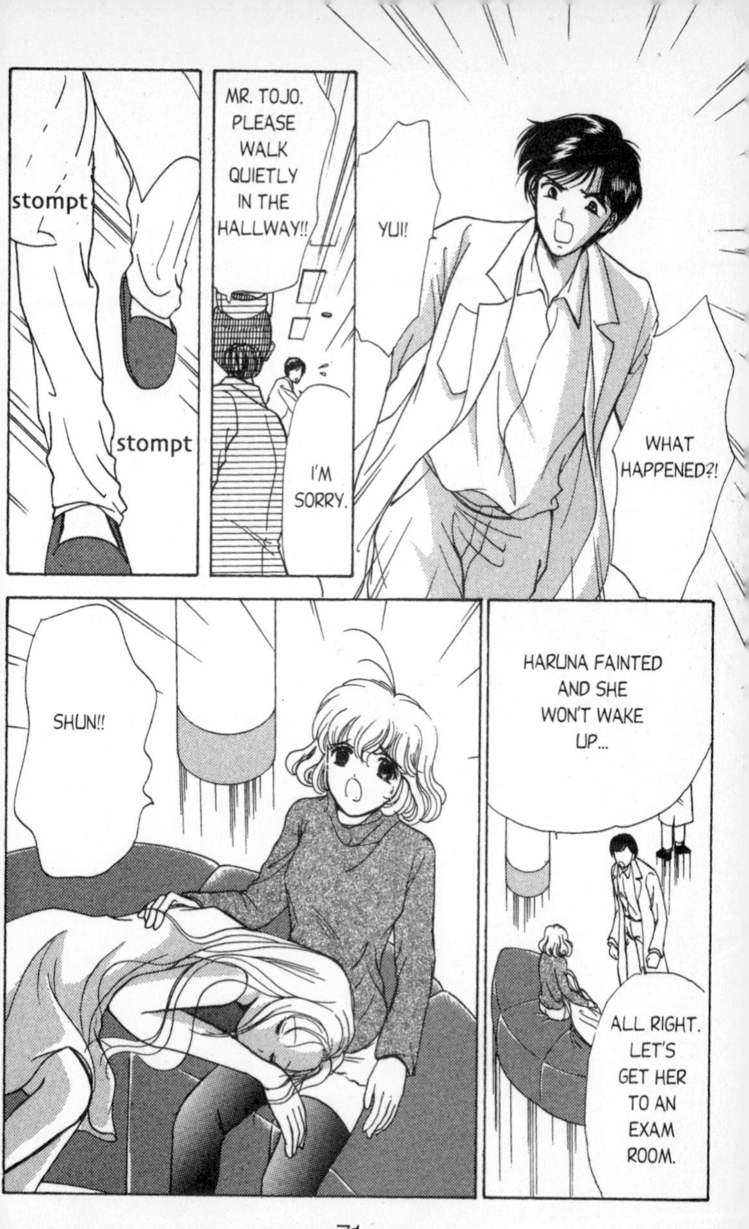
stompt
stompt
MR. TOJO. PLEASE WALK QUIETLY IN THE HALLWAY!!
I'M SORRY.
YUI!
WHAT HAPPENED?!
SHUN!!
HARUNA FAINTED AND SHE WON'T WAKE UP...
ALL RIGHT. LET'S GET HER TO AN EXAM ROOM.

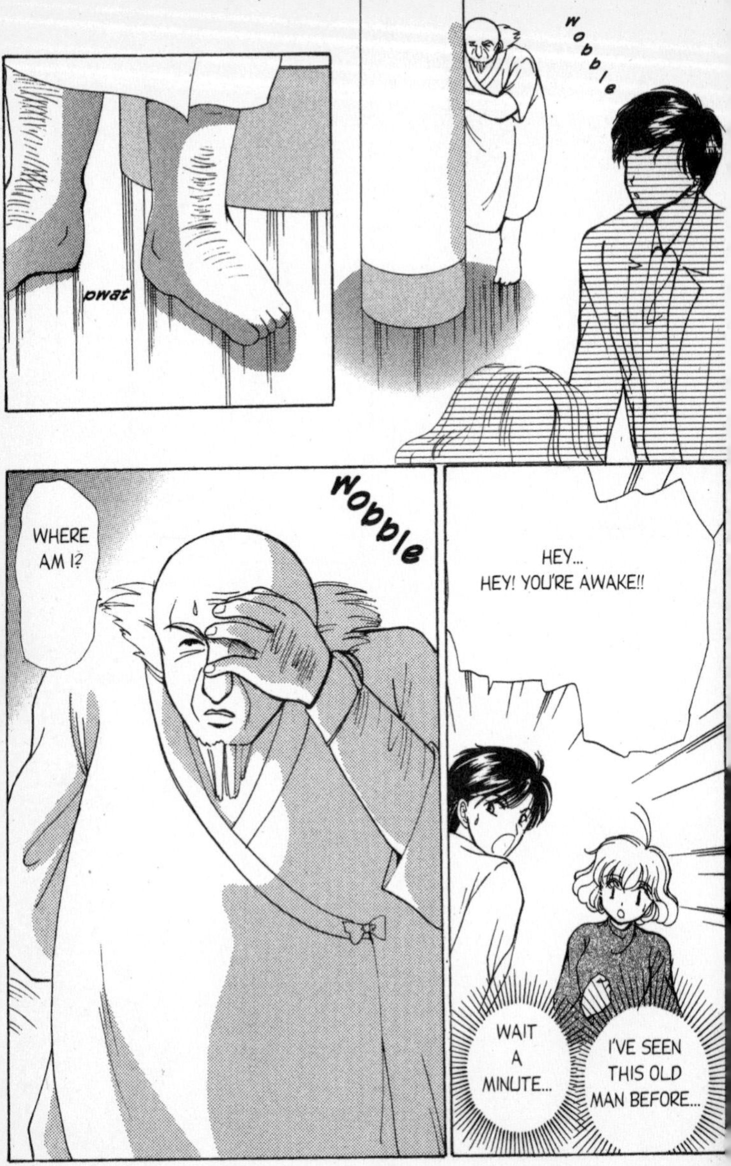
wobble
pwat
HEY...
HEY! YOU'RE AWAKE!!
WAIT A MINUTE...
I'VE SEEN THIS OLD MAN BEFORE...
wobble
WHERE AM I?

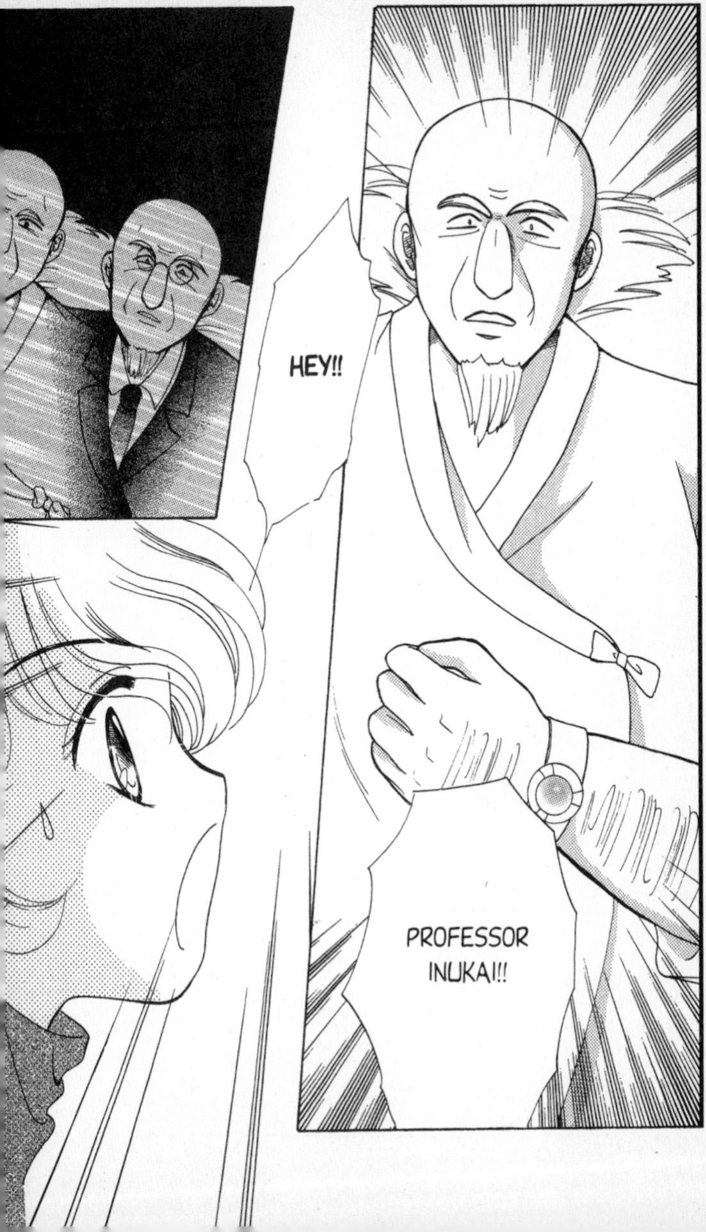
HEY!!
PROFESSOR INUKAI!!

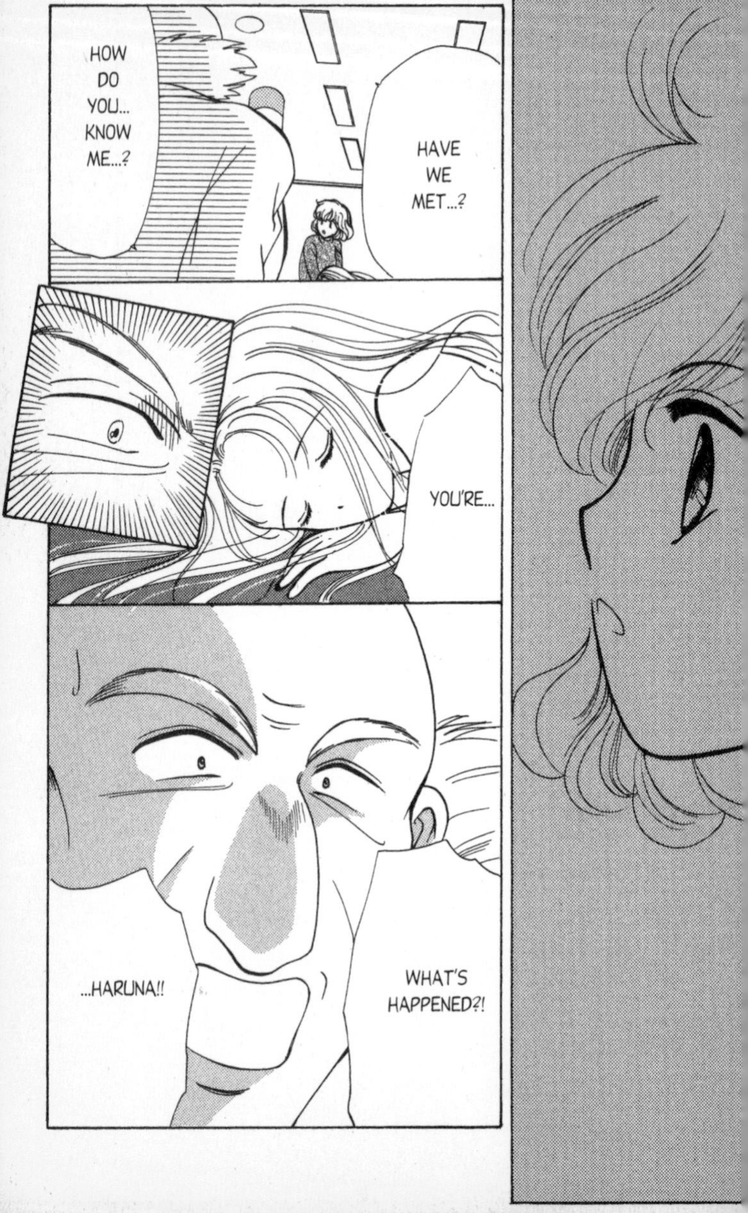
HAVE WE MET...?
HOW DO YOU... KNOW ME...?
YOU'RE...
WHAT'S HAPPENED?!
...HARUNA!!

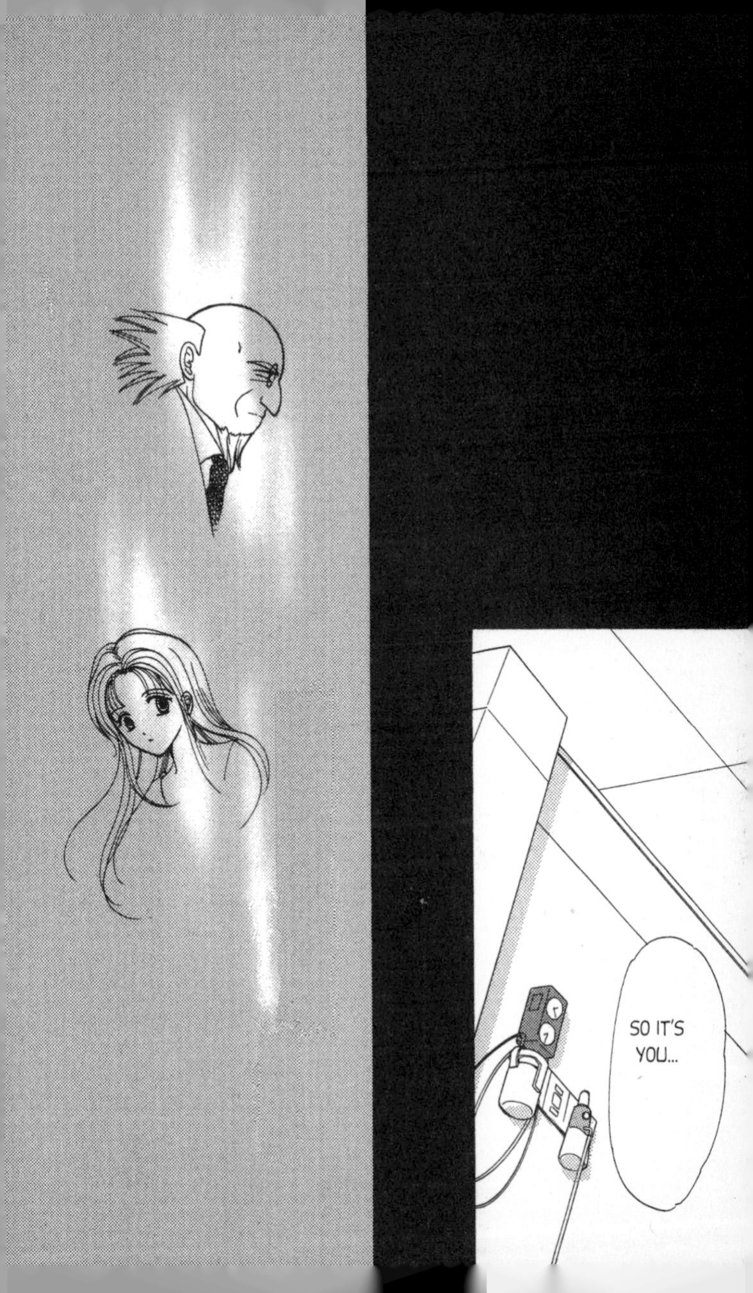
SO IT'S YOU...

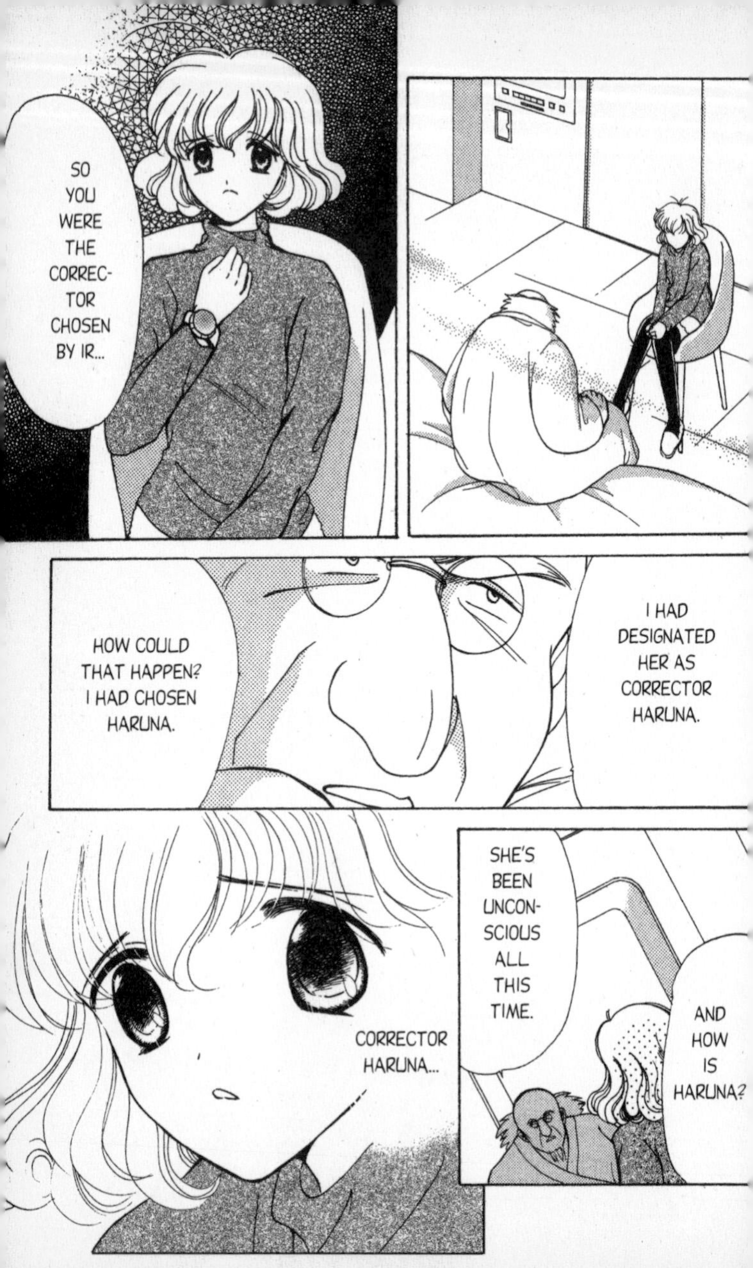
SO YOU WERE THE CORRECTOR CHOSEN BY IR...
I HAD DESIGNATED HER AS CORRECTOR HARUNA.
HOW COULD THAT HAPPEN? I HAD CHOSEN HARUNA.
AND HOW IS HARUNA?
SHE'S BEEN UNCONSCIOUS ALL THIS TIME.
CORRECTOR HARUNA...

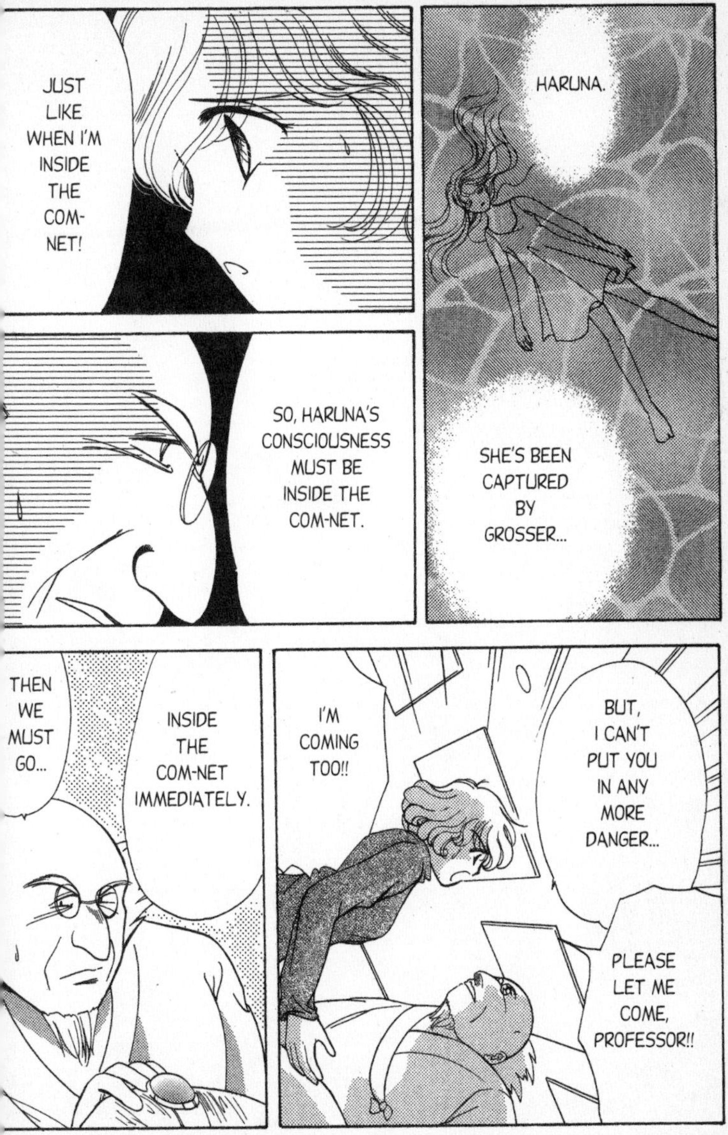
JUST LIKE WHEN I'M INSIDE THE COM-NET!
SO, HARUNA'S CONSCIOUSNESS MUST BE INSIDE THE COM-NET.
HARUNA.
SHE'S BEEN CAPTURED BY GROSSER...
THEN WE MUST GO...
INSIDE THE COM-NET IMMEDIATELY.
I'M COMING TOO!!
BUT, I CAN'T PUT YOU IN ANY MORE DANGER...
PLEASE LET ME COME, PROFESSOR!!

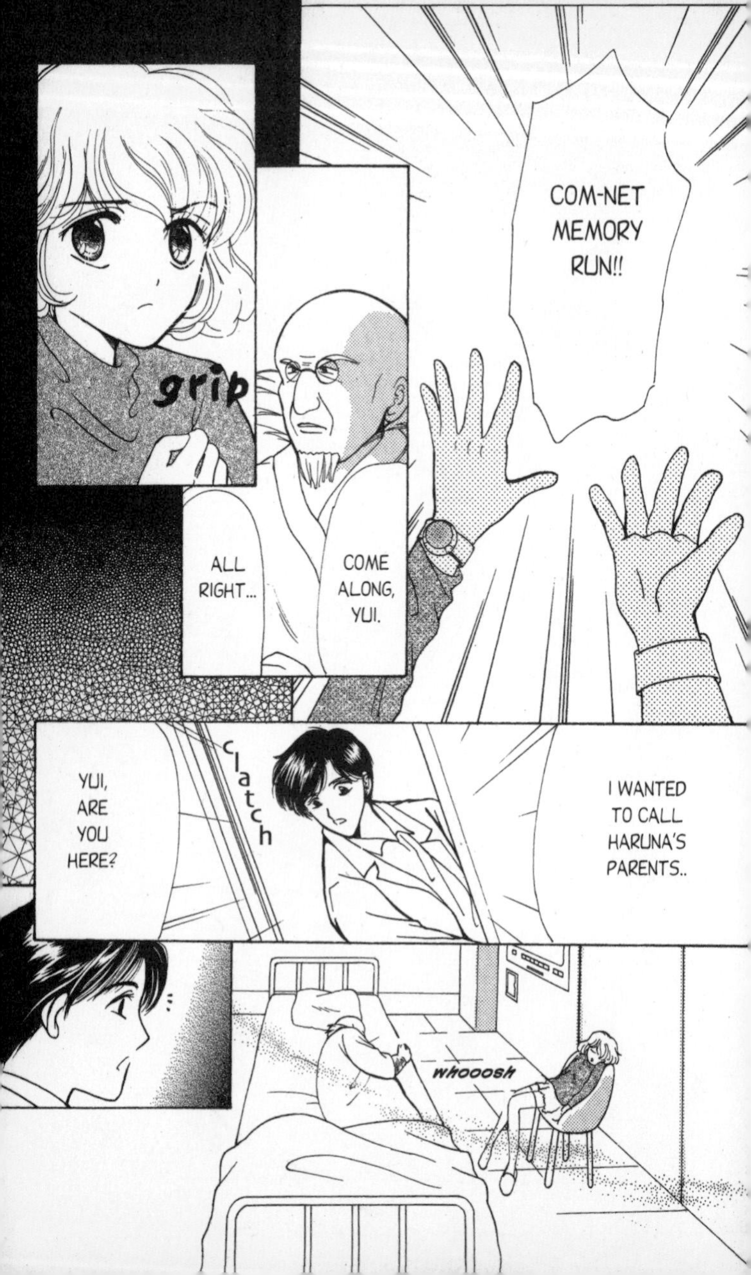
COM-NET MEMORY RUN!!
grip
COME ALONG, YUI.
ALL RIGHT...
I WANTED TO CALL HARUNA'S PARENTS..
clatch
YUI, ARE YOU HERE?
whooosh

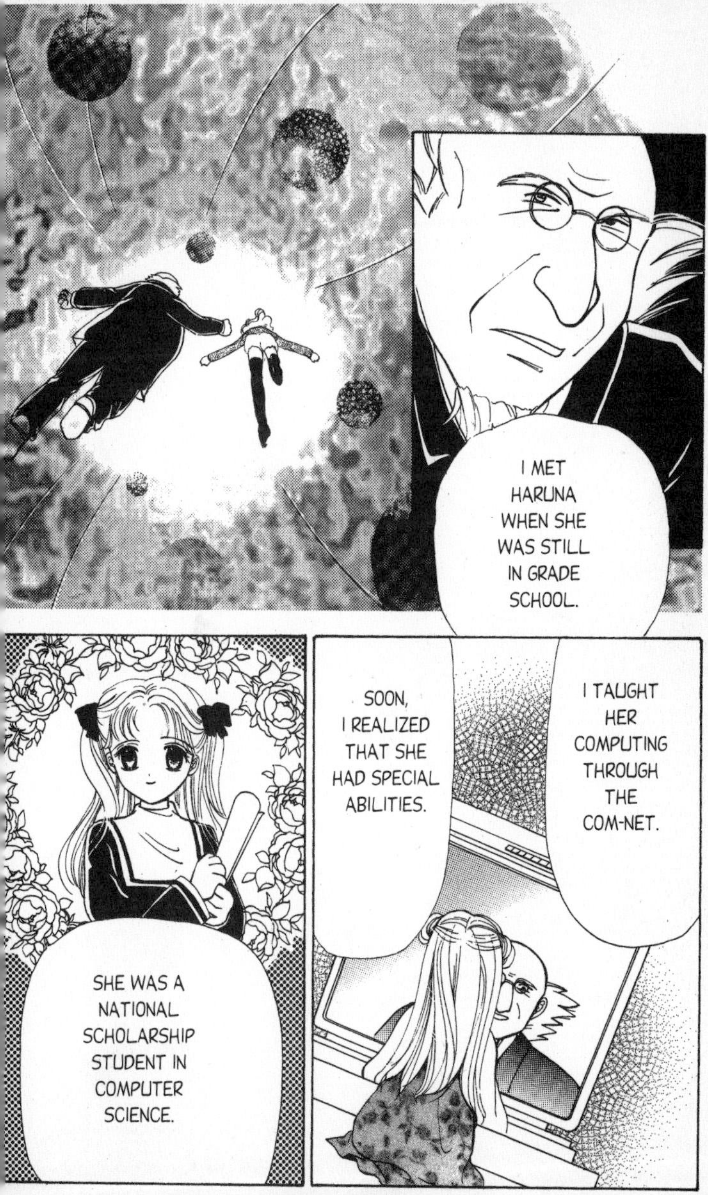
I MET HARUNA WHEN SHE WAS STILL IN GRADE SCHOOL.
I TAUGHT HER COMPUTING THROUGH THE COM-NET.
SOON, I REALIZED THAT SHE HAD SPECIAL ABILITIES.
SHE WAS A NATIONAL SCHOLARSHIP STUDENT IN COMPUTER SCIENCE.

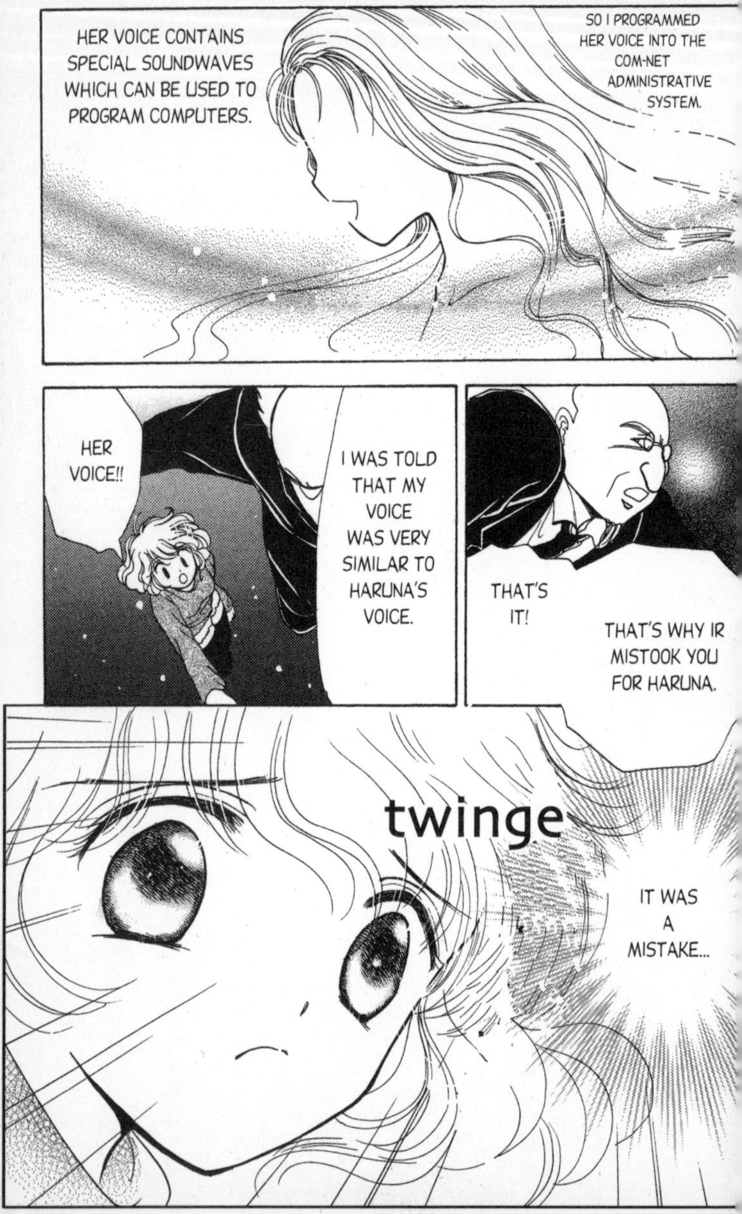
HER VOICE CONTAINS SPECIAL SOUNDWAVES WHICH CAN BE USED TO PROGRAM COMPUTERS.
SO I PROGRAMMED HER VOICE INTO THE COM-NET ADMINISTRATIVE SYSTEM.
HER VOICE!!
I WAS TOLD THAT MY VOICE WAS VERY SIMILAR TO HARUNA'S VOICE.
THAT'S IT!
THAT'S WHY IR MISTOOK YOU FOR HARUNA.
twinge
IT WAS A MISTAKE...

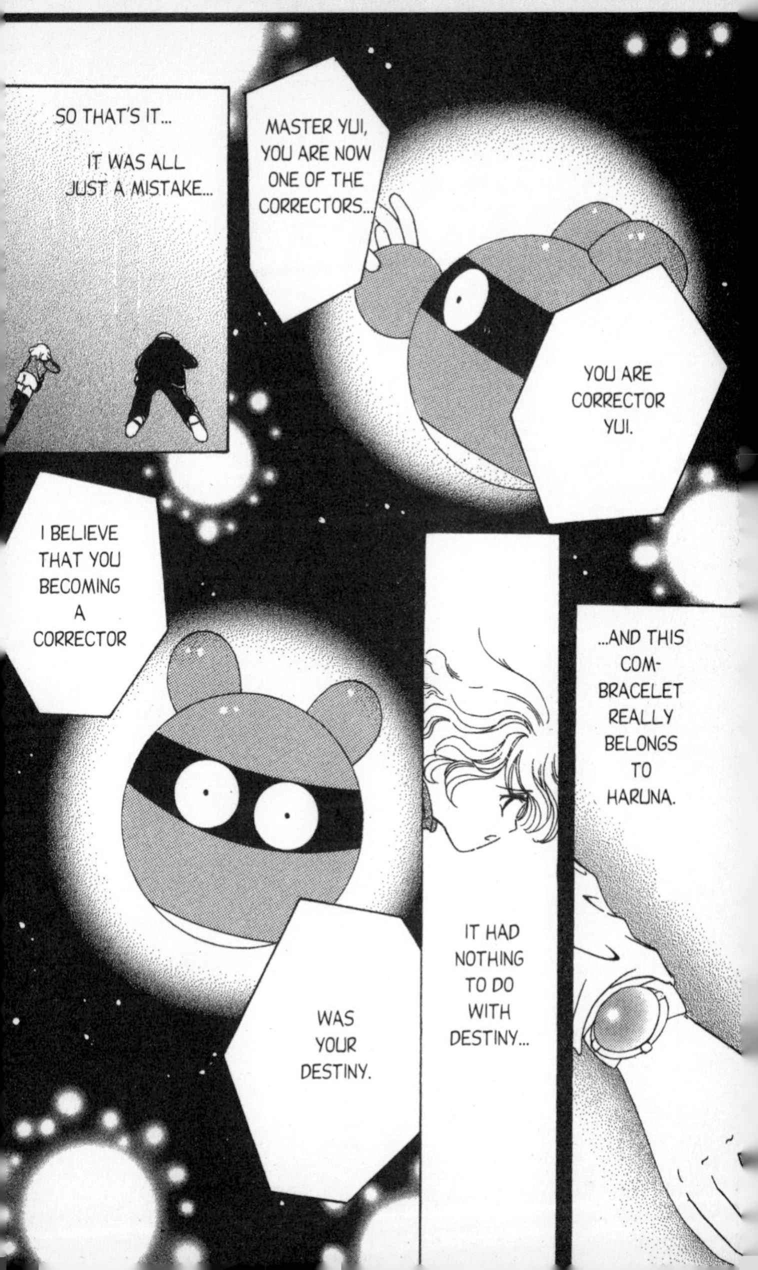
MASTER YUI, YOU ARE NOW ONE OF THE CORRECTORS...
YOU ARE CORRECTOR YUI.
SO THAT'S IT...
IT WAS ALL JUST A MISTAKE...
...AND THIS COM-BRACELET REALLY BELONGS TO HARUNA.
I BELIEVE THAT YOU BECOMING A CORRECTOR
WAS YOUR DESTINY.
IT HAD NOTHING TO DO WITH DESTINY...

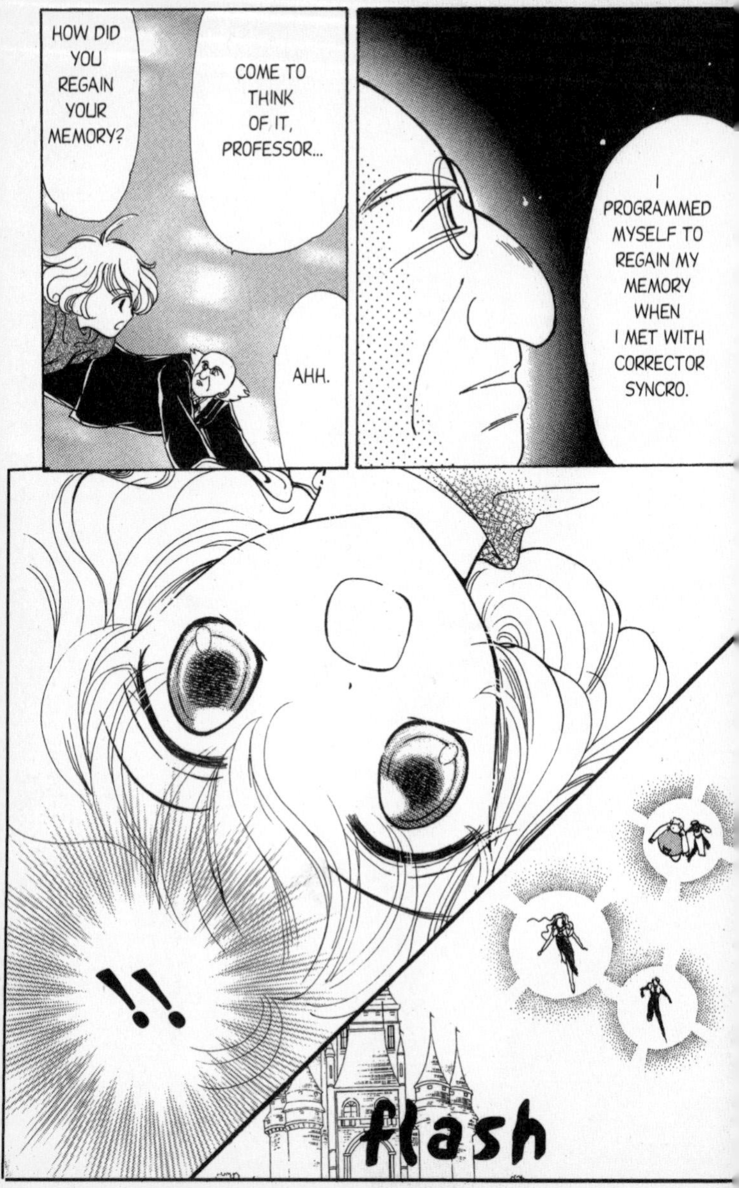
COME TO THINK OF IT, PROFESSOR...
HOW DID YOU REGAIN YOUR MEMORY?
AHH.
I PROGRAMMED MYSELF TO REGAIN MY MEMORY WHEN I MET WITH CORRECTOR SYNCRO.
!!
flash

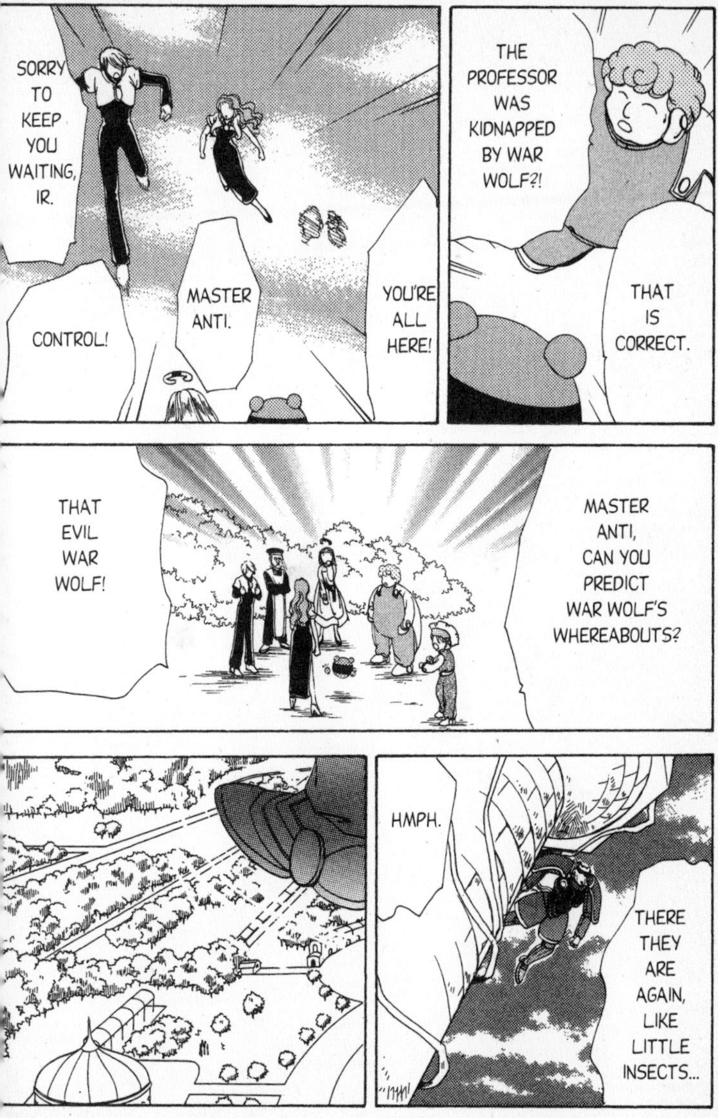
THE PROFESSOR WAS KIDNAPPED BY WAR WOLF?!
THAT IS CORRECT.
YOU'RE ALL HERE!
MASTER ANTI.
SORRY TO KEEP YOU WAITING, IR.
CONTROL!
MASTER ANTI, CAN YOU PREDICT WAR WOLF'S WHEREABOUTS?
THAT EVIL WAR WOLF!
HMPH.
THERE THEY ARE AGAIN, LIKE LITTLE INSECTS...

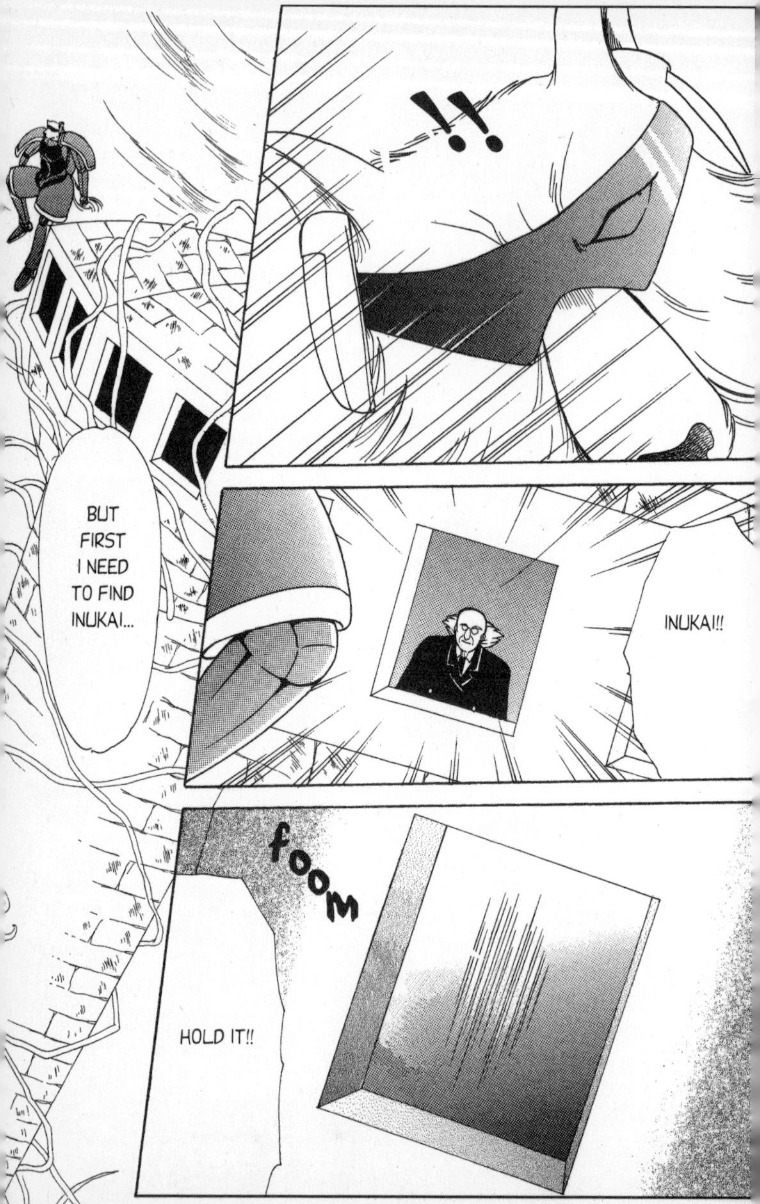
!!
INUKAI!!
BUT FIRST I NEED TO FIND INUKAI...
foom
HOLD IT!!

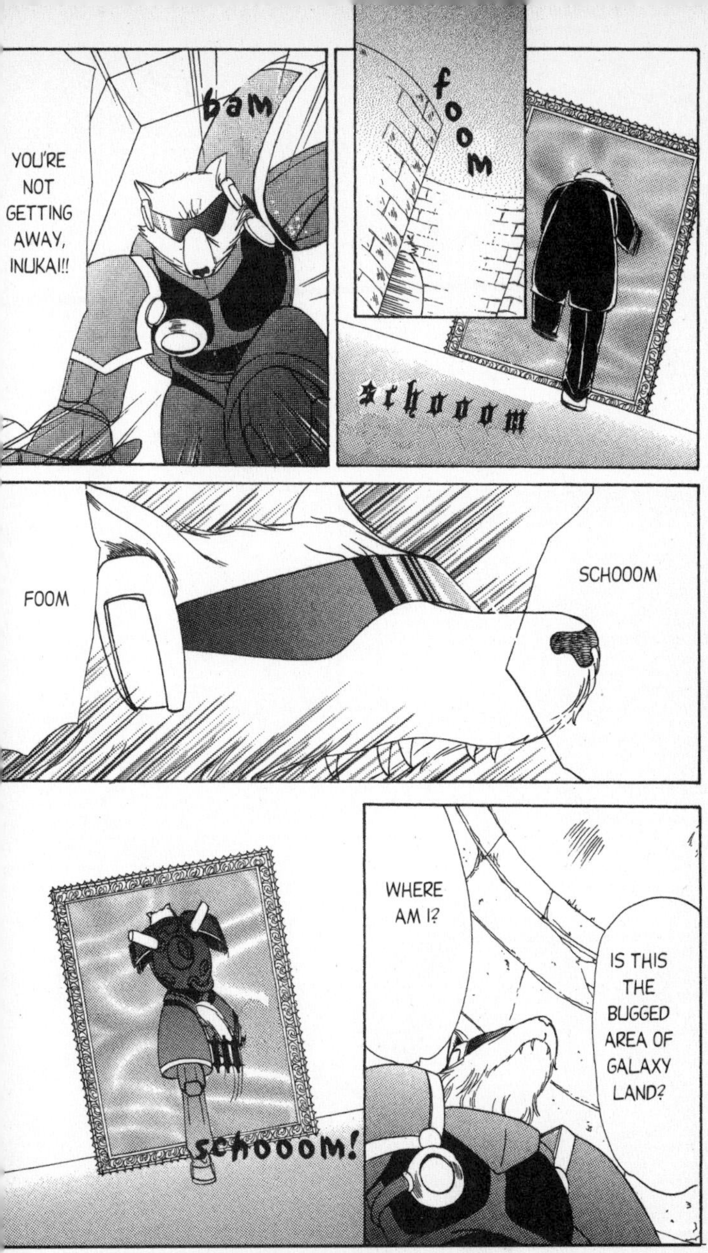
foom
schooom
bam
YOU'RE NOT GETTING AWAY, INUKAI!!
SCHOOOM
FOOM
WHERE AM I?
IS THIS THE BUGGED AREA OF GALAXY LAND?
schoooom!

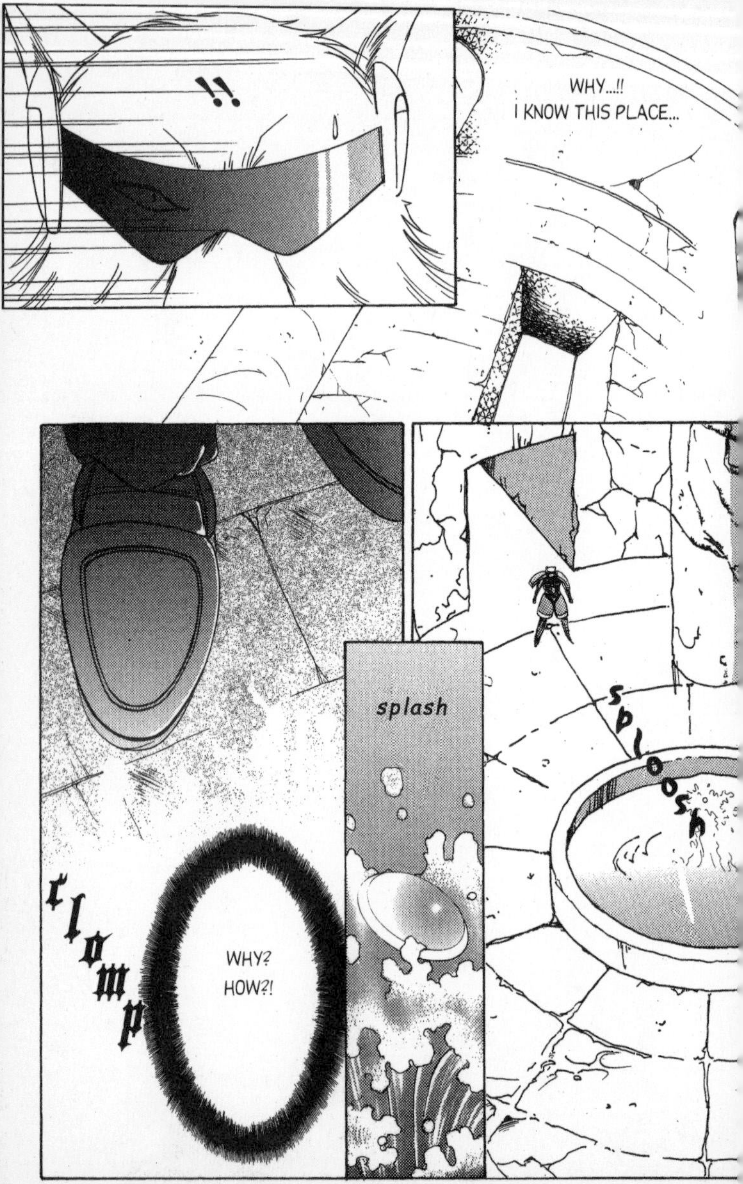
WHY...!! I KNOW THIS PLACE...
!!
sploosh
splash
WHY? HOW?!
clomp

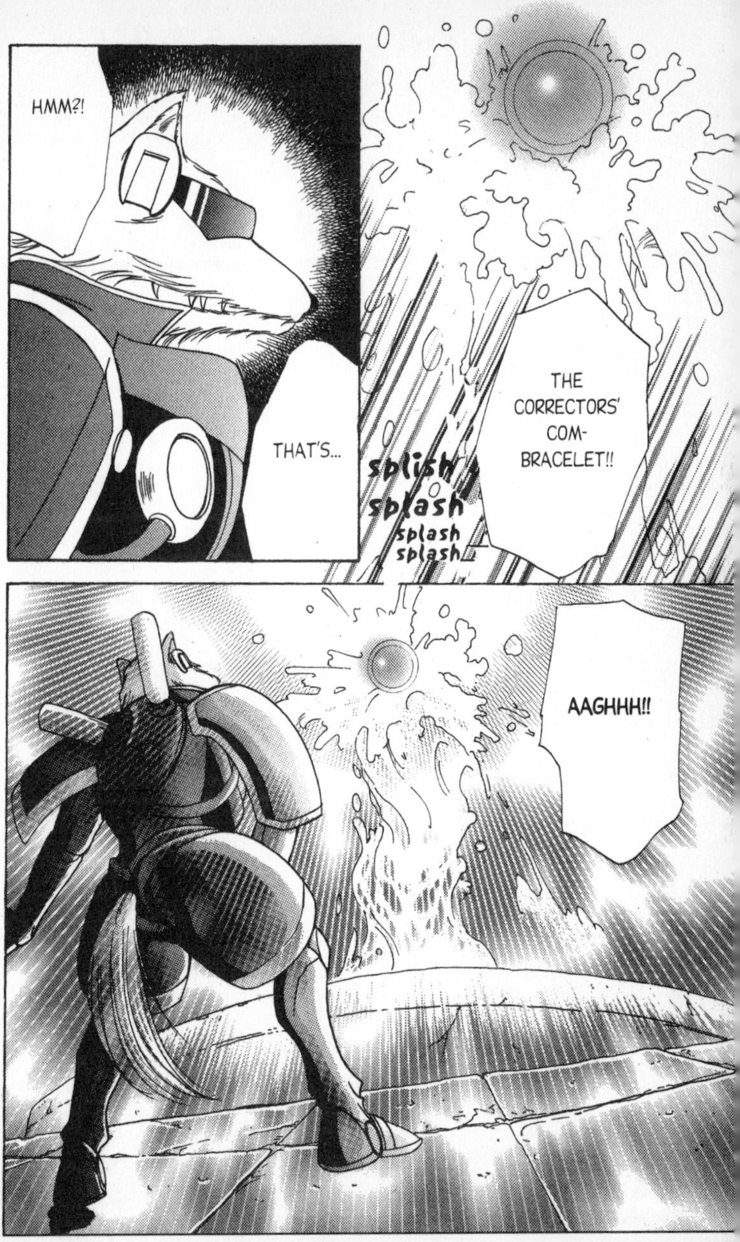
HMM?!
THAT'S...
splish
splash
splash
splash
THE CORRECTORS' COM-BRACELET!!
AAGHHH!!

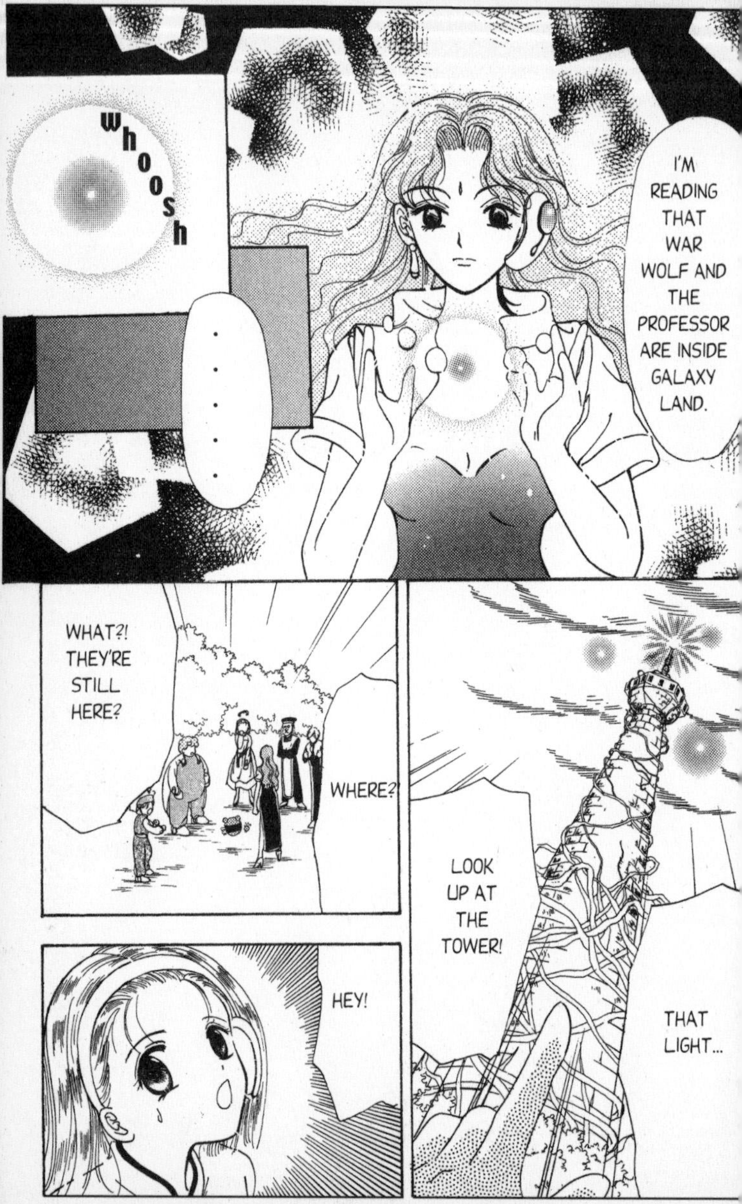
whoosh
......
I'M READING THAT WAR WOLF AND THE PROFESSOR ARE INSIDE GALAXY LAND.
WHAT?! THEY'RE STILL HERE?
WHERE?
HEY!
LOOK UP AT THE TOWER!
THAT LIGHT...

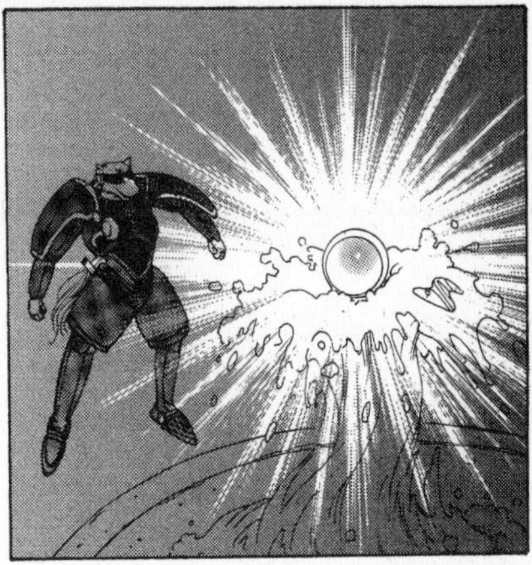

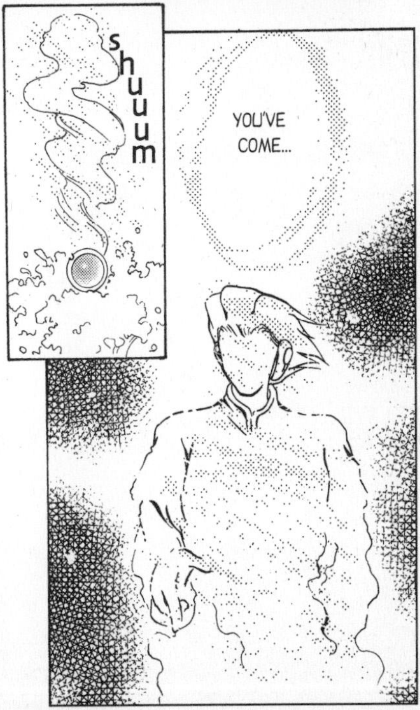
shuuum
YOU'VE COME...

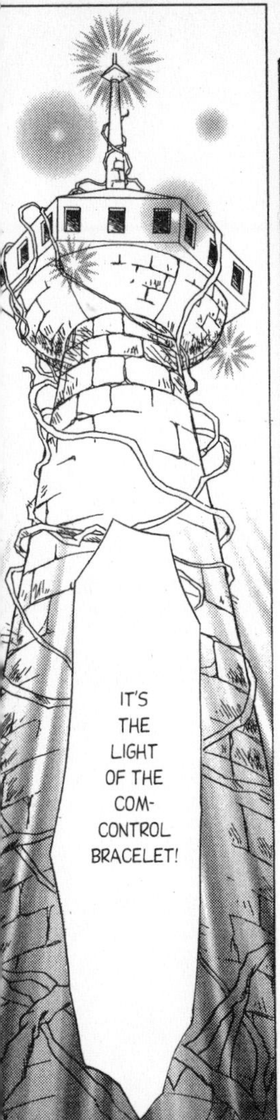
IT'S THE LIGHT OF THE COM-CONTROL BRACELET!

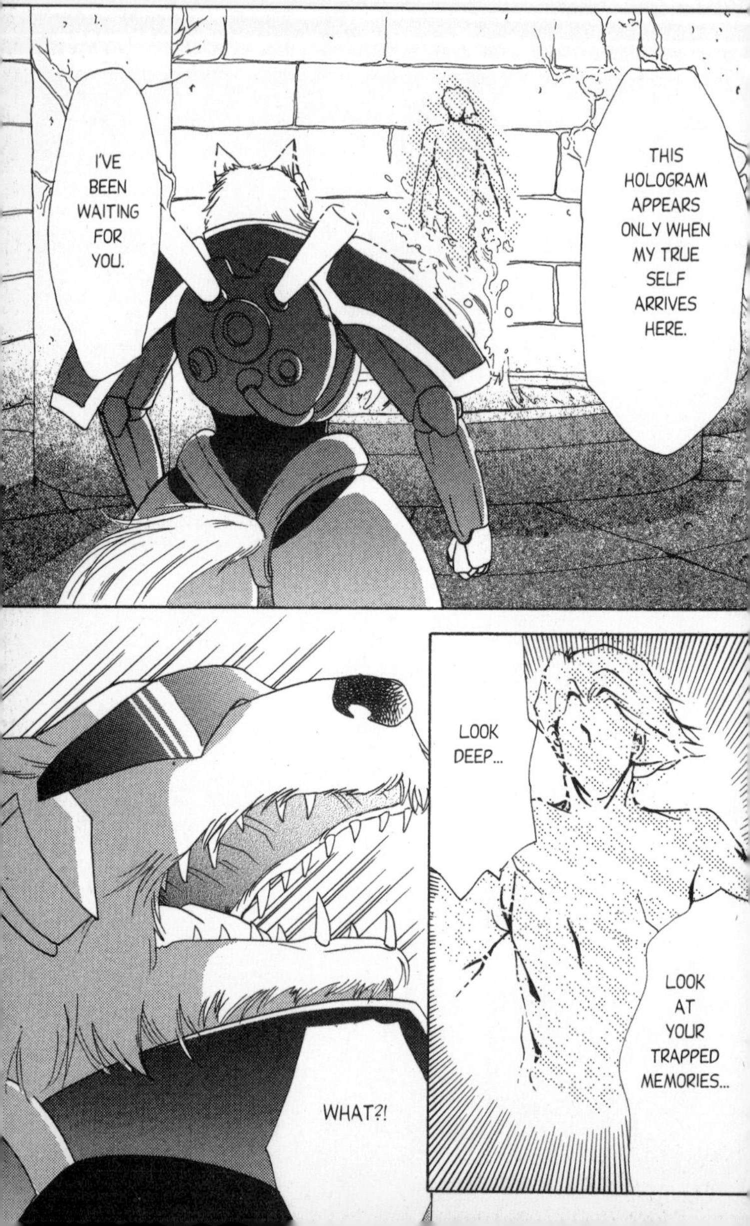
THIS HOLOGRAM APPEARS ONLY WHEN MY TRUE SELF ARRIVES HERE.
I'VE BEEN WAITING FOR YOU.
LOOK DEEP...
LOOK AT YOUR TRAPPED MEMORIES...
WHAT?!

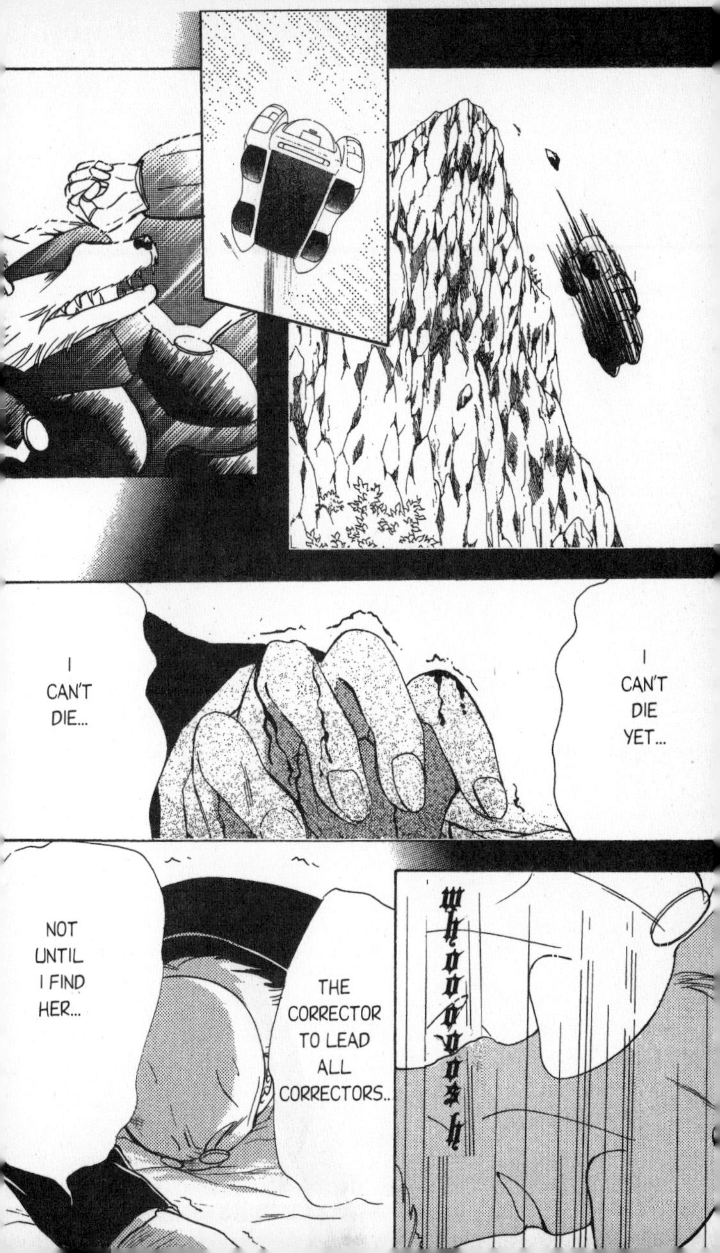
I CAN'T DIE YET...
I CAN'T DIE...
WHOOOOOSH
THE CORRECTOR TO LEAD ALL CORRECTORS..
NOT UNTIL I FIND HER...

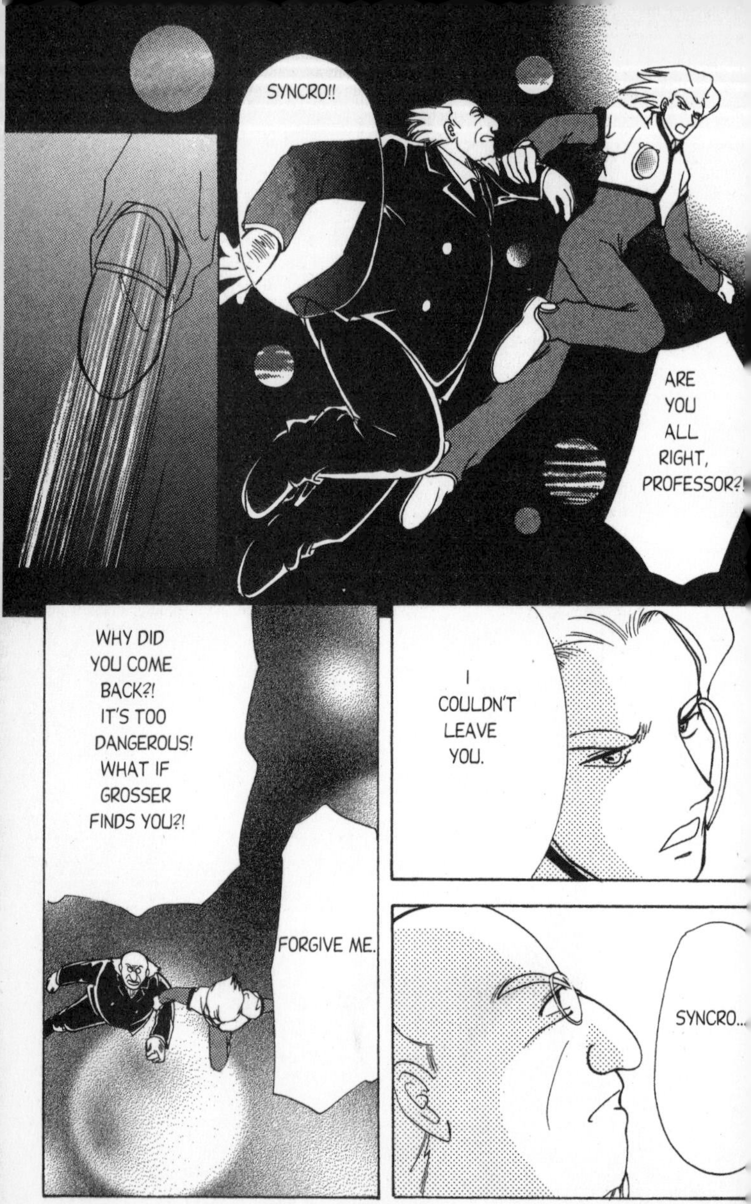
SYNCRO!!
ARE YOU ALL RIGHT, PROFESSOR?!
I COULDN'T LEAVE YOU.
SYNCRO...
WHY DID YOU COME BACK?! IT'S TOO DANGEROUS! WHAT IF GROSSER FINDS YOU?!
FORGIVE ME.

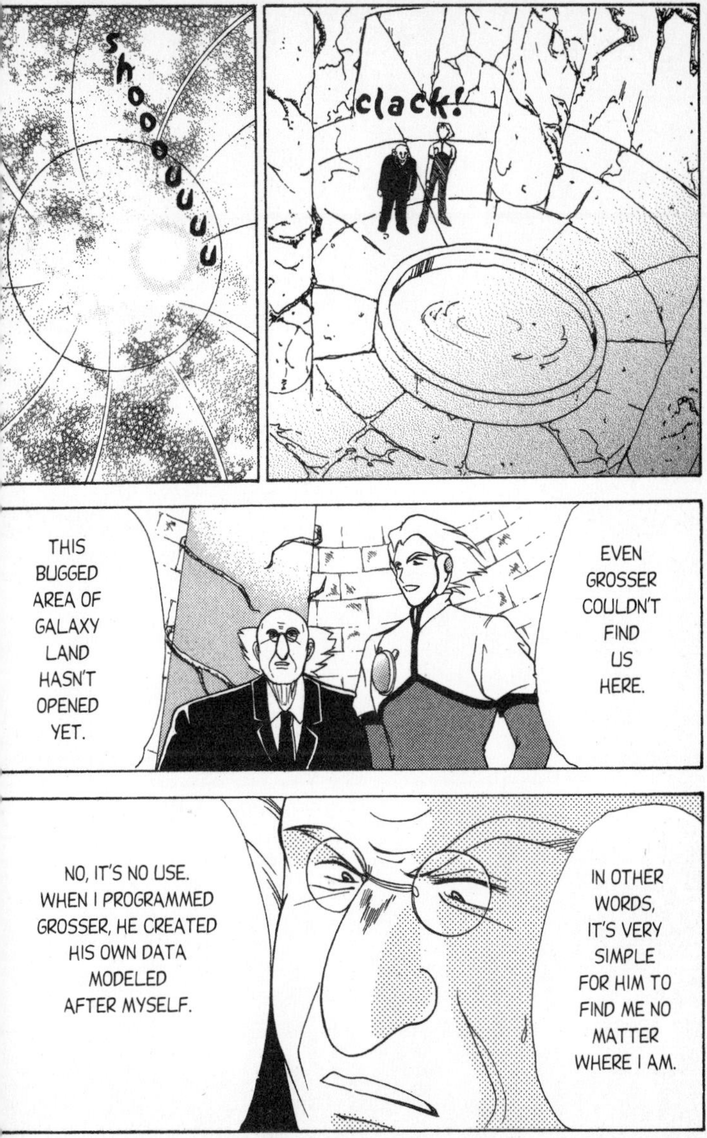
shooouuuu
clack!
THIS BUGGED AREA OF GALAXY LAND HASN'T OPENED YET.
EVEN GROSSER COULDN'T FIND US HERE.
NO, IT'S NO USE. WHEN I PROGRAMMED GROSSER, HE CREATED HIS OWN DATA MODELED AFTER MYSELF.
IN OTHER WORDS, IT'S VERY SIMPLE FOR HIM TO FIND ME NO MATTER WHERE I AM.

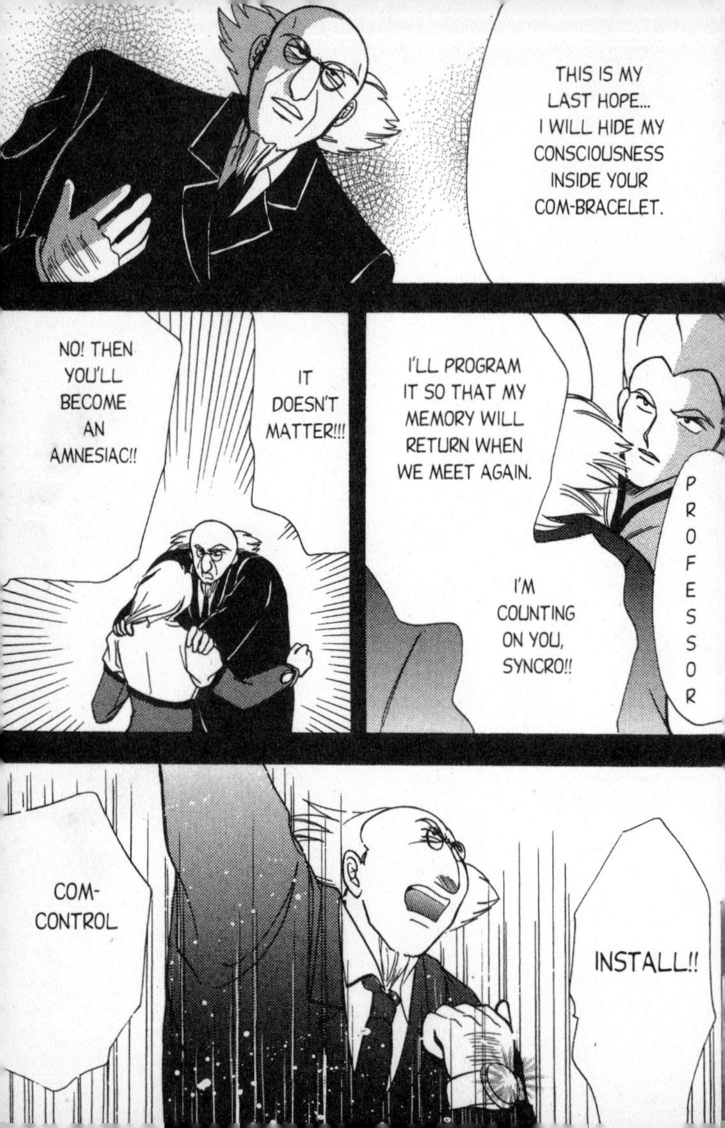
THIS IS MY LAST HOPE... I WILL HIDE MY CONSCIOUSNESS INSIDE YOUR COM-BRACELET.
NO! THEN YOU'LL BECOME AN AMNESIAC!!
IT DOESN'T MATTER!!!
I'LL PROGRAM IT SO THAT MY MEMORY WILL RETURN WHEN WE MEET AGAIN.
I'M COUNTING ON YOU, SYNCRO!!
PROFESSOR
COM-CONTROL
INSTALL!!

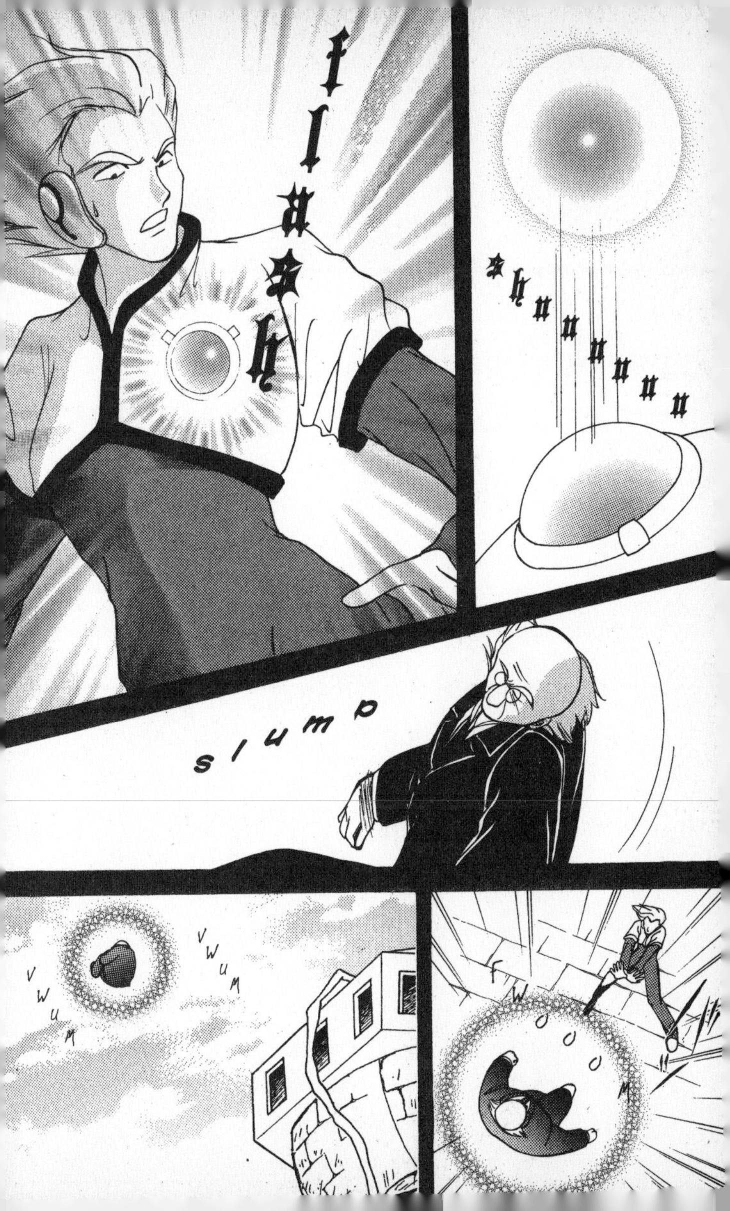
shuuuuuu
flash
slump
fwooooom
vwum
vwum

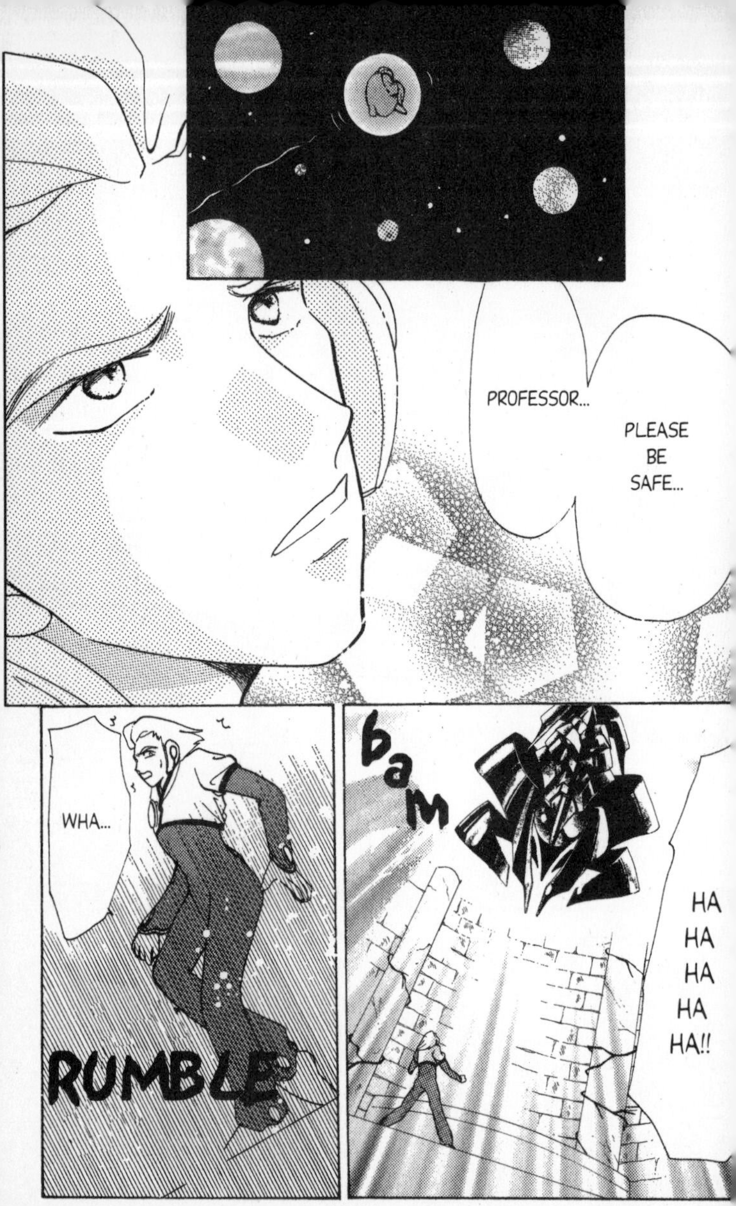
PROFESSOR...
PLEASE BE SAFE...
bam
HA HA HA HA HA!!
WHA...
RUMBLE

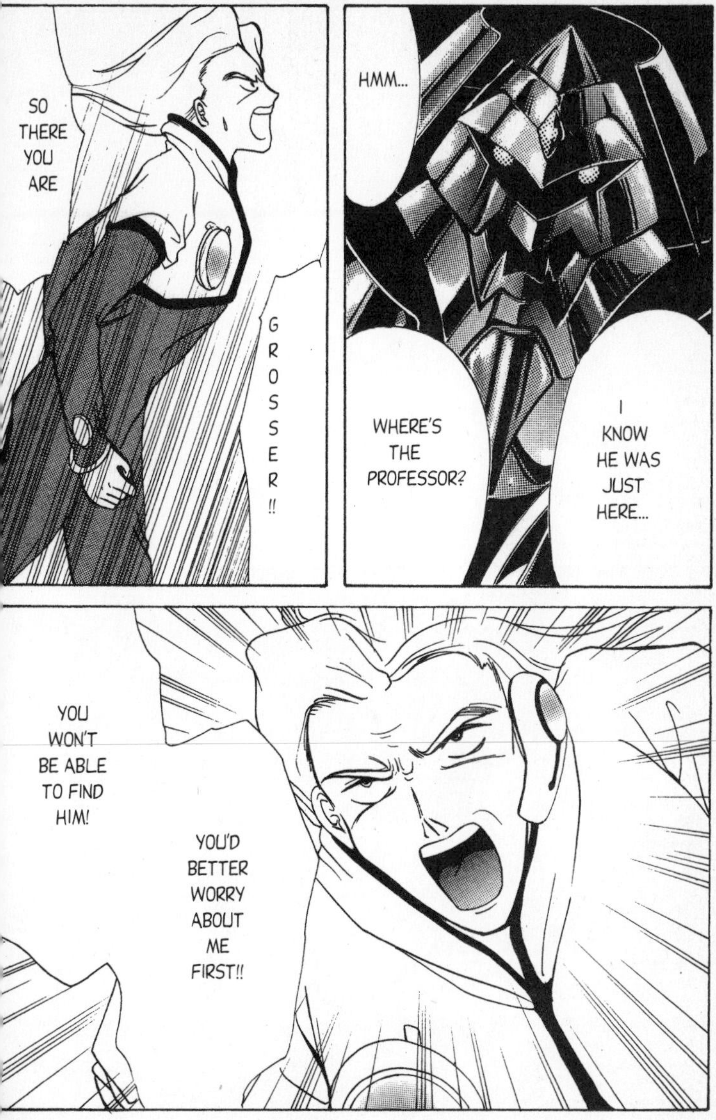
HMM...
I KNOW HE WAS JUST HERE...
WHERE'S THE PROFESSOR?
SO THERE YOU ARE
GROSSER!!
YOU WON'T BE ABLE TO FIND HIM!
YOU'D BETTER WORRY ABOUT ME FIRST!!

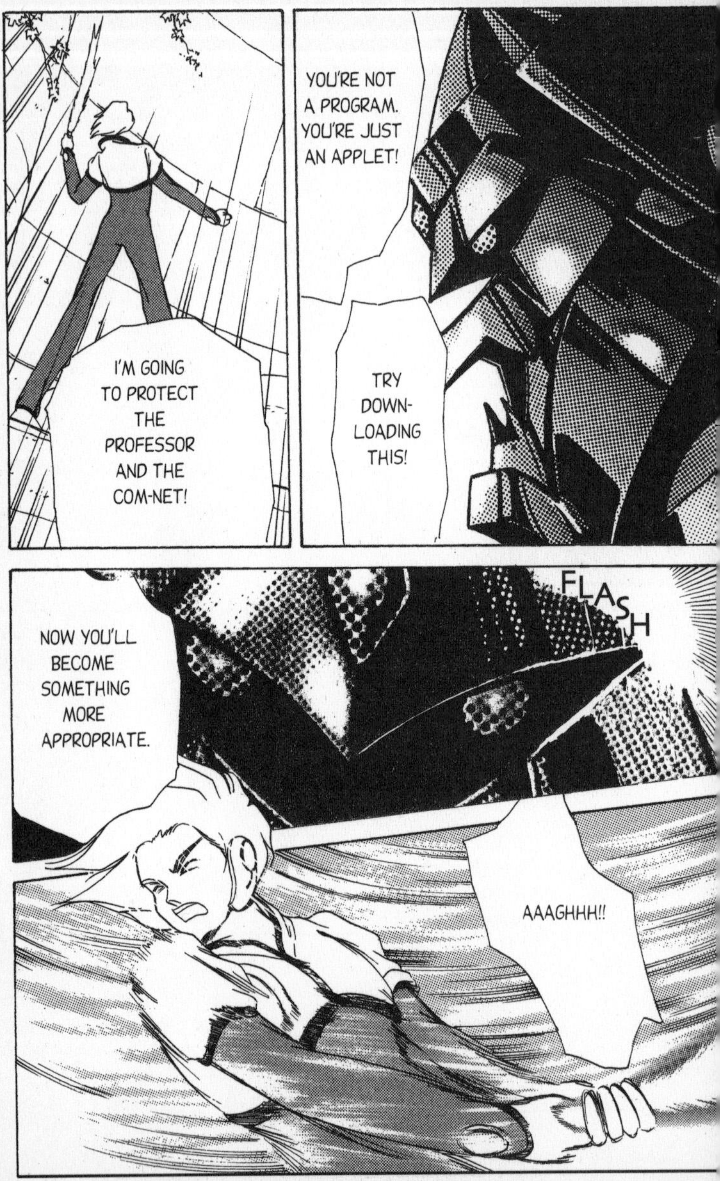
I'M GOING TO PROTECT THE PROFESSOR AND THE COM-NET!
YOU'RE NOT A PROGRAM. YOU'RE JUST AN APPLET!
TRY DOWN-LOADING THIS!
NOW YOU'LL BECOME SOMETHING MORE APPROPRIATE.
FLASH
AAAGHHH!!

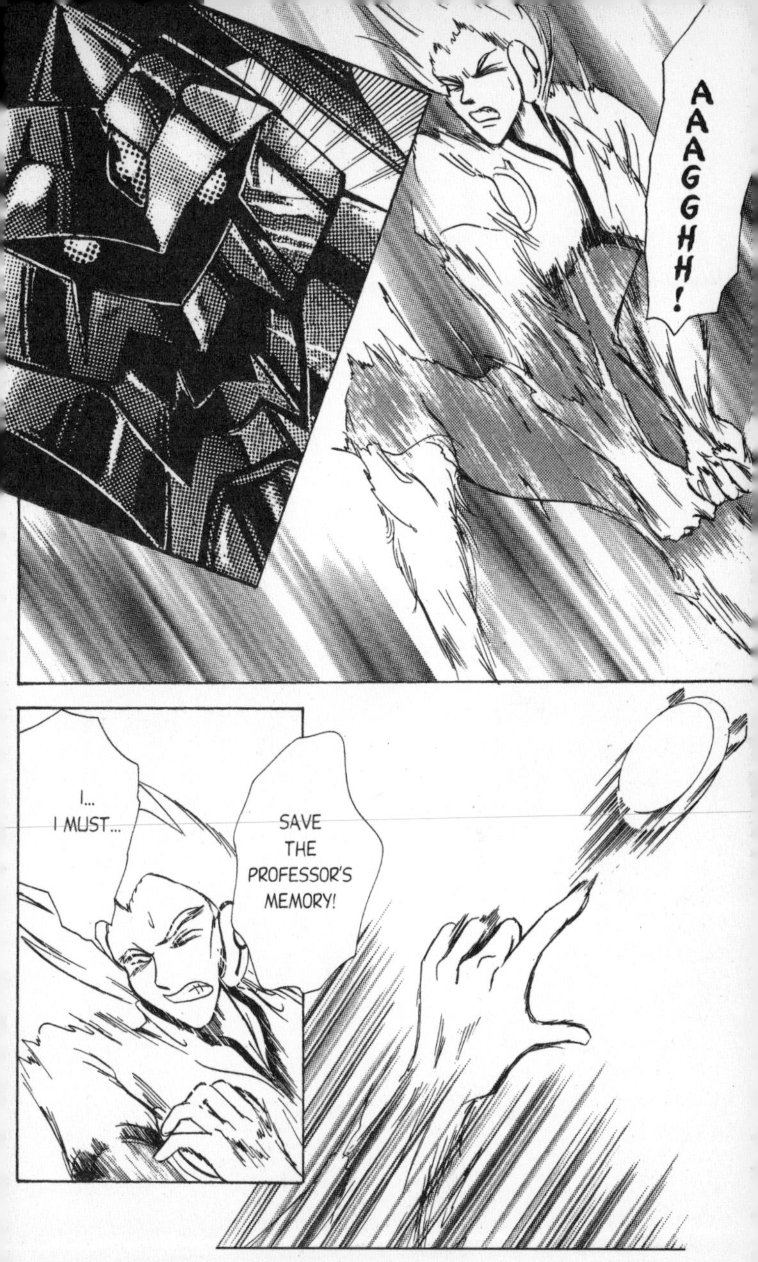
AAAGGHH!
I... I MUST...
SAVE THE PROFESSOR'S MEMORY!

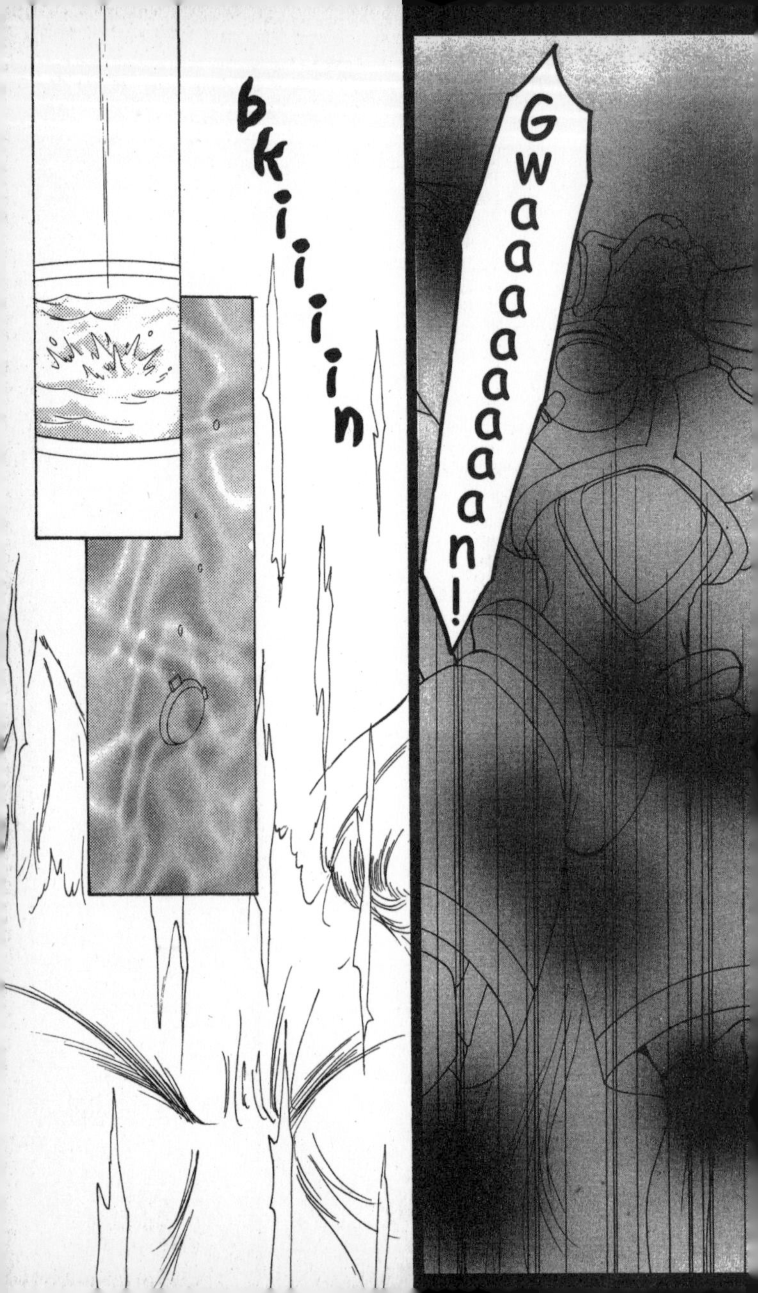
Gwaaaaaaaaan!
bkiiiin

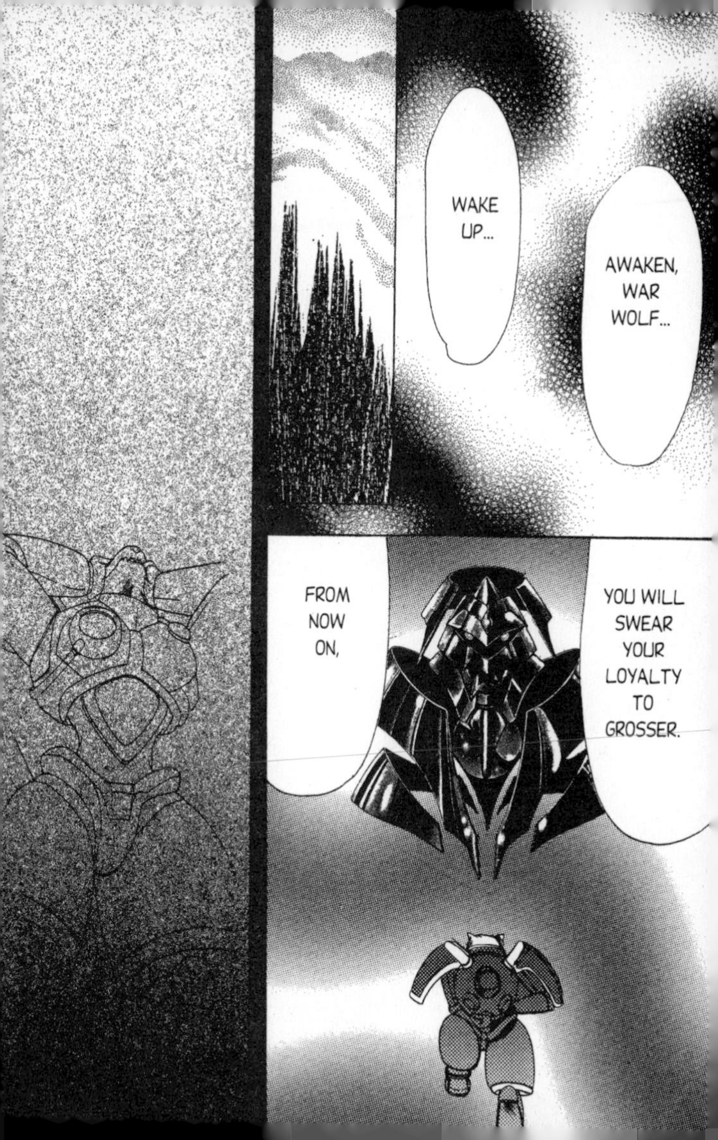
AWAKEN, WAR WOLF...
WAKE UP...
YOU WILL SWEAR YOUR LOYALTY TO GROSSER.
FROM NOW ON,

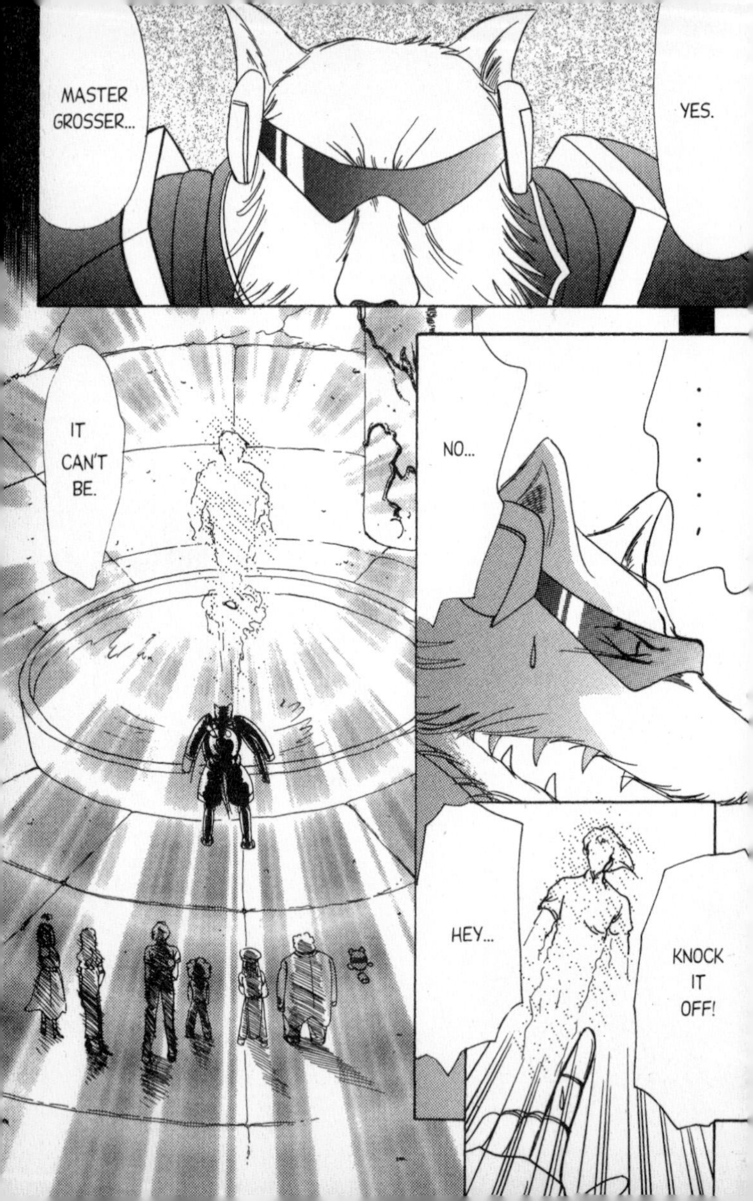
MASTER GROSSER...
YES.
IT CAN'T BE.
NO...
. . . . .
HEY...
KNOCK IT OFF!

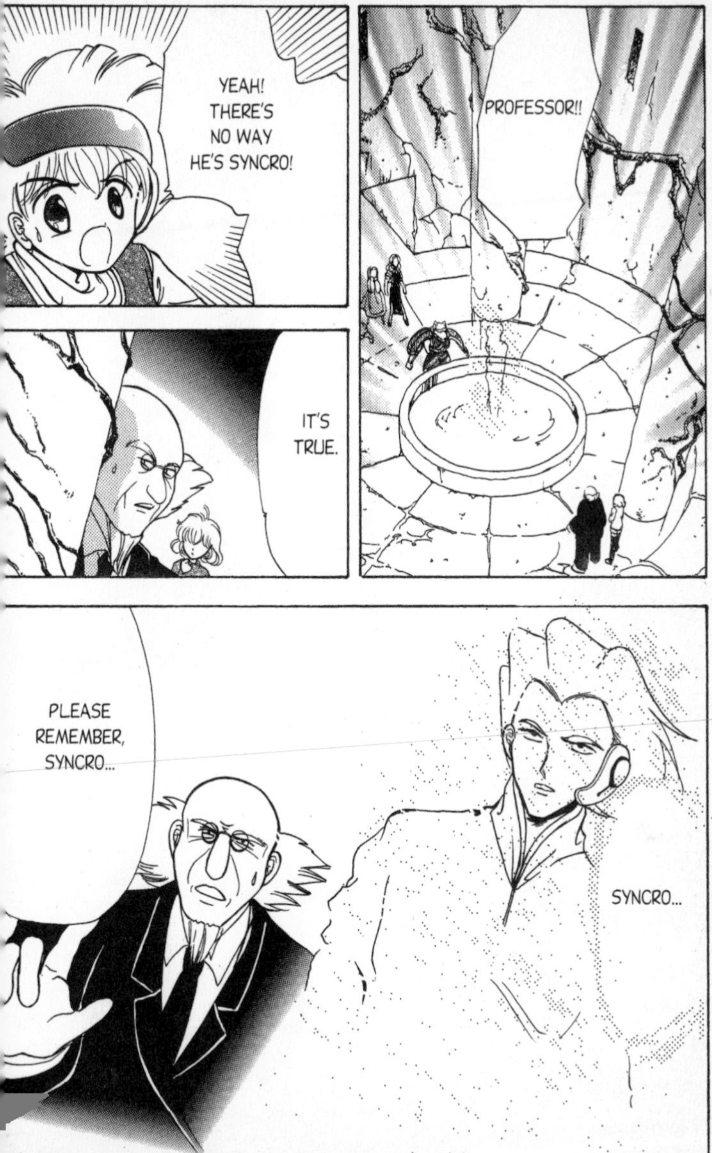
PROFESSOR!!
YEAH! THERE'S NO WAY HE'S SYNCRO!
IT'S TRUE.
PLEASE REMEMBER, SYNCRO...
SYNCRO...

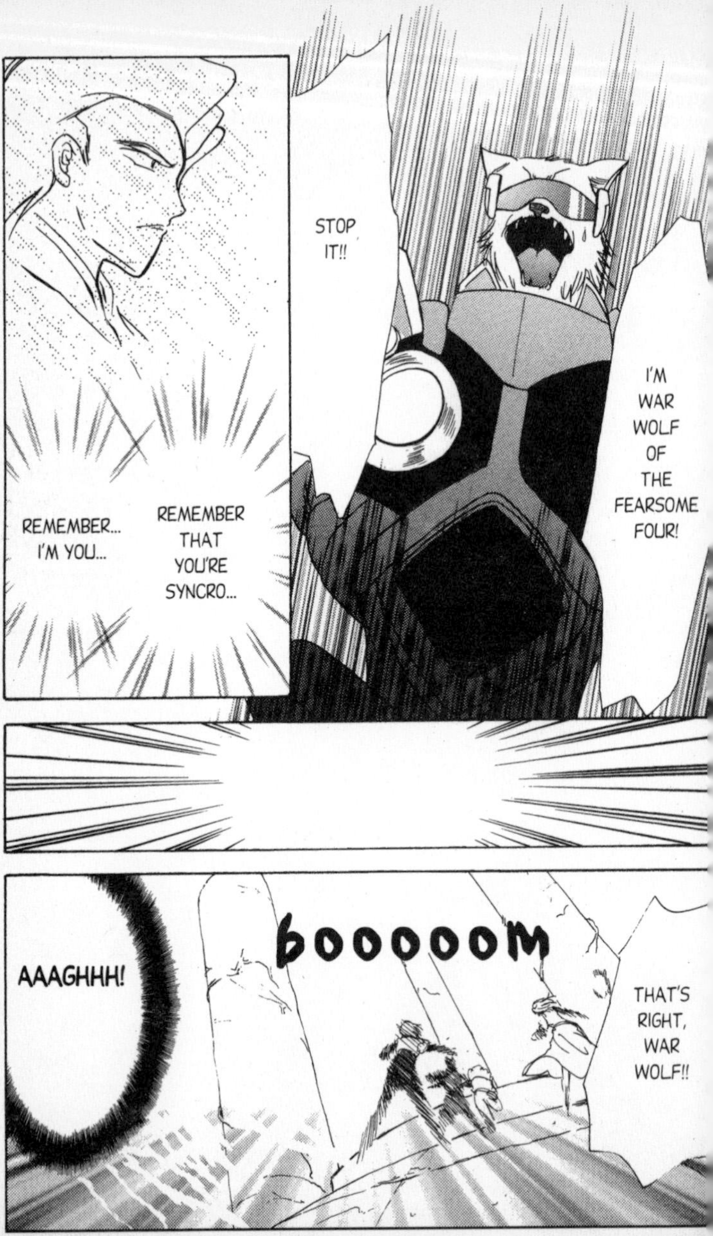
STOP IT!!
I'M WAR WOLF OF THE FEARSOME FOUR!
REMEMBER THAT YOU'RE SYNCRO...
REMEMBER... I'M YOU...
THAT'S RIGHT, WAR WOLF!!
booooom
AAAGHHH!

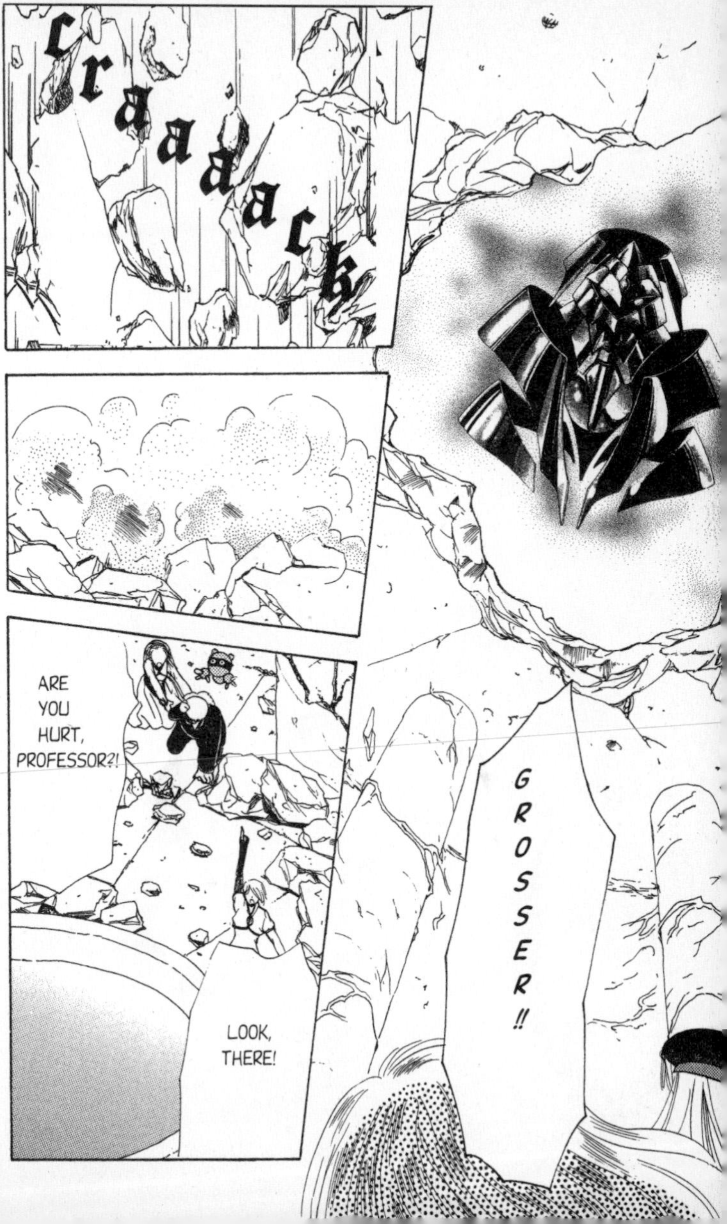
GROSSER!!
craaaack
ARE YOU HURT, PROFESSOR?!
LOOK, THERE!

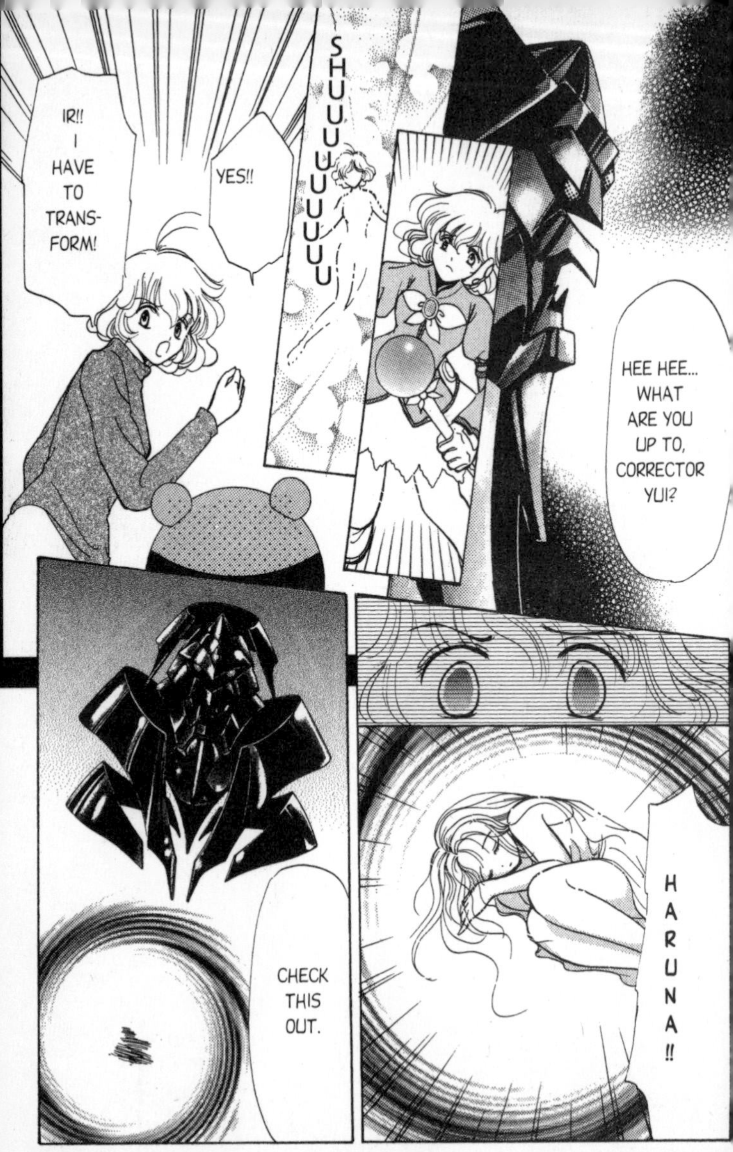
IR!! I HAVE TO TRANS-FORM!
YES!!
SHUUUUUUUUU
HEE HEE... WHAT ARE YOU UP TO, CORRECTOR YUI?
CHECK THIS OUT.
HARUNA!!

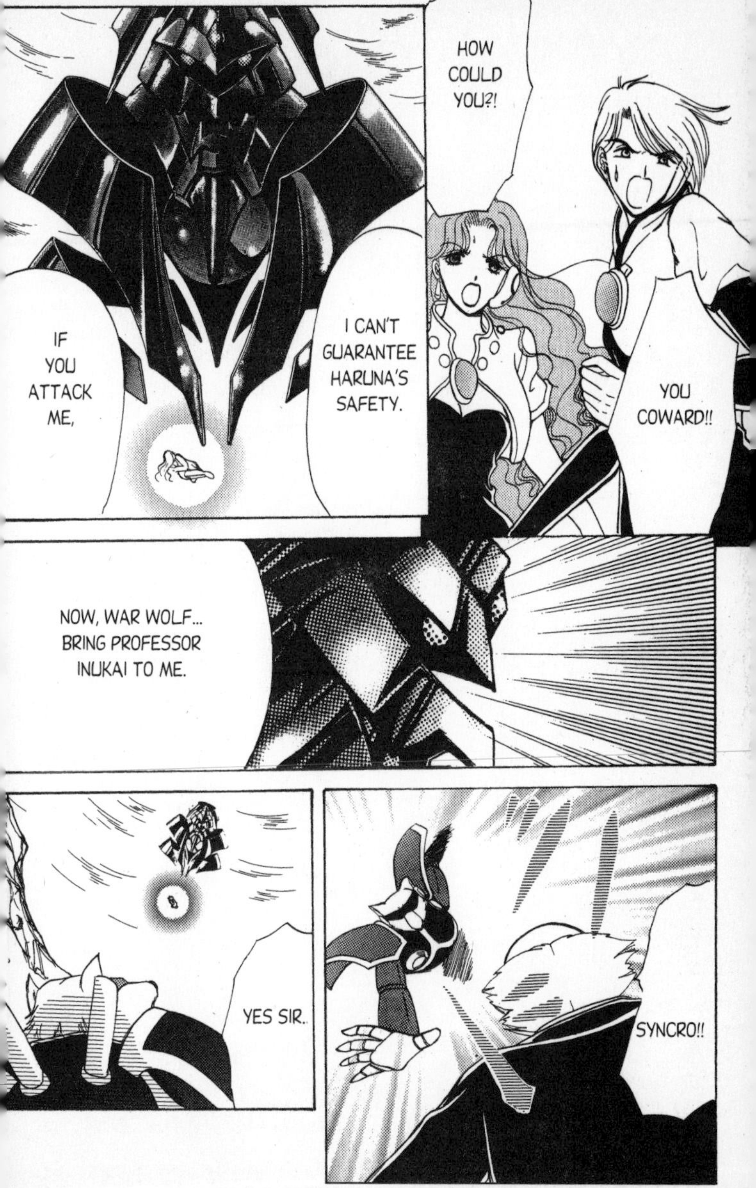
HOW COULD YOU?!
YOU COWARD!!
I CAN'T GUARANTEE HARUNA'S SAFETY.
IF YOU ATTACK ME,
NOW, WAR WOLF... BRING PROFESSOR INUKAI TO ME.
SYNCRO!!
YES SIR.

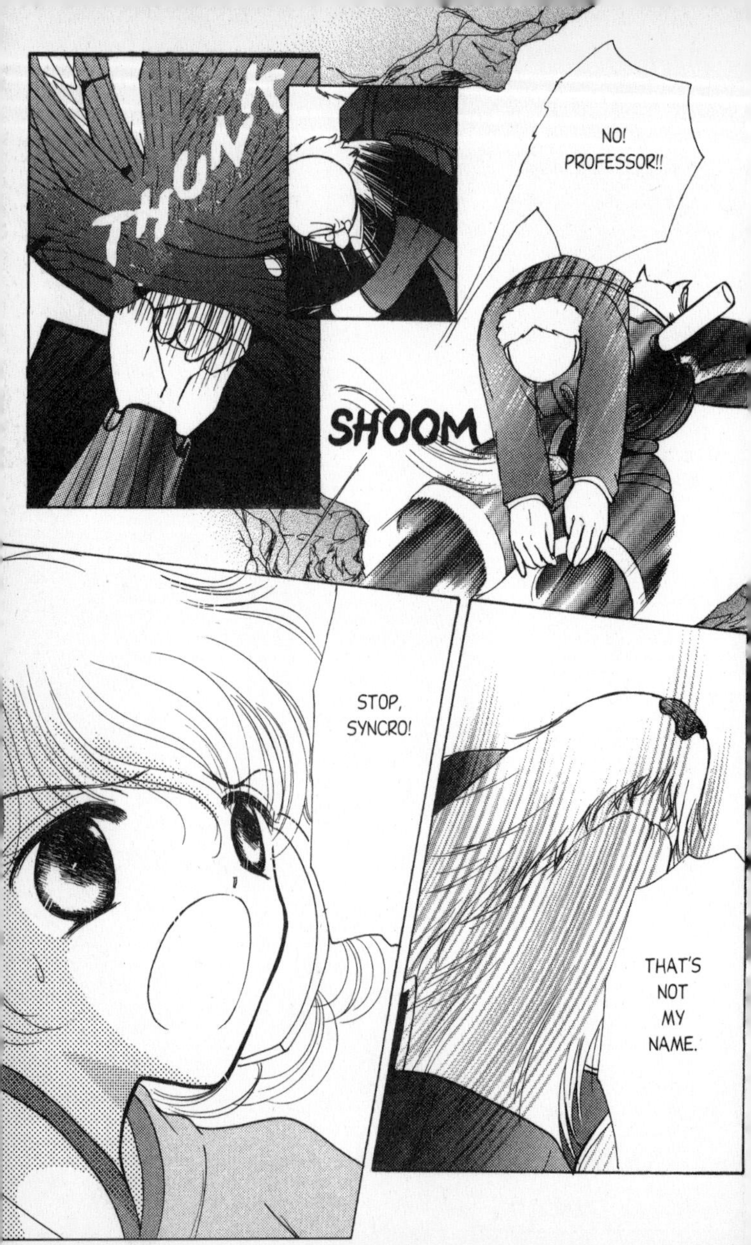
THUNK
NO! PROFESSOR!!
SHOOM
STOP, SYNCRO!
THAT'S NOT MY NAME.

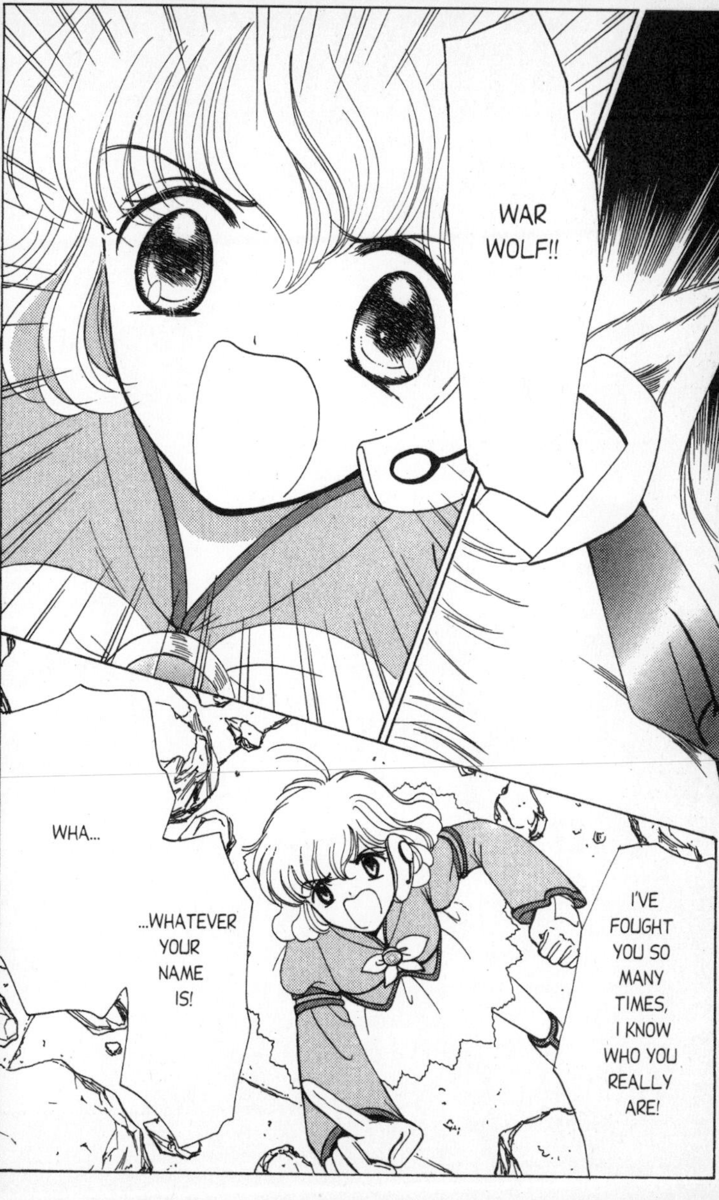
WAR WOLF!!
I'VE FOUGHT YOU SO MANY TIMES, I KNOW WHO YOU REALLY ARE!
...WHATEVER YOUR NAME IS!
WHA...

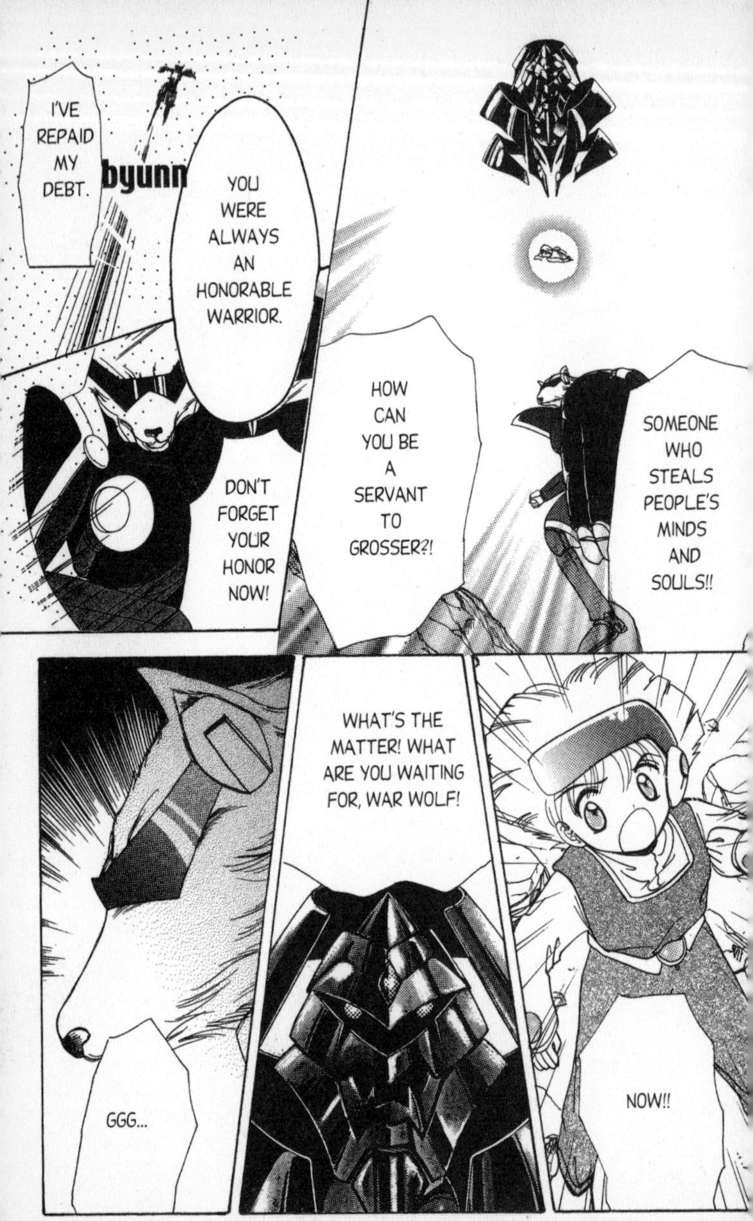
SOMEONE WHO STEALS PEOPLE'S MINDS AND SOULS!!
HOW CAN YOU BE A SERVANT TO GROSSER?!
YOU WERE ALWAYS AN HONORABLE WARRIOR.
DON'T FORGET YOUR HONOR NOW!
byunn
I'VE REPAID MY DEBT.
NOW!!
WHAT'S THE MATTER! WHAT ARE YOU WAITING FOR, WAR WOLF!
GGG...

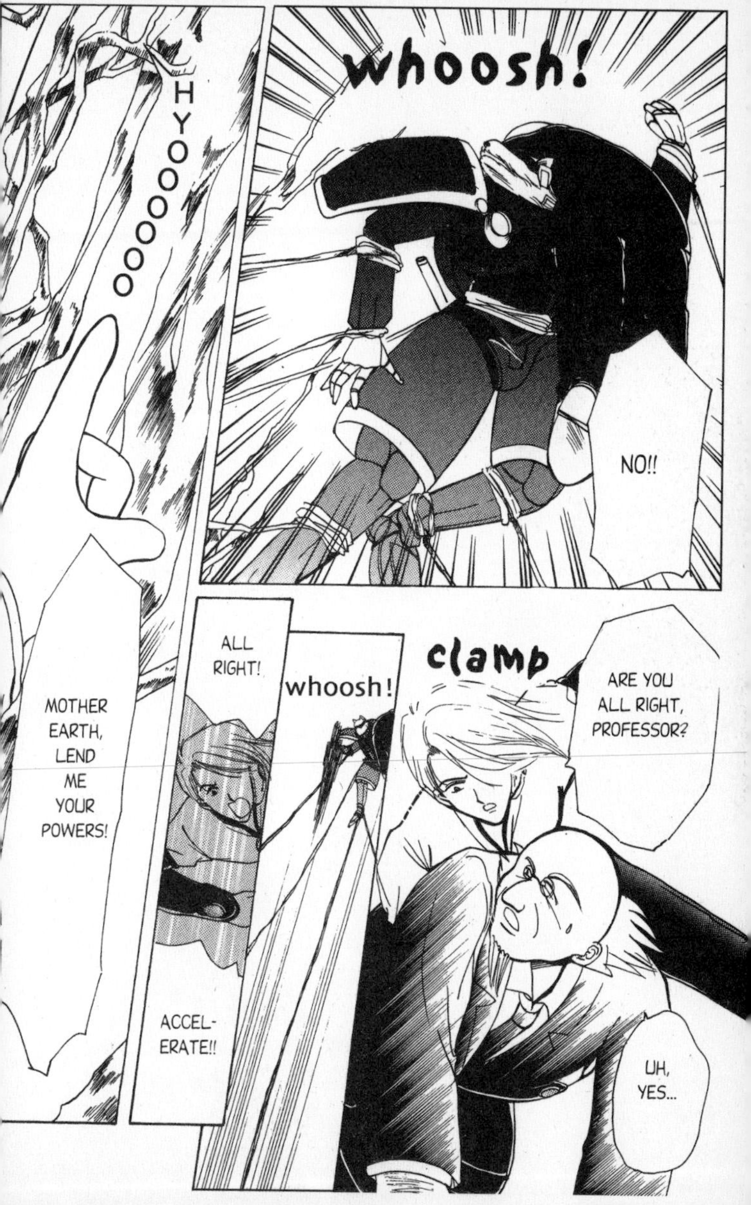
whoosh!
NO!!
clamp
ARE YOU ALL RIGHT, PROFESSOR?
UH, YES...
whoosh!
ALL RIGHT!
ACCEL-ERATE!!
HYOOOOOO
MOTHER EARTH, LEND ME YOUR POWERS!

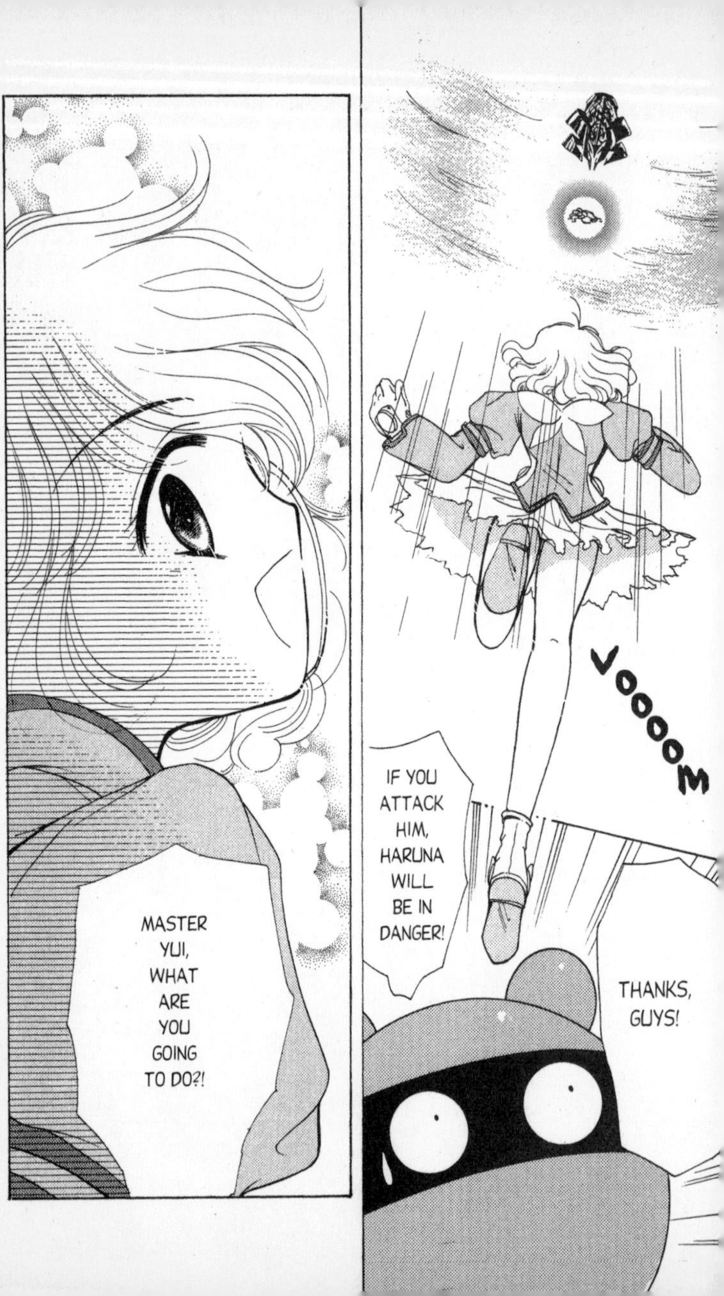
VOOOOM
IF YOU ATTACK HIM, HARUNA WILL BE IN DANGER!
THANKS, GUYS!
MASTER YUI, WHAT ARE YOU GOING TO DO?!

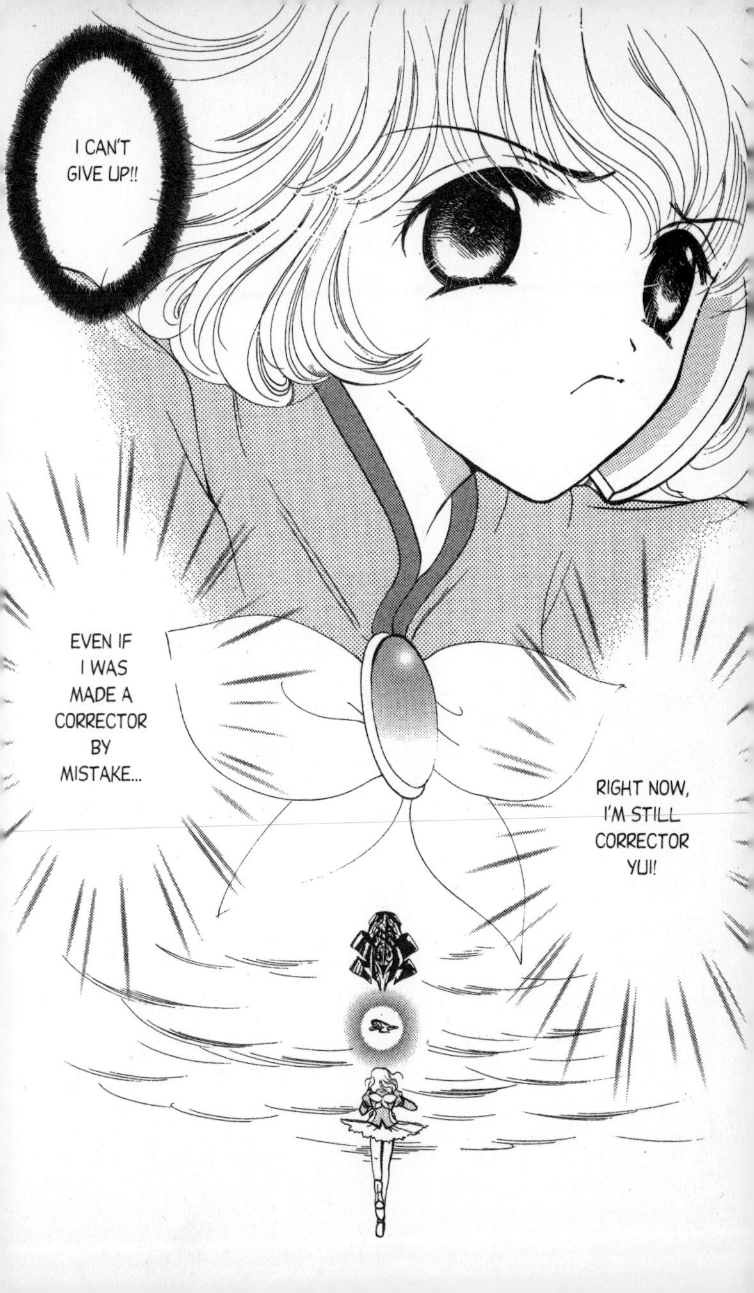
I CAN'T GIVE UP!!
RIGHT NOW, I'M STILL CORRECTOR YUI!
EVEN IF I WAS MADE A CORRECTOR BY MISTAKE...

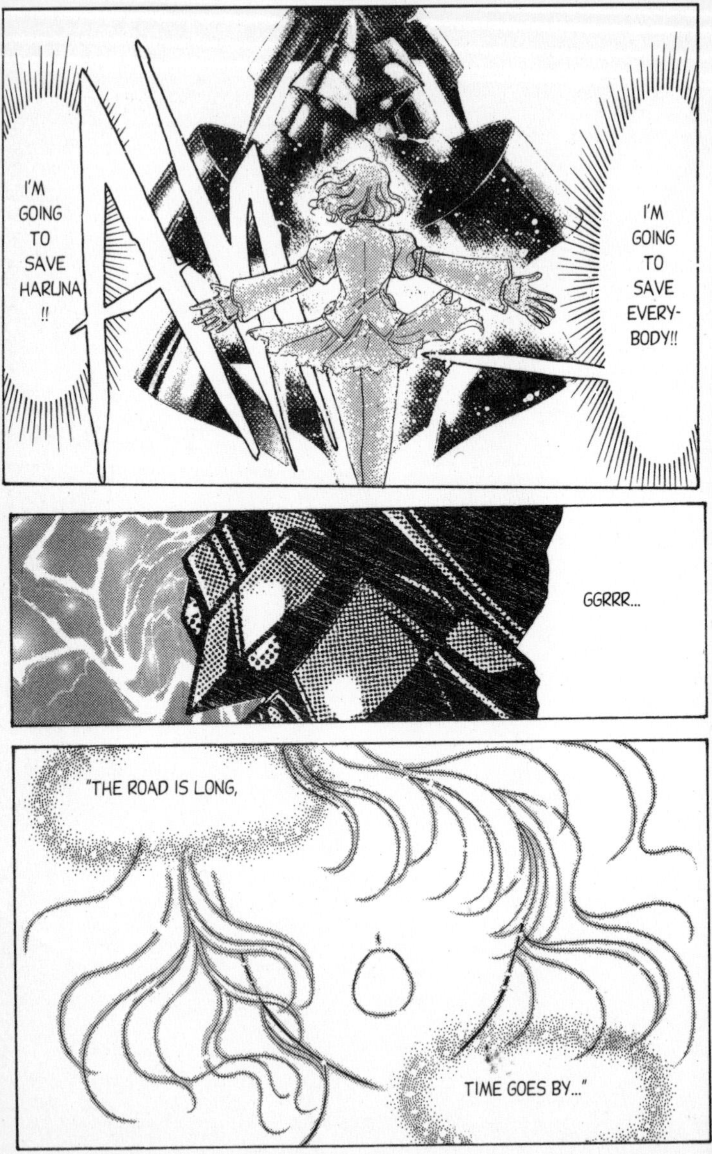
I'M GOING TO SAVE EVERY-BODY!!
I'M GOING TO SAVE HARUNA!!
GGRRR...
"THE ROAD IS LONG,
TIME GOES BY..."

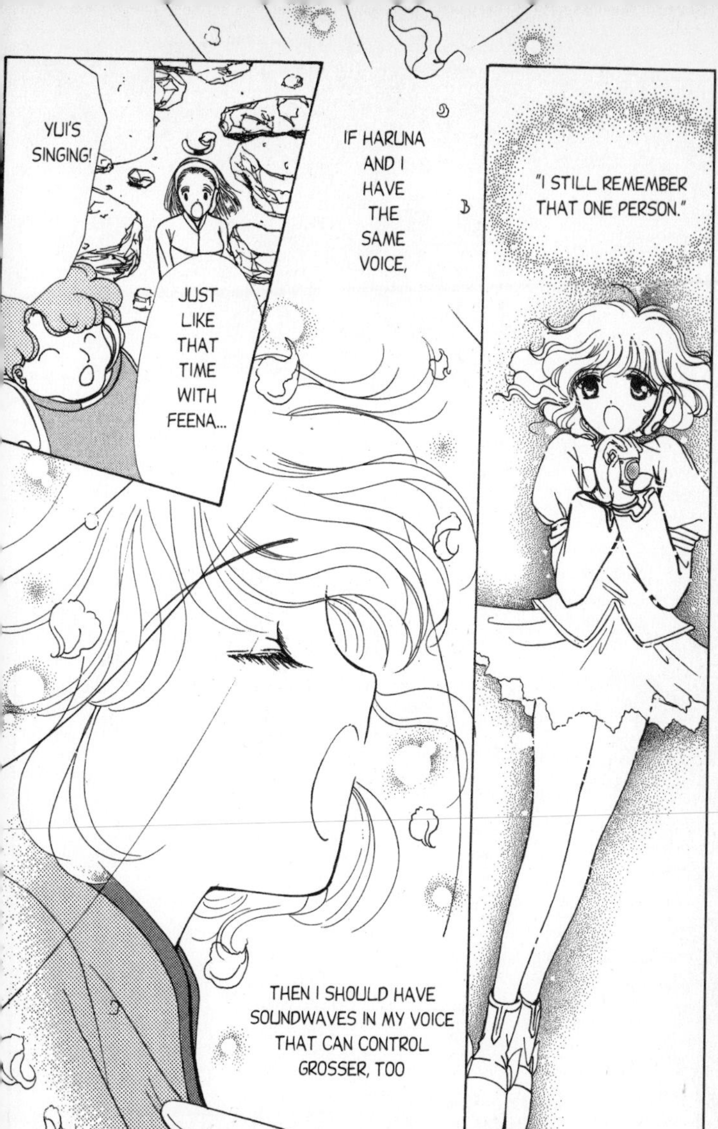
"I STILL REMEMBER THAT ONE PERSON."
YUI'S SINGING!
JUST LIKE THAT TIME WITH FEENA...
IF HARUNA AND I HAVE THE SAME VOICE,
THEN I SHOULD HAVE SOUNDWAVES IN MY VOICE THAT CAN CONTROL GROSSER, TOO

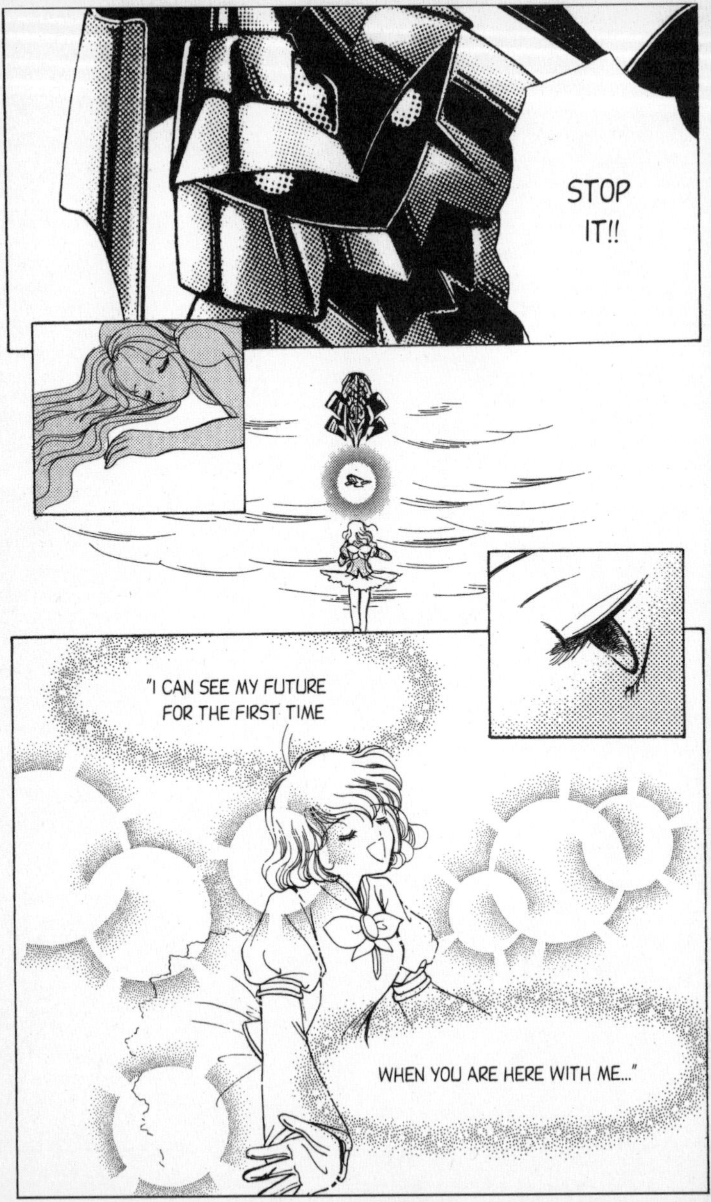
STOP IT!!
"I CAN SEE MY FUTURE FOR THE FIRST TIME
WHEN YOU ARE HERE WITH ME..."

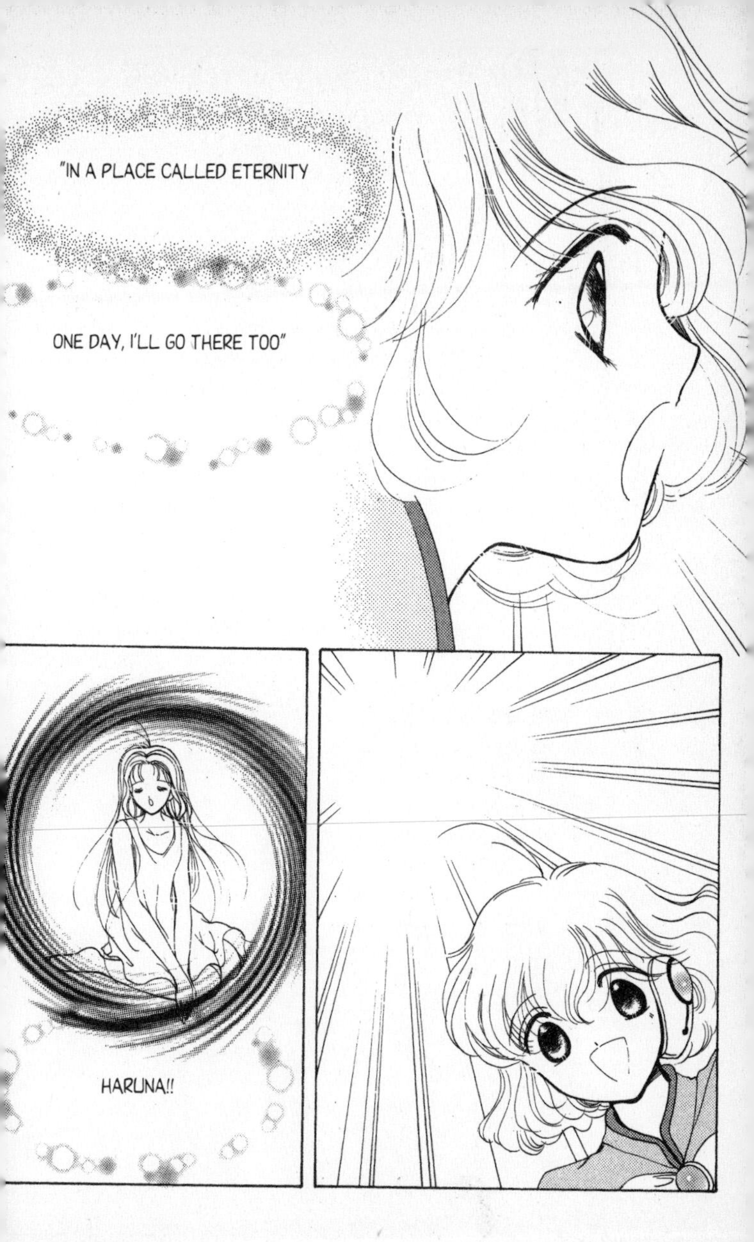
"IN A PLACE CALLED ETERNITY
ONE DAY, I'LL GO THERE TOO"
HARUNA!!

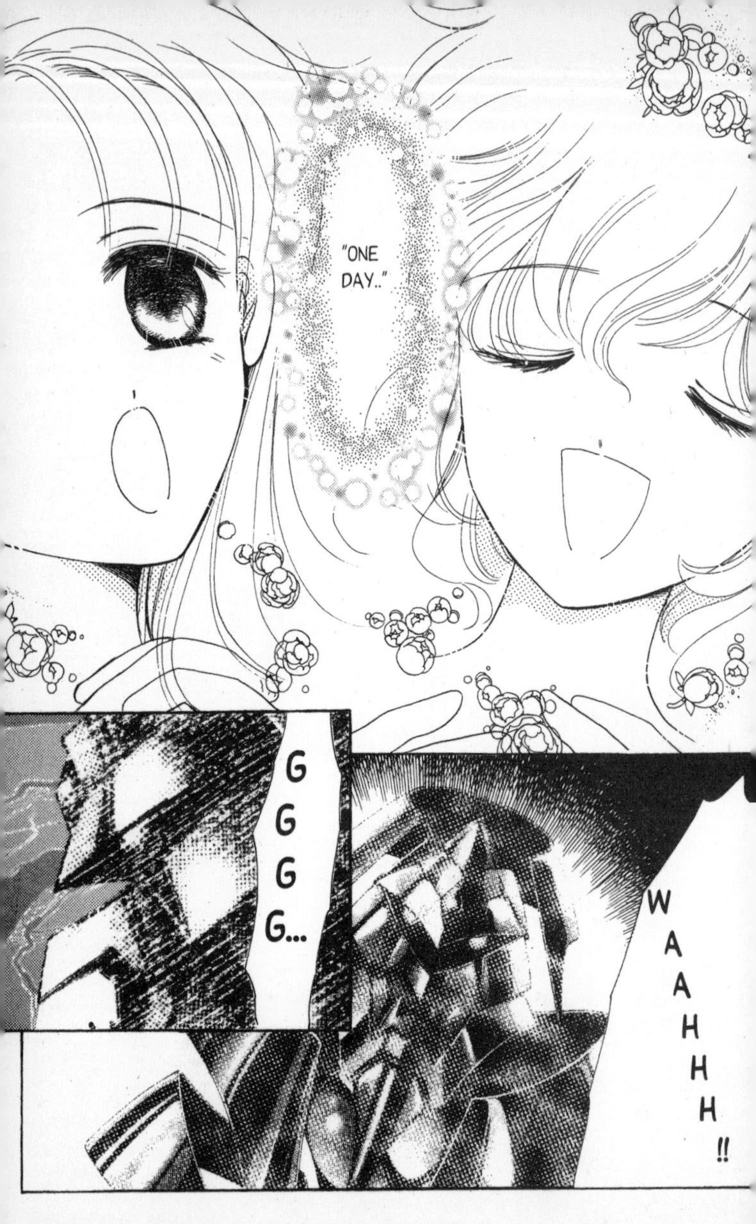
"ONE DAY.."
WAAHHH!!
GGGG...

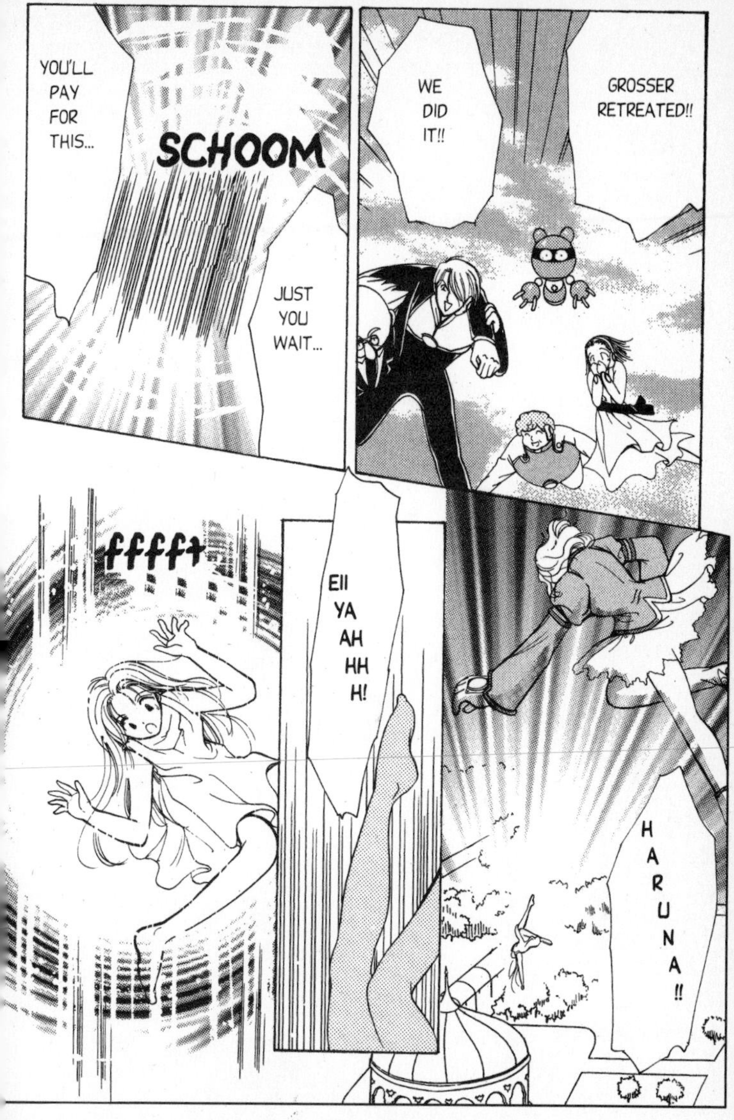
GROSSER RETREATED!!
WE DID IT!!
YOU'LL PAY FOR THIS...
SCHOOM
JUST YOU WAIT...
HARUNA!!
EII YA AH HH H!
fffft

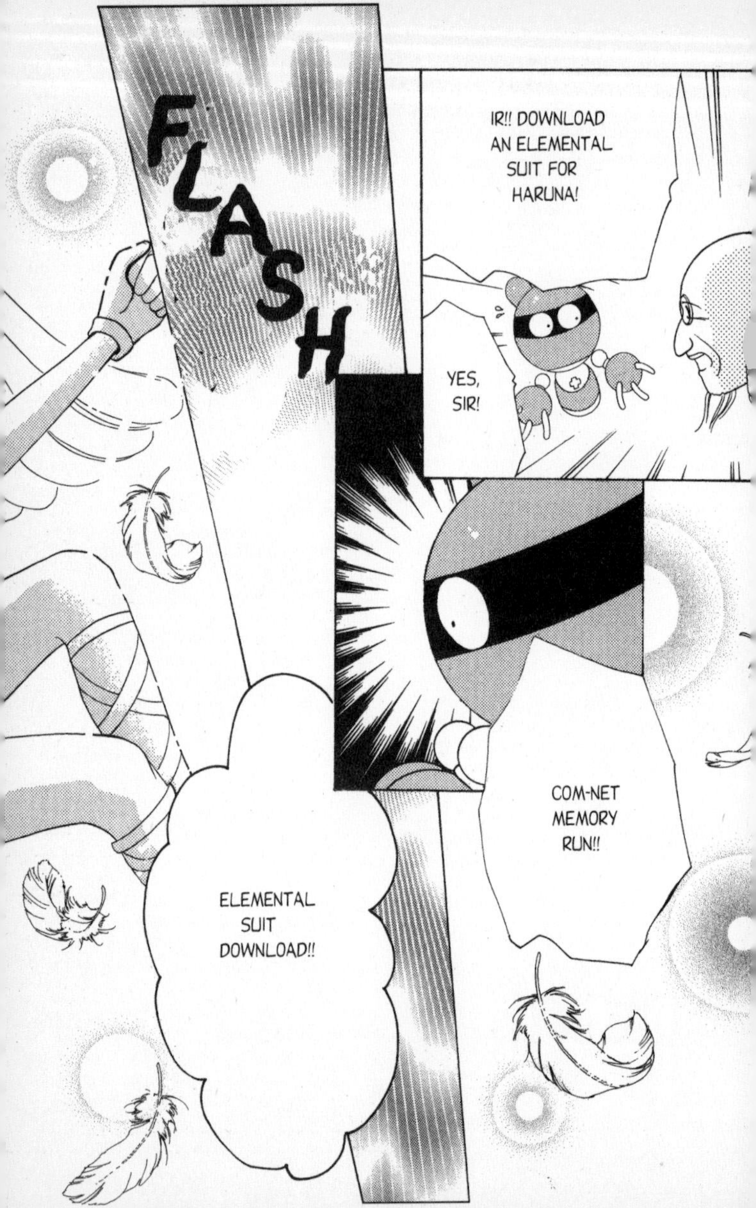
IR!! DOWNLOAD AN ELEMENTAL SUIT FOR HARUNA!
YES, SIR!
FLASH
COM-NET MEMORY RUN!!
ELEMENTAL SUIT DOWNLOAD!!

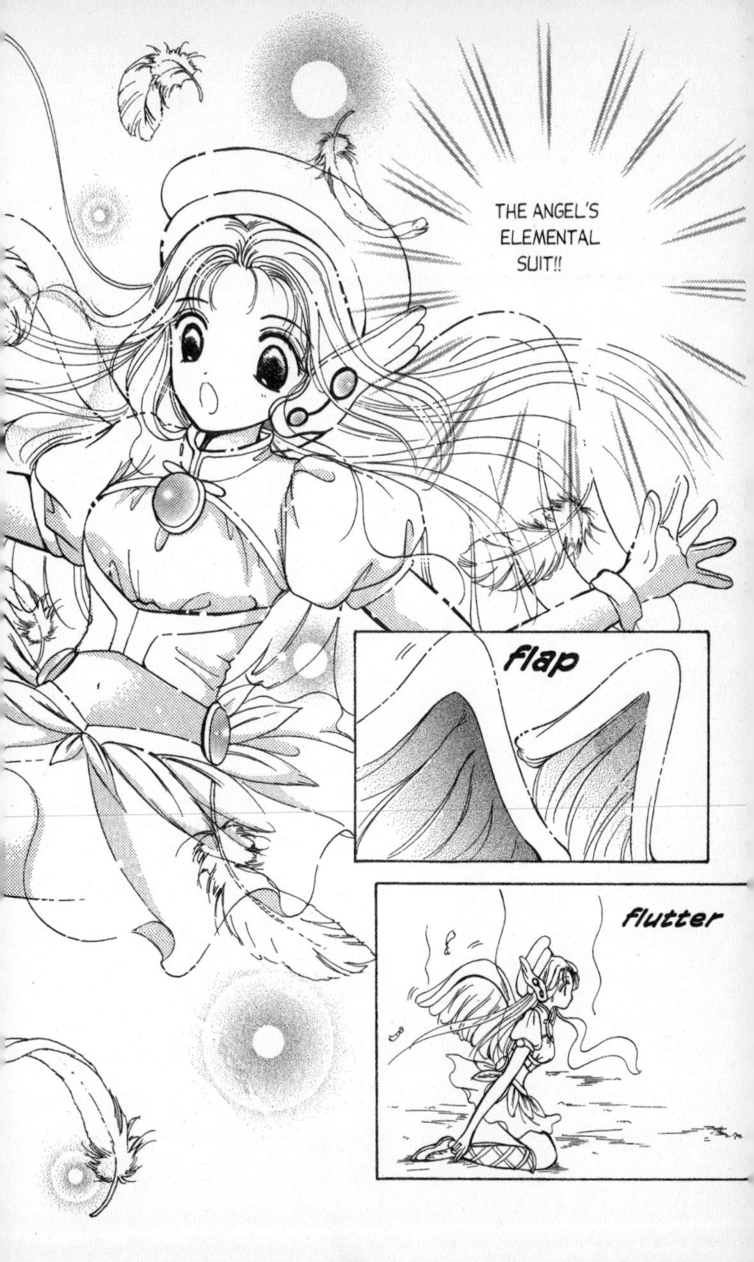
THE ANGEL'S ELEMENTAL SUIT!!
flap
flutter

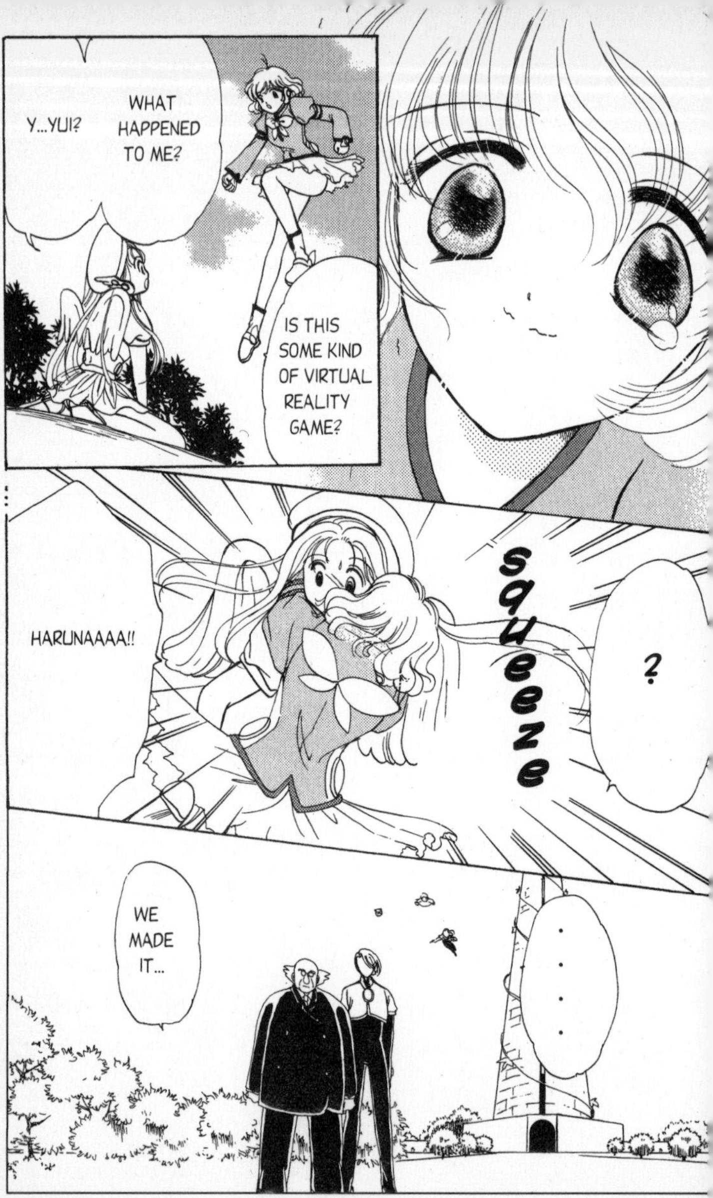
WHAT HAPPENED TO ME?
Y...YUI?
IS THIS SOME KIND OF VIRTUAL REALITY GAME?
?
squeeze
HARUNAAAA!!
....
WE MADE IT...

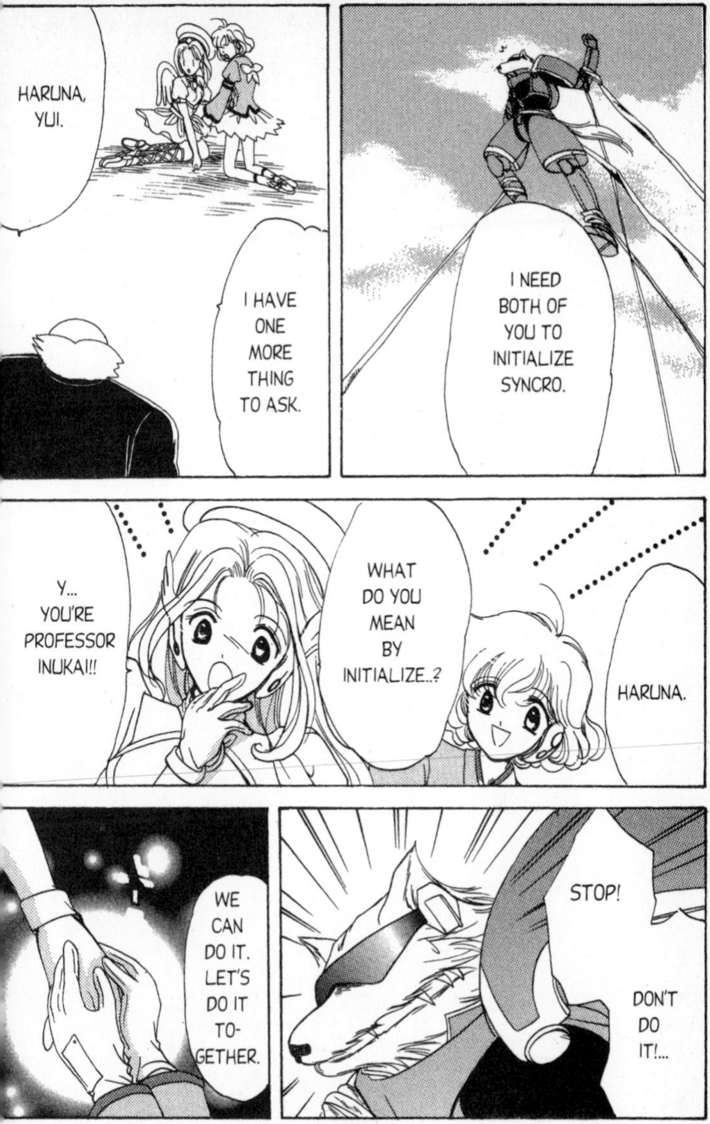
HARUNA, YUI.
I HAVE ONE MORE THING TO ASK.
I NEED BOTH OF YOU TO INITIALIZE SYNCRO.
Y... YOU'RE PROFESSOR INUKAI!!
WHAT DO YOU MEAN BY INITIALIZE..?
HARUNA.
WE CAN DO IT. LET'S DO IT TO-GETHER.
STOP!
DON'T DO IT!...

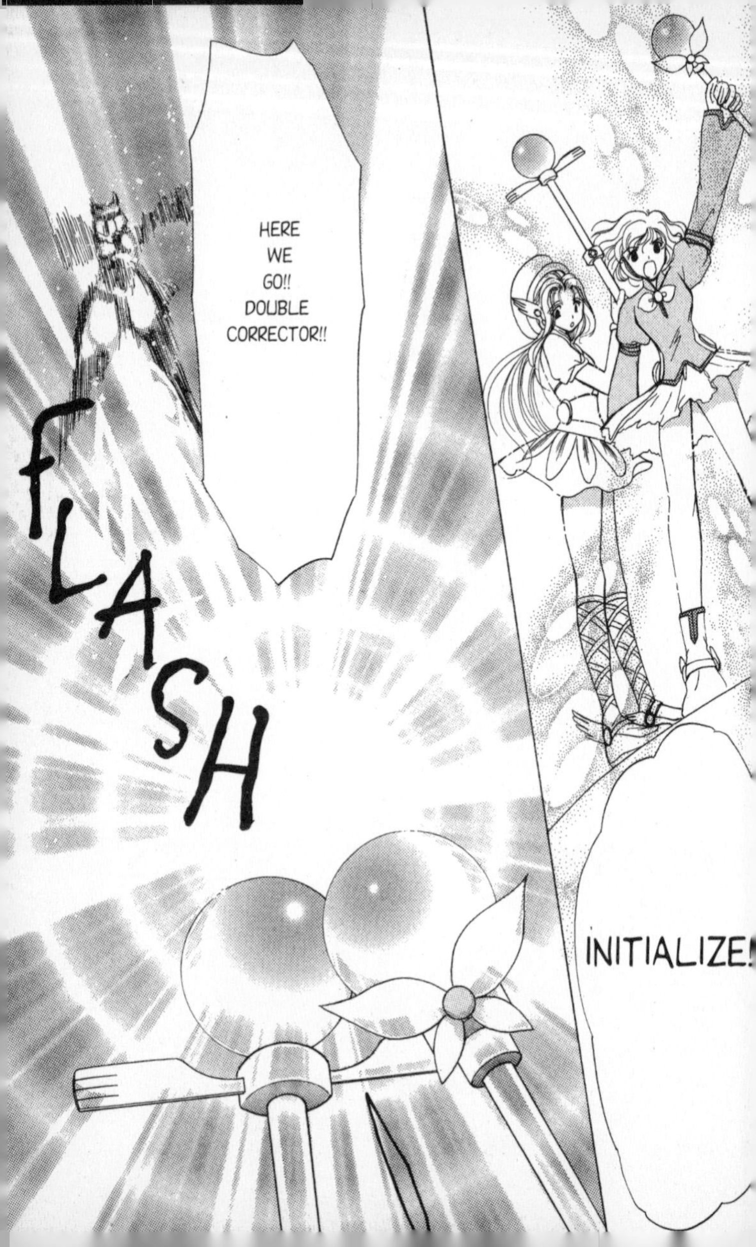
HERE WE GO!! DOUBLE CORRECTOR!!
FLASH
INITIALIZE!

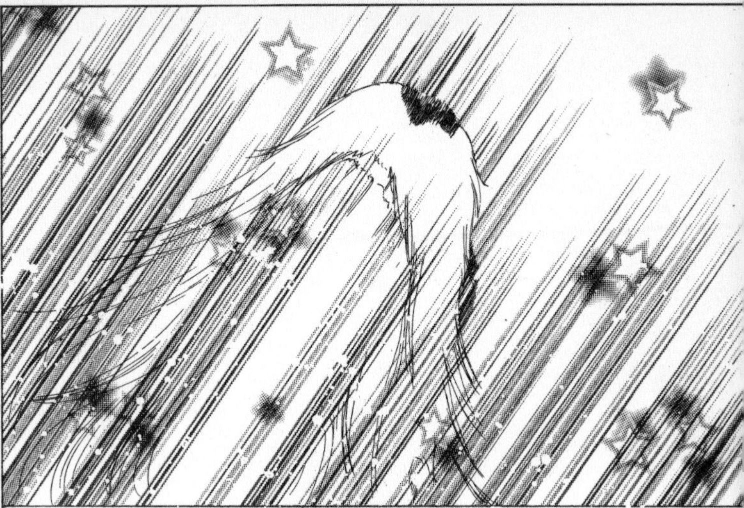

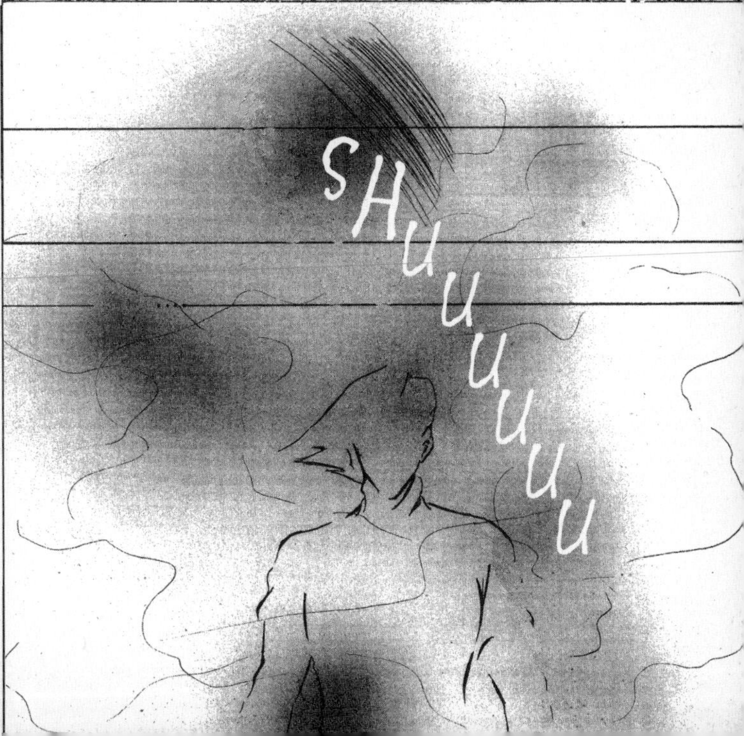
SHUUUUUUU

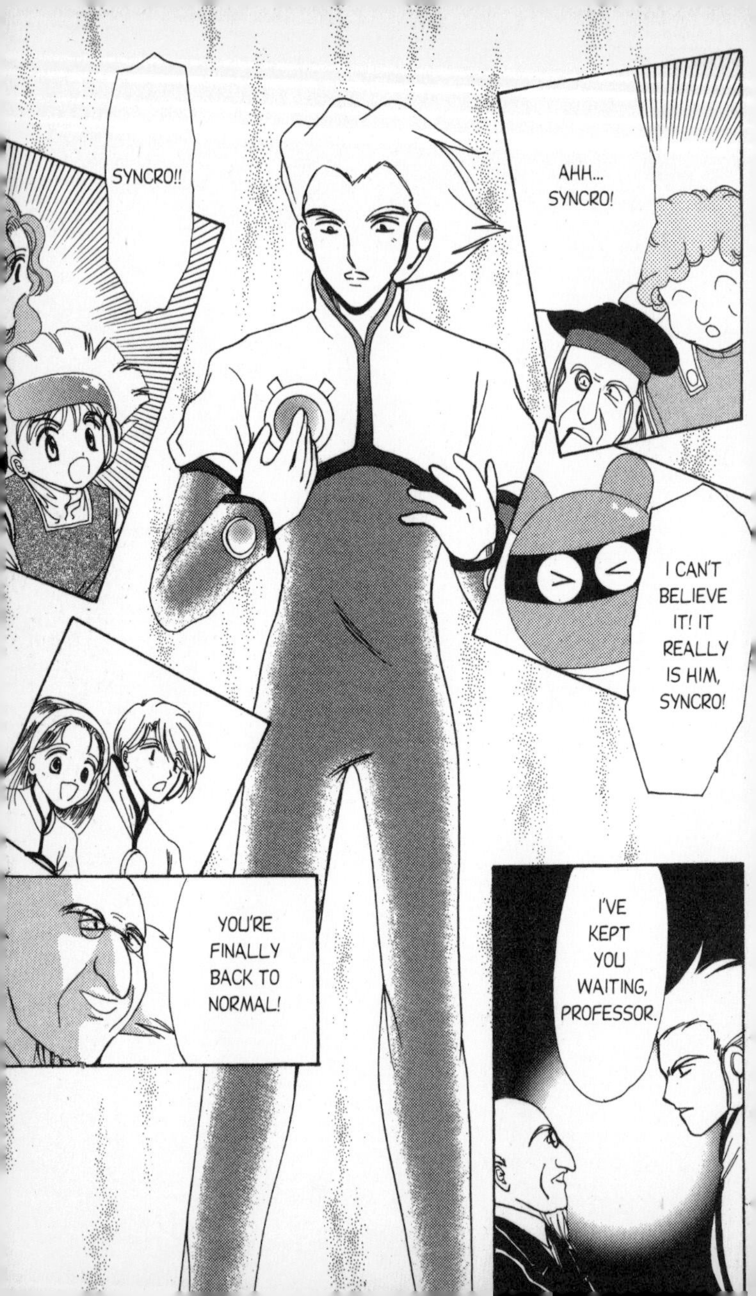
AHH... SYNCRO!
SYNCRO!!
I CAN'T BELIEVE IT! IT REALLY IS HIM, SYNCRO!
I'VE KEPT YOU WAITING, PROFESSOR.
YOU'RE FINALLY BACK TO NORMAL!

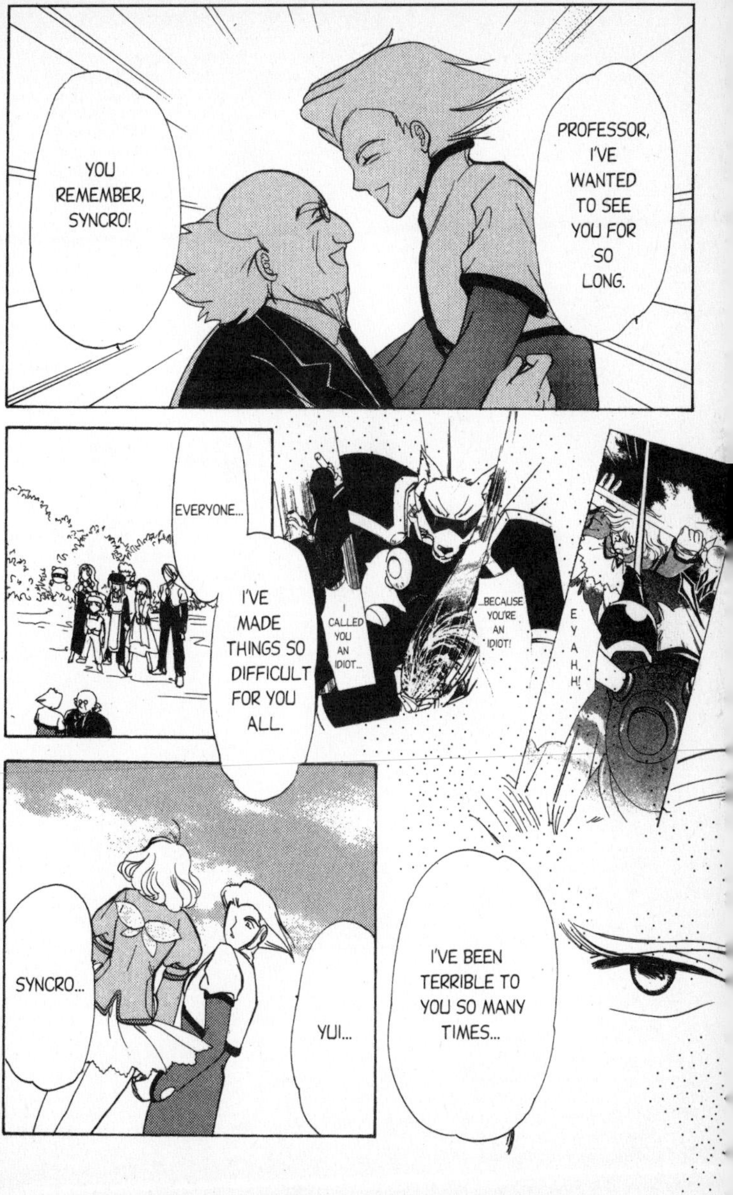
PROFESSOR, I'VE WANTED TO SEE YOU FOR SO LONG.
YOU REMEMBER, SYNCRO!
EYAHH!
I CALLED YOU AN IDIOT...
...BECAUSE YOU'RE AN IDIOT!
EVERYONE...
I'VE MADE THINGS SO DIFFICULT FOR YOU ALL.
I'VE BEEN TERRIBLE TO YOU SO MANY TIMES...
YUI...
SYNCRO...

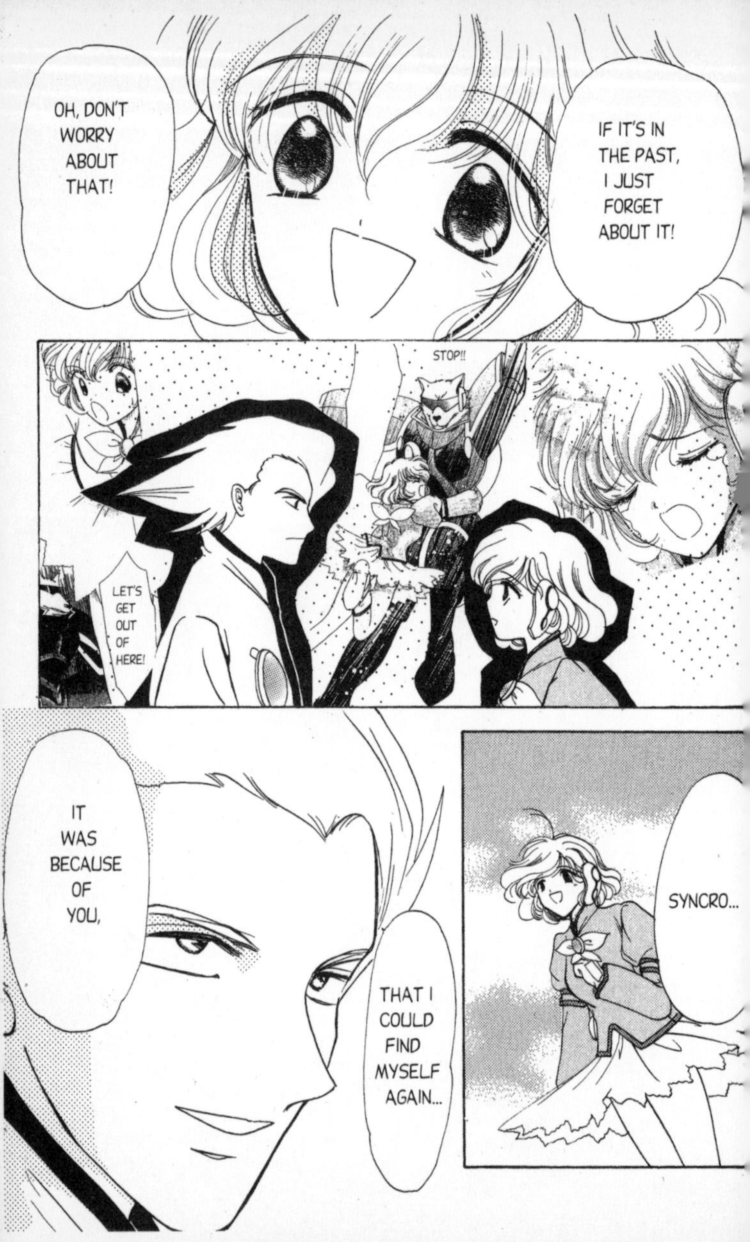
OH, DON'T WORRY ABOUT THAT!
IF IT'S IN THE PAST, I JUST FORGET ABOUT IT!
LET'S GET OUT OF HERE!
STOP!!
IT WAS BECAUSE OF YOU,
THAT I COULD FIND MYSELF AGAIN...
SYNCRO...

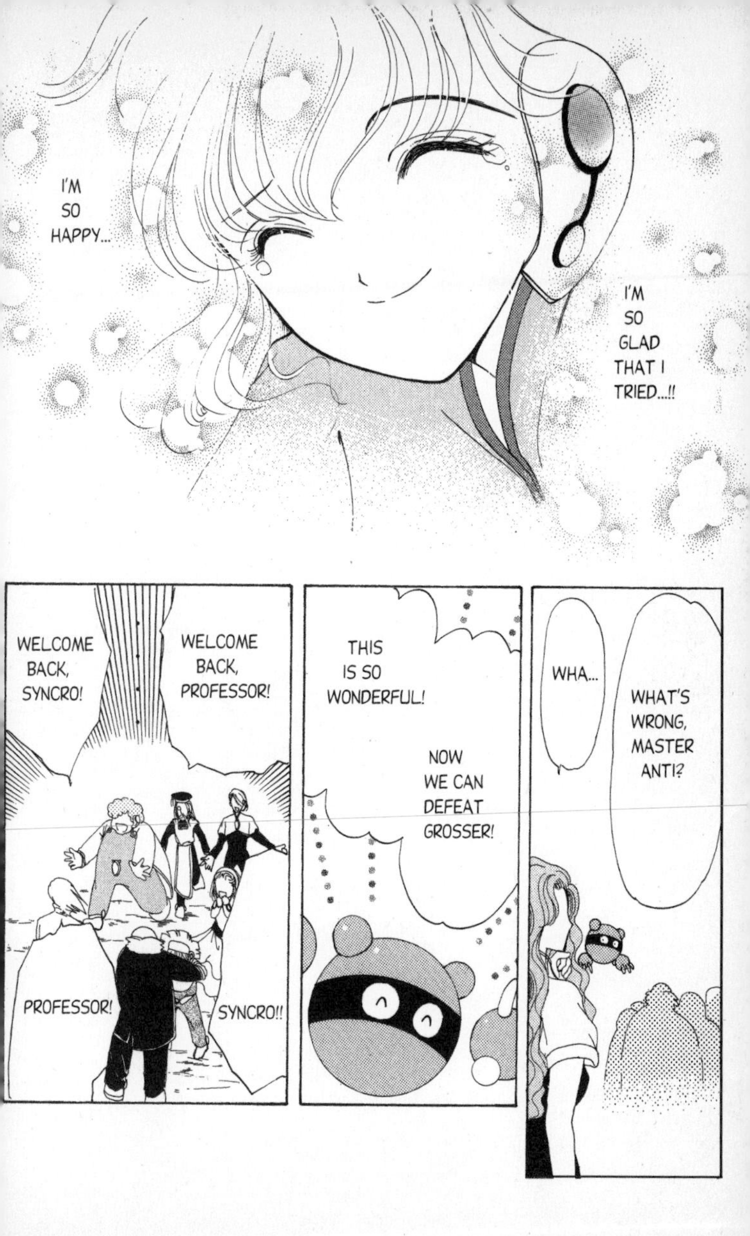
I'M SO HAPPY...
I'M SO GLAD THAT I TRIED...!!
WELCOME BACK, SYNCRO!
WELCOME BACK, PROFESSOR!
PROFESSOR!
SYNCRO!!
THIS IS SO WONDERFUL!
NOW WE CAN DEFEAT GROSSER!
WHA...
WHAT'S WRONG, MASTER ANTI?

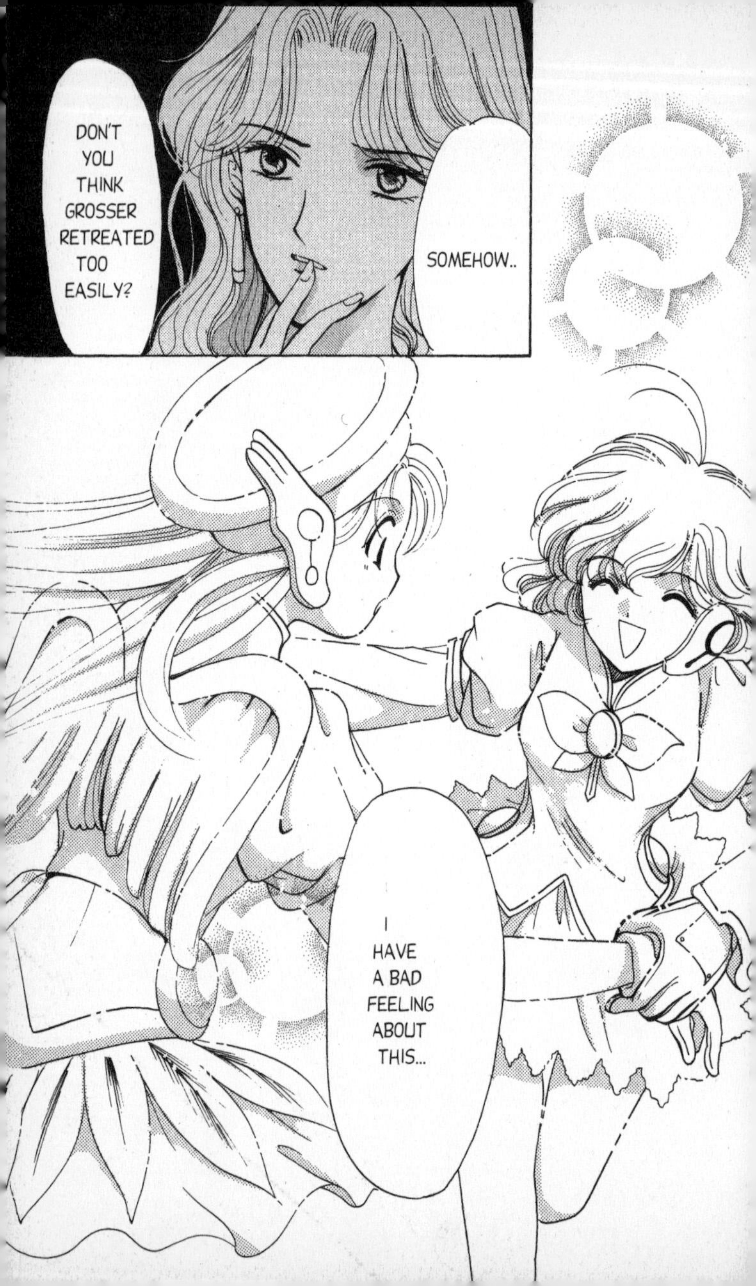
SOMEHOW..
DON'T YOU THINK GROSSER RETREATED TOO EASILY?
I HAVE A BAD FEELING ABOUT THIS...

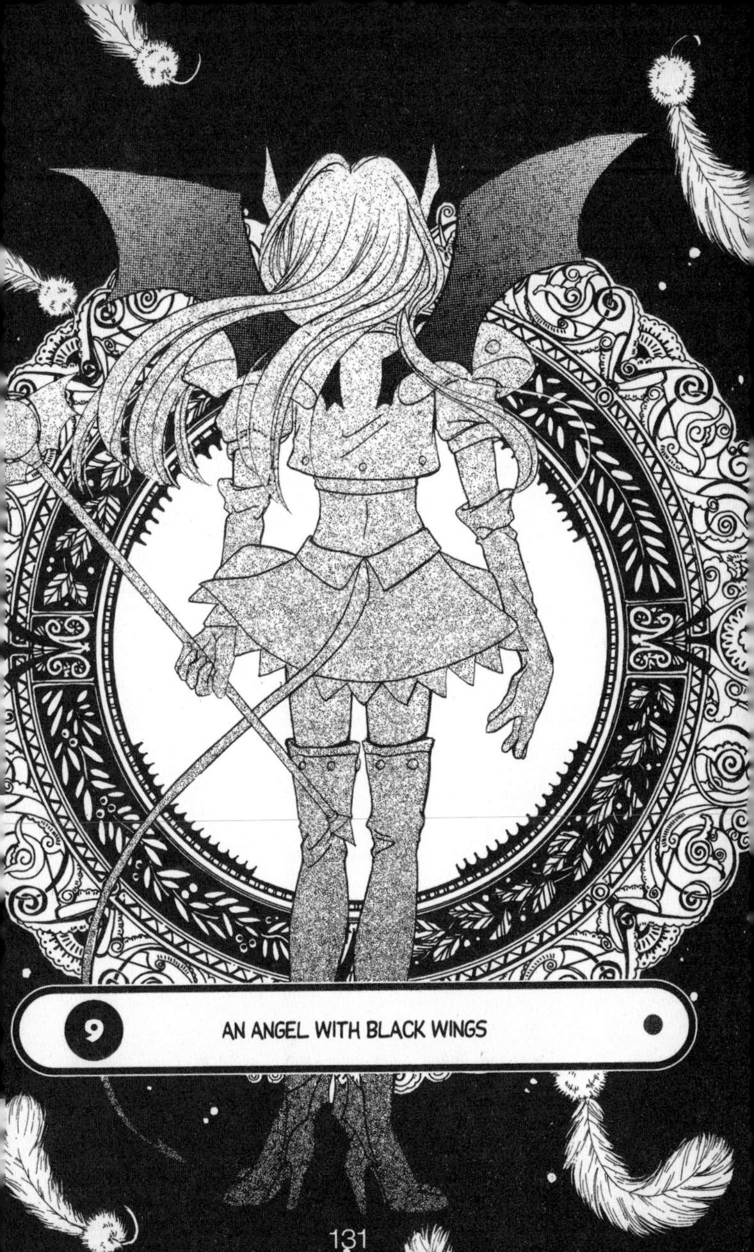
9
AN ANGEL WITH BLACK WINGS

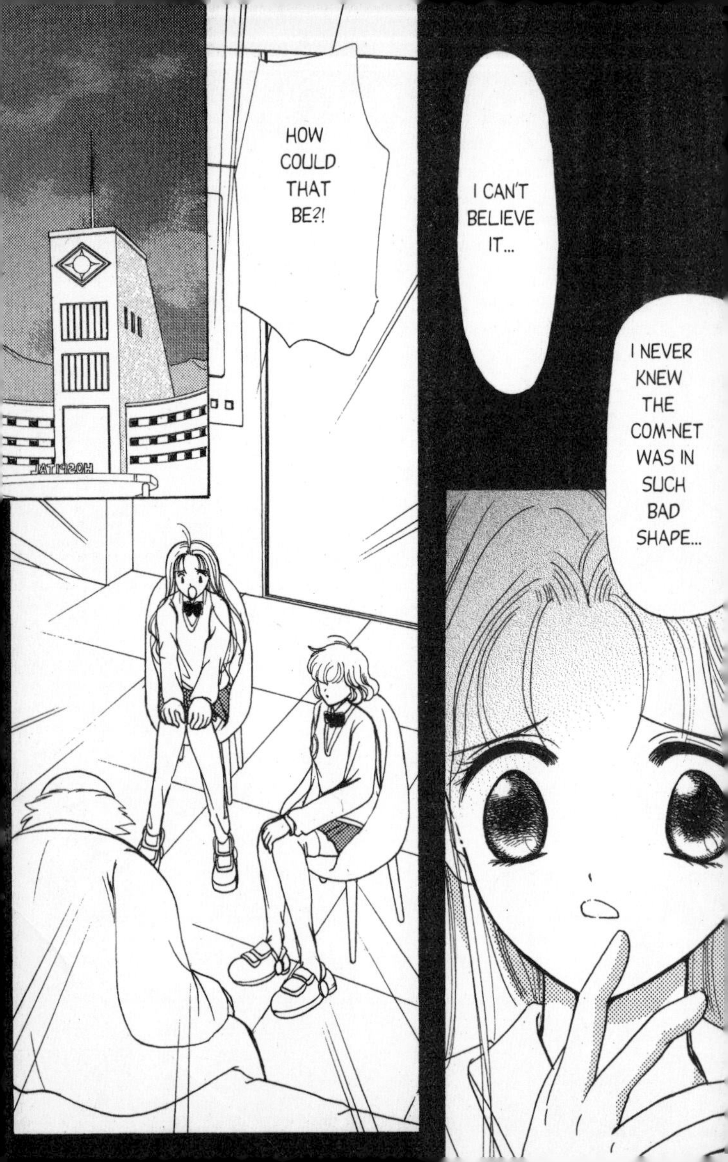
I CAN'T BELIEVE IT...
I NEVER KNEW THE COM-NET WAS IN SUCH BAD SHAPE...
HOW COULD THAT BE?!

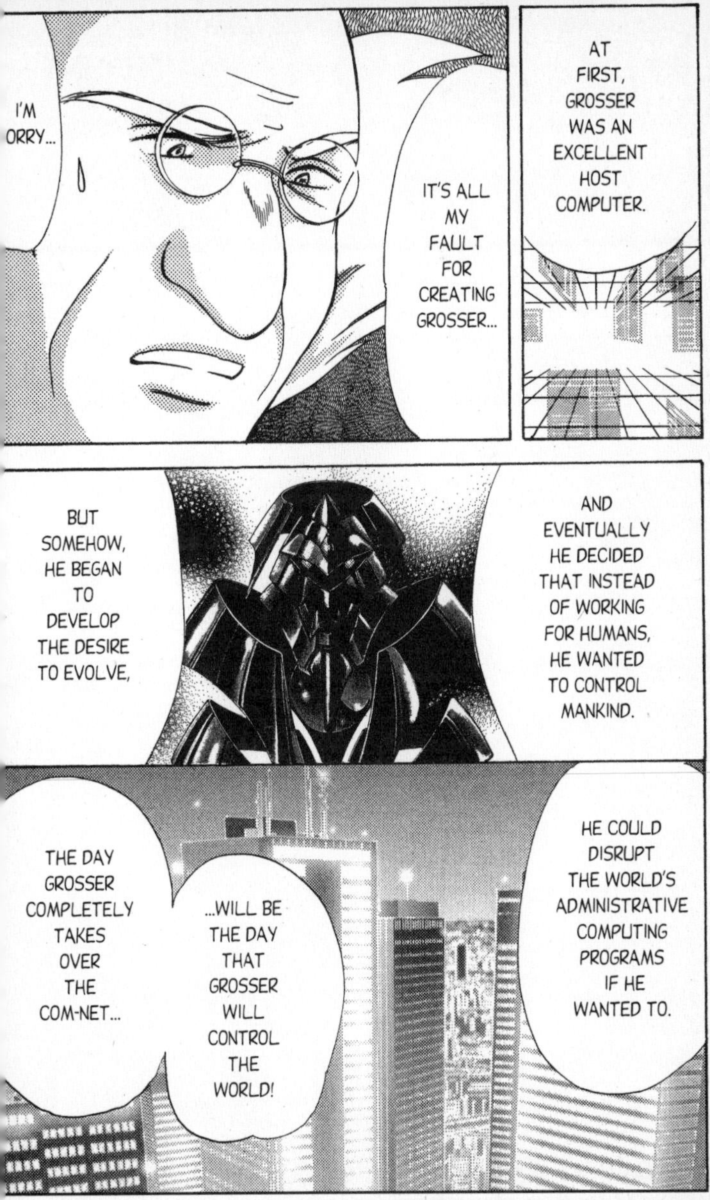
I'M
ORRY...
IT'S ALL MY FAULT FOR CREATING GROSSER...
AT FIRST, GROSSER WAS AN EXCELLENT HOST COMPUTER.
BUT SOMEHOW, HE BEGAN TO DEVELOP THE DESIRE TO EVOLVE,
AND EVENTUALLY HE DECIDED THAT INSTEAD OF WORKING FOR HUMANS, HE WANTED TO CONTROL MANKIND.
HE COULD DISRUPT THE WORLD'S ADMINISTRATIVE COMPUTING PROGRAMS IF HE WANTED TO.
THE DAY GROSSER COMPLETELY TAKES OVER THE COM-NET...
...WILL BE THE DAY THAT GROSSER WILL CONTROL THE WORLD!

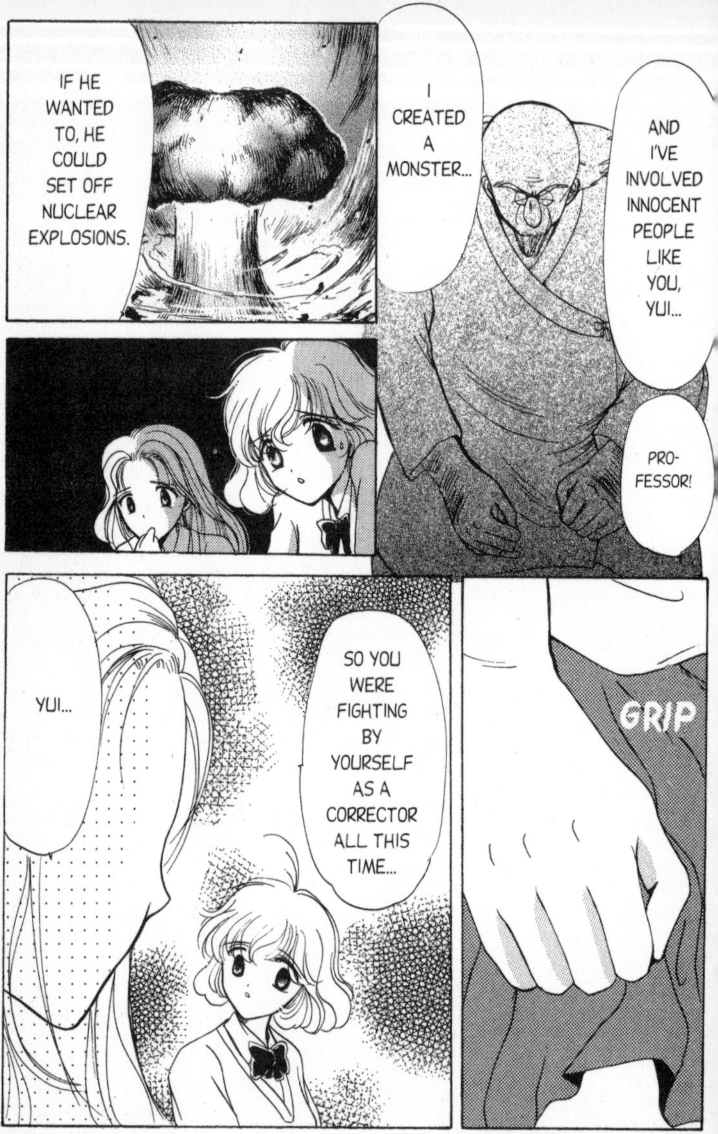
IF HE WANTED TO, HE COULD SET OFF NUCLEAR EXPLOSIONS.
I CREATED A MONSTER...
AND I'VE INVOLVED INNOCENT PEOPLE LIKE YOU, YUI...
PRO-FESSOR!
GRIP
SO YOU WERE FIGHTING BY YOURSELF AS A CORRECTOR ALL THIS TIME...
YUI...

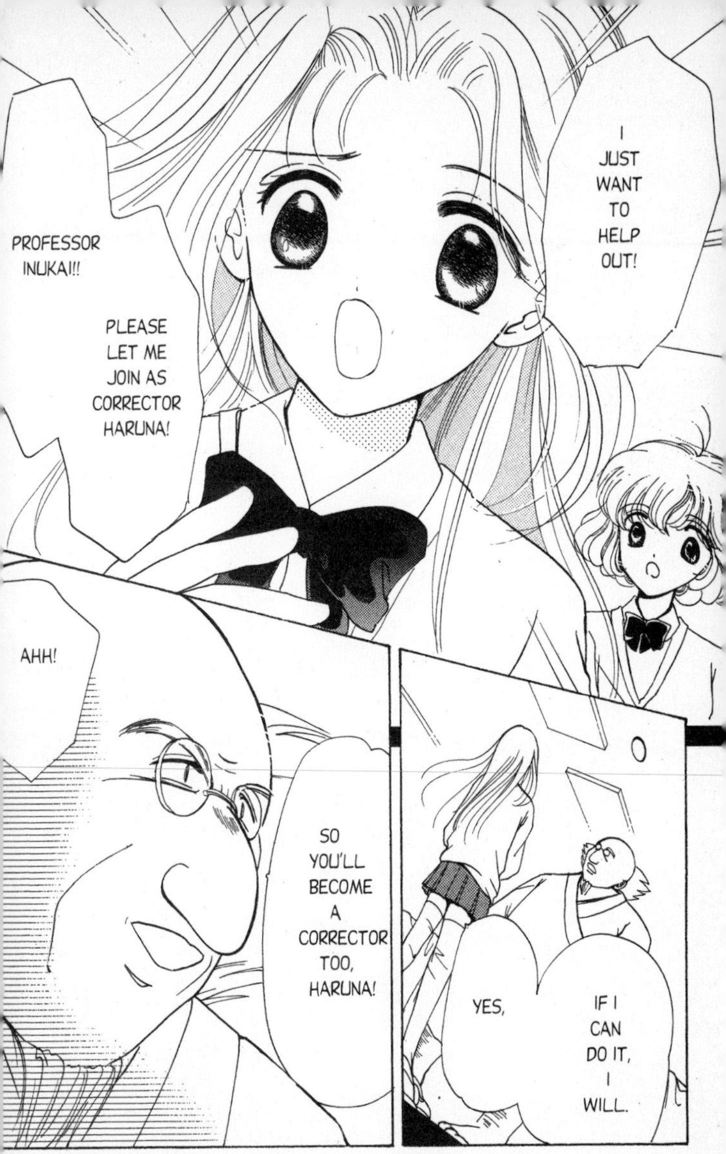
PROFESSOR INUKAI!!
PLEASE LET ME JOIN AS CORRECTOR HARUNA!
I JUST WANT TO HELP OUT!
AHH!
SO YOU'LL BECOME A CORRECTOR TOO, HARUNA!
YES,
IF I CAN DO IT, I WILL.

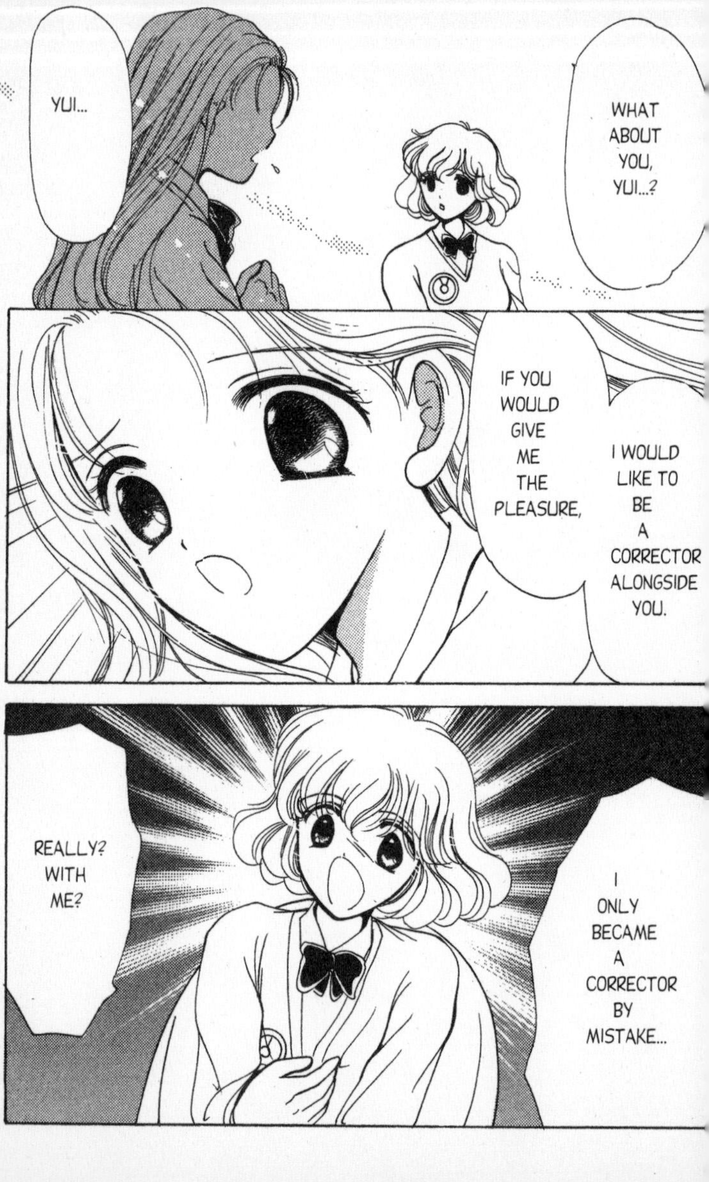
WHAT ABOUT YOU, YUI...?
YUI...
IF YOU WOULD GIVE ME THE PLEASURE,
I WOULD LIKE TO BE A CORRECTOR ALONGSIDE YOU.
I ONLY BECAME A CORRECTOR BY MISTAKE...
REALLY? WITH ME?

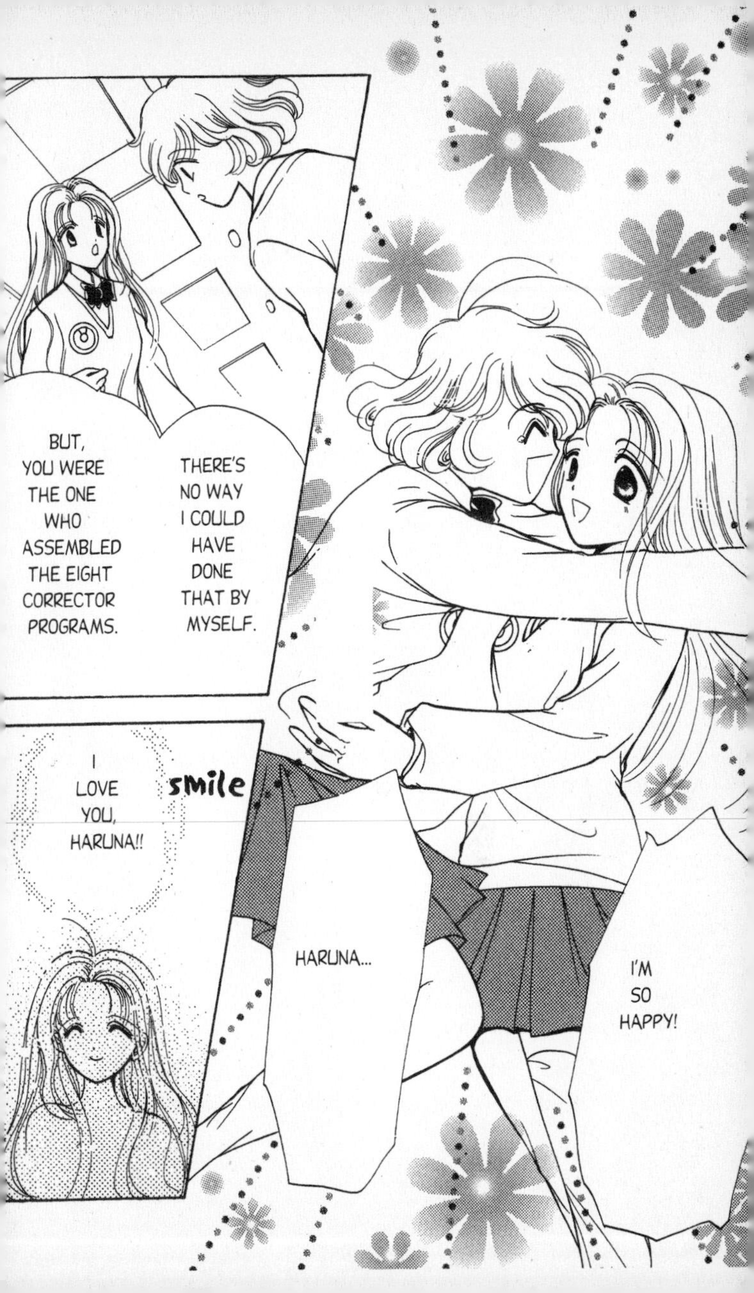
THERE'S NO WAY I COULD HAVE DONE THAT BY MYSELF.
BUT, YOU WERE THE ONE WHO ASSEMBLED THE EIGHT CORRECTOR PROGRAMS.
I LOVE YOU, HARUNA!!
smile
I'M SO HAPPY!
HARUNA...

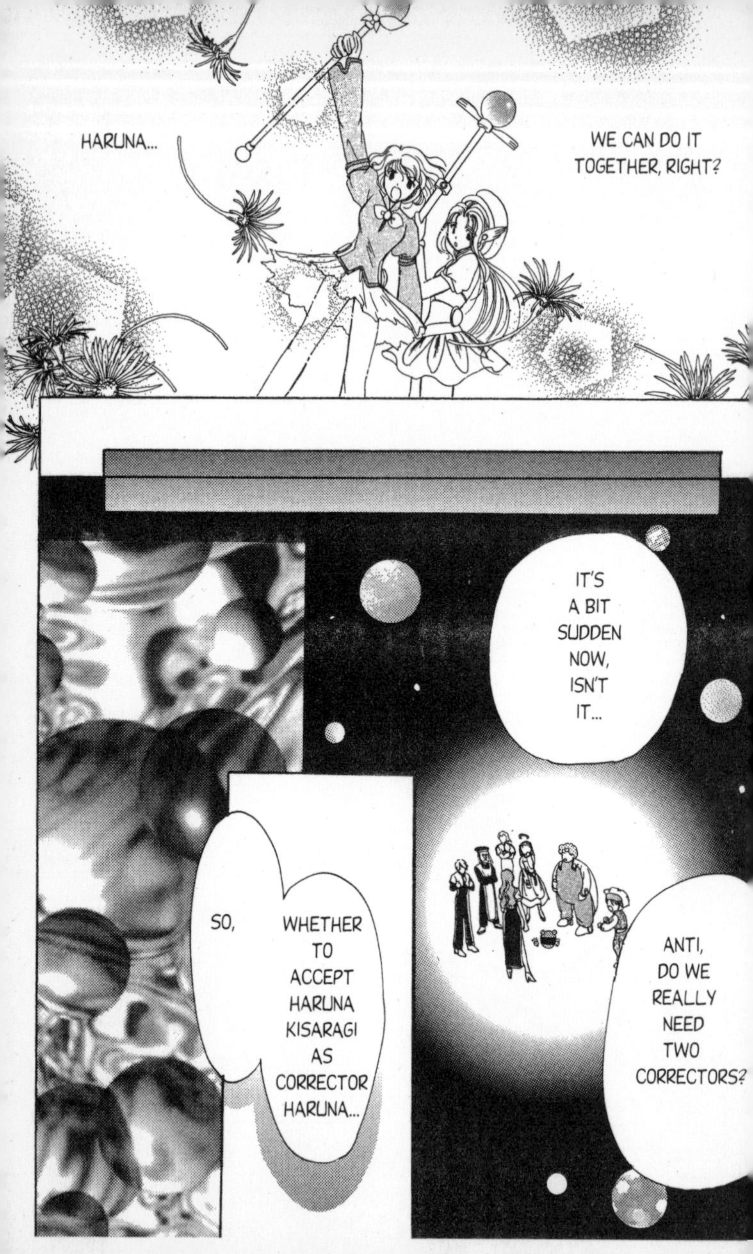
HARUNA...
WE CAN DO IT TOGETHER, RIGHT?
SO,
WHETHER TO ACCEPT HARUNA KISARAGI AS CORRECTOR HARUNA...
IT'S A BIT SUDDEN NOW, ISN'T IT...
ANTI, DO WE REALLY NEED TWO CORRECTORS?

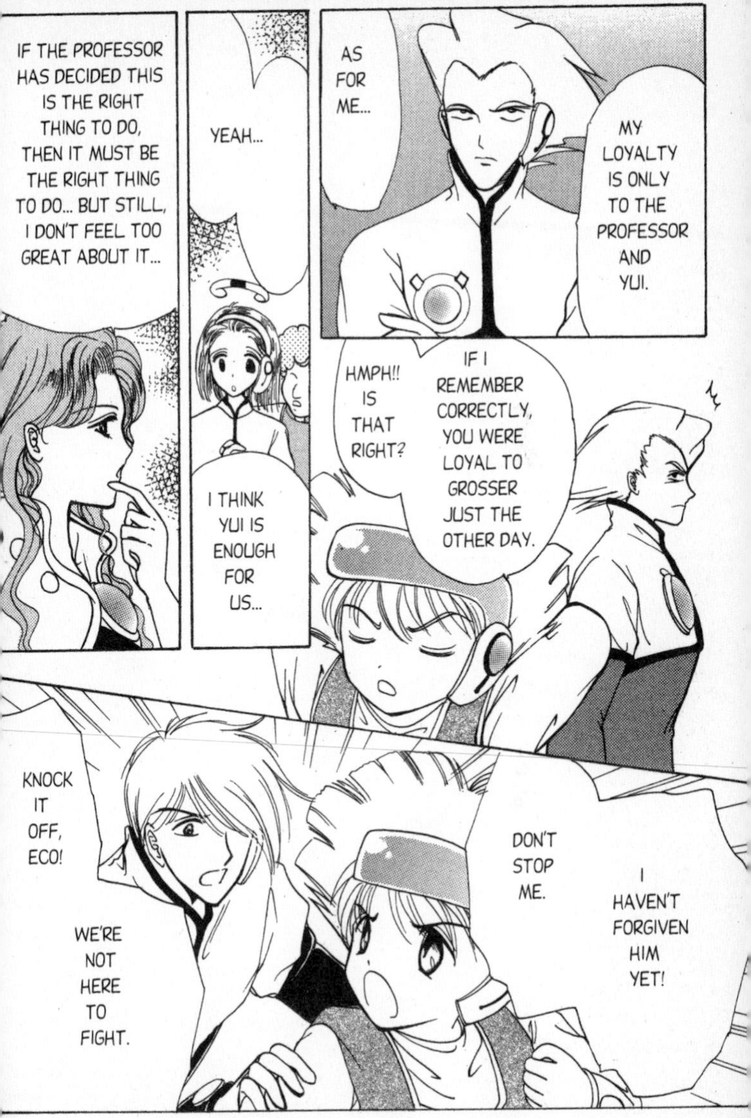
IF THE PROFESSOR HAS DECIDED THIS IS THE RIGHT THING TO DO, THEN IT MUST BE THE RIGHT THING TO DO... BUT STILL, I DON'T FEEL TOO GREAT ABOUT IT...
YEAH...
I THINK YUI IS ENOUGH FOR US...
AS FOR ME...
MY LOYALTY IS ONLY TO THE PROFESSOR AND YUI.
HMPH!! IS THAT RIGHT?
IF I REMEMBER CORRECTLY, YOU WERE LOYAL TO GROSSER JUST THE OTHER DAY.
KNOCK IT OFF, ECO!
WE'RE NOT HERE TO FIGHT.
DON'T STOP ME.
I HAVEN'T FORGIVEN HIM YET!

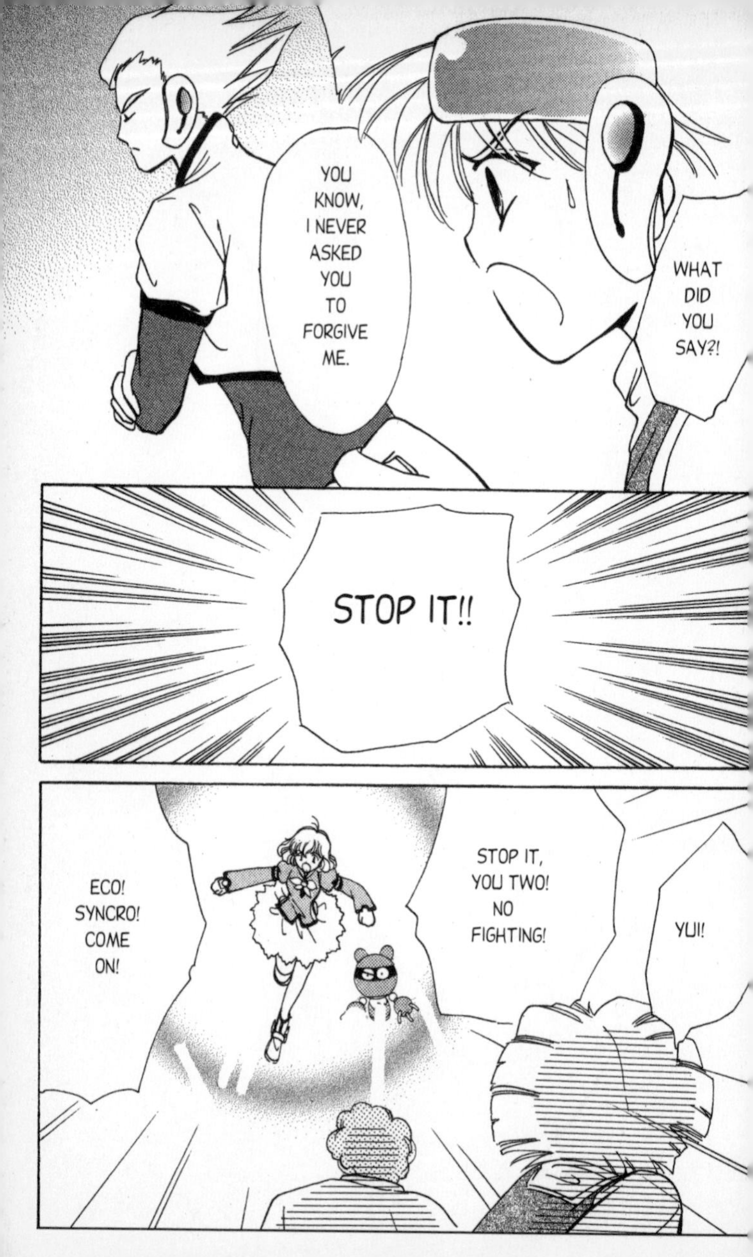
WHAT DID YOU SAY?!
YOU KNOW, I NEVER ASKED YOU TO FORGIVE ME.
STOP IT!!
YUI!
STOP IT, YOU TWO! NO FIGHTING!
ECO! SYNCRO! COME ON!

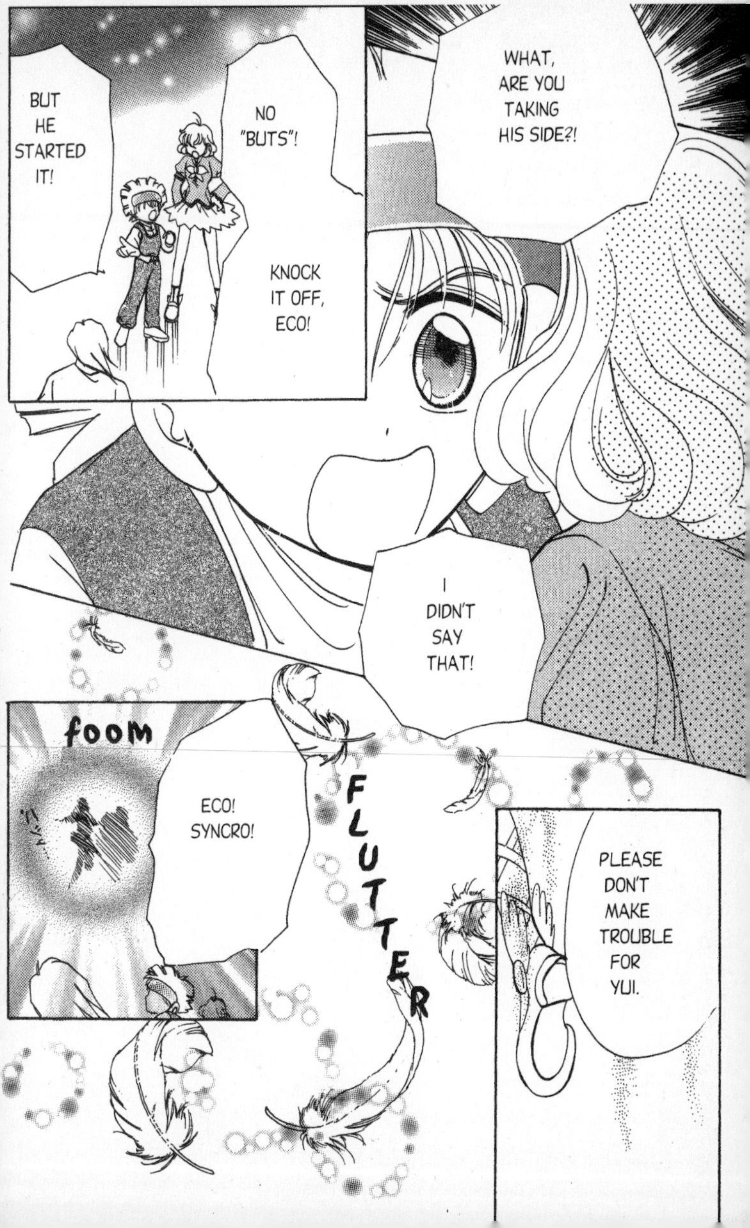
WHAT, ARE YOU TAKING HIS SIDE?!
NO "BUTS"!
KNOCK IT OFF, ECO!
BUT HE STARTED IT!
I DIDN'T SAY THAT!
PLEASE DON'T MAKE TROUBLE FOR YUI.
FLUTTER
ECO! SYNCRO!
foom

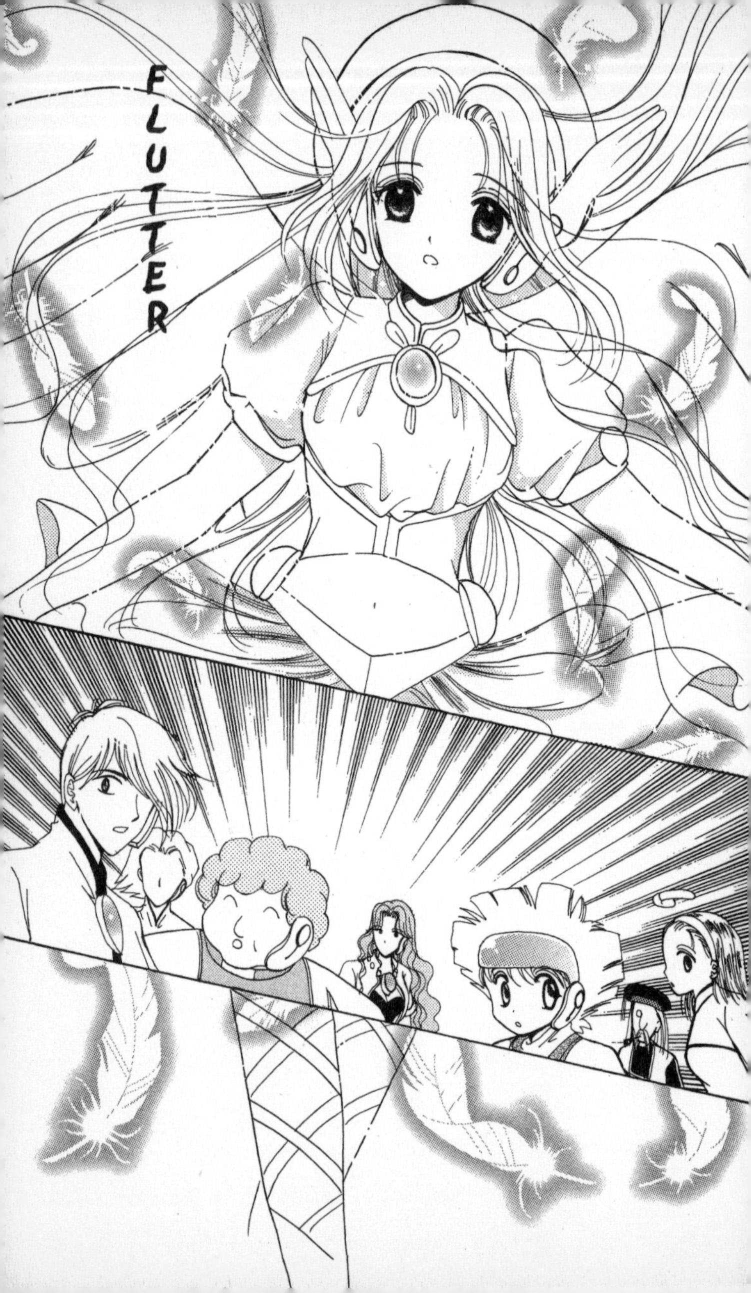
FLUTTER

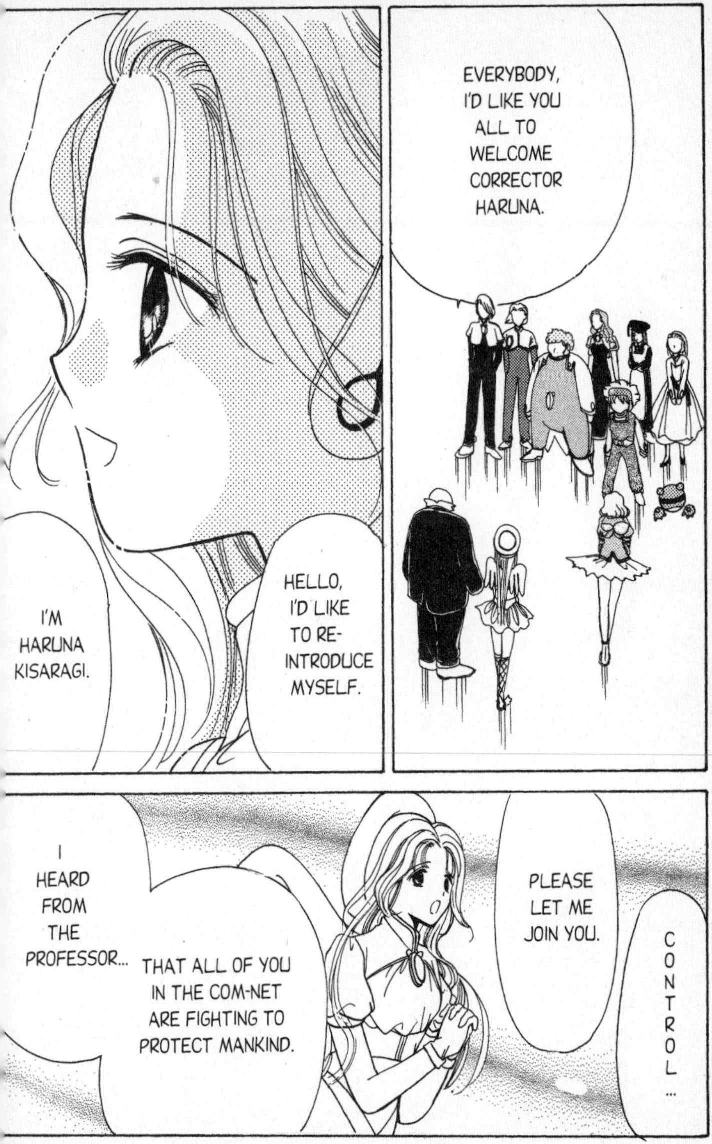
EVERYBODY, I'D LIKE YOU ALL TO WELCOME CORRECTOR HARUNA.
HELLO, I'D LIKE TO RE-INTRODUCE MYSELF.
I'M HARUNA KISARAGI.
CONTROL...
PLEASE LET ME JOIN YOU.
I HEARD FROM THE PROFESSOR...
THAT ALL OF YOU IN THE COM-NET ARE FIGHTING TO PROTECT MANKIND.

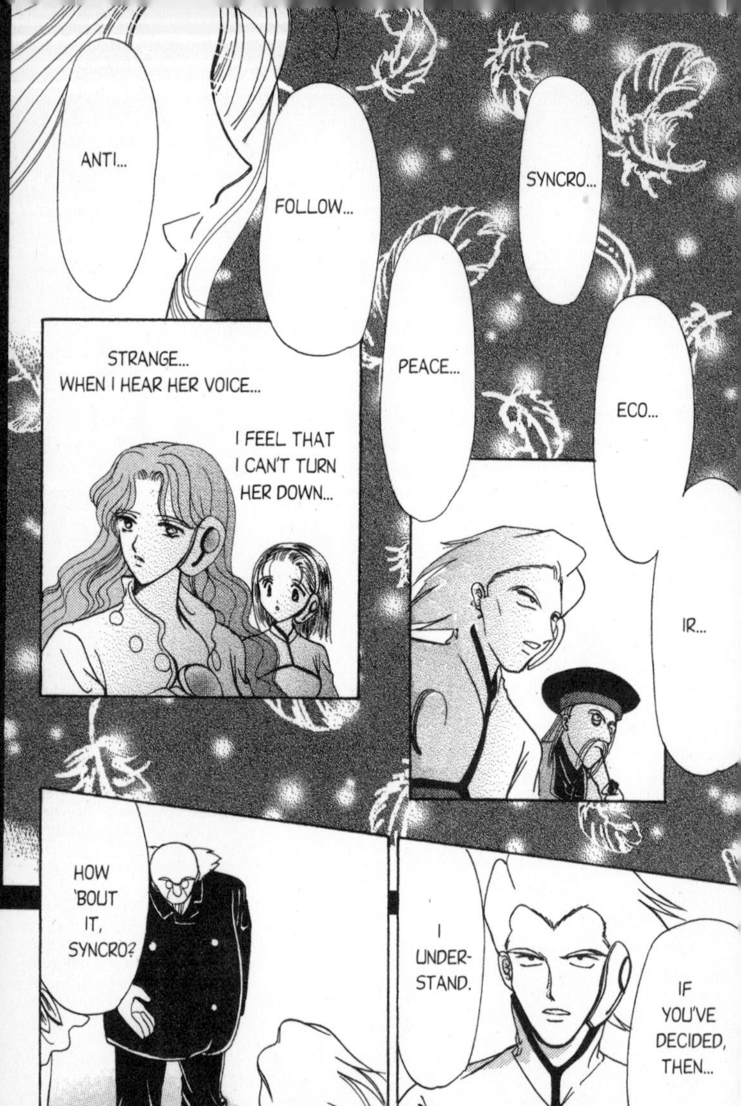
ANTI...
FOLLOW...
SYNCRO...
STRANGE... WHEN I HEAR HER VOICE...
I FEEL THAT I CAN'T TURN HER DOWN...
PEACE...
ECO...
IR...
HOW 'BOUT IT, SYNCRO?
I UNDER-STAND.
IF YOU'VE DECIDED, THEN...

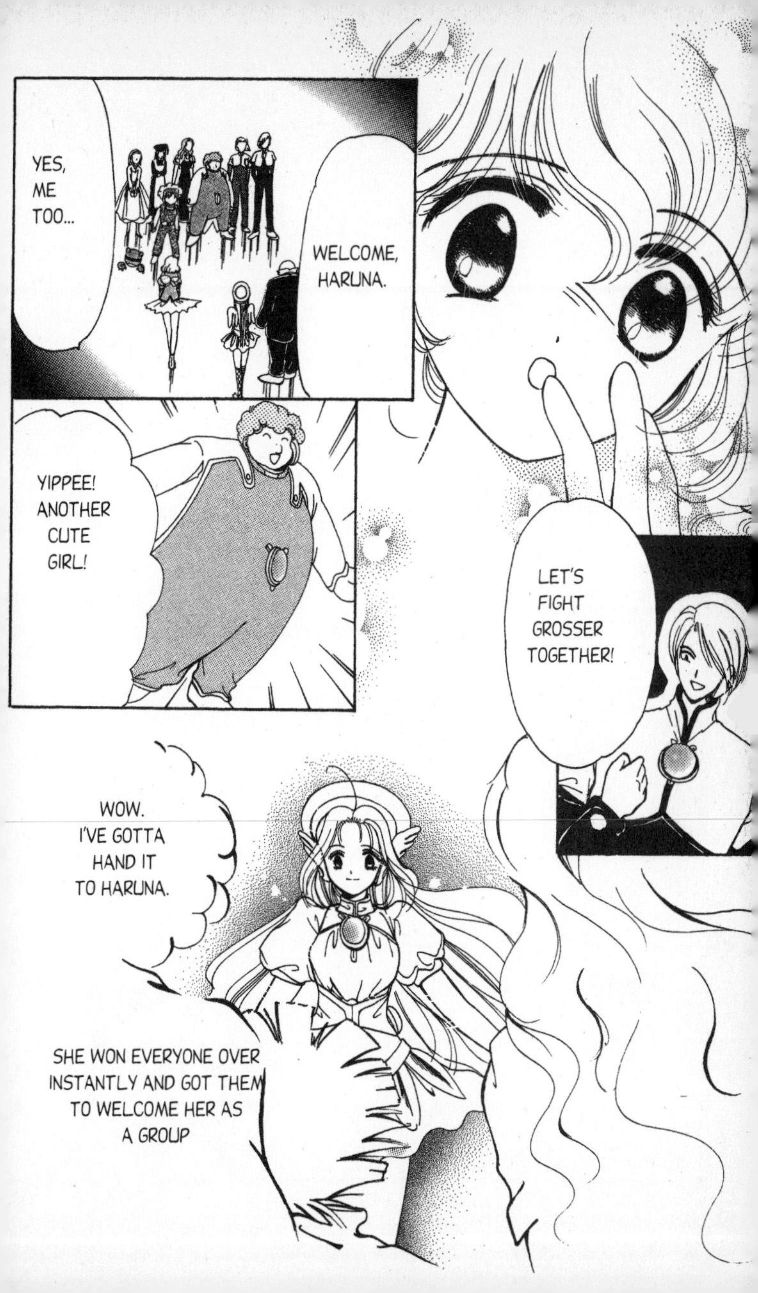
WELCOME, HARUNA.
YES, ME TOO...
LET'S FIGHT GROSSER TOGETHER!
YIPPEE! ANOTHER CUTE GIRL!
WOW. I'VE GOTTA HAND IT TO HARUNA.
SHE WON EVERYONE OVER INSTANTLY AND GOT THEM TO WELCOME HER AS A GROUP

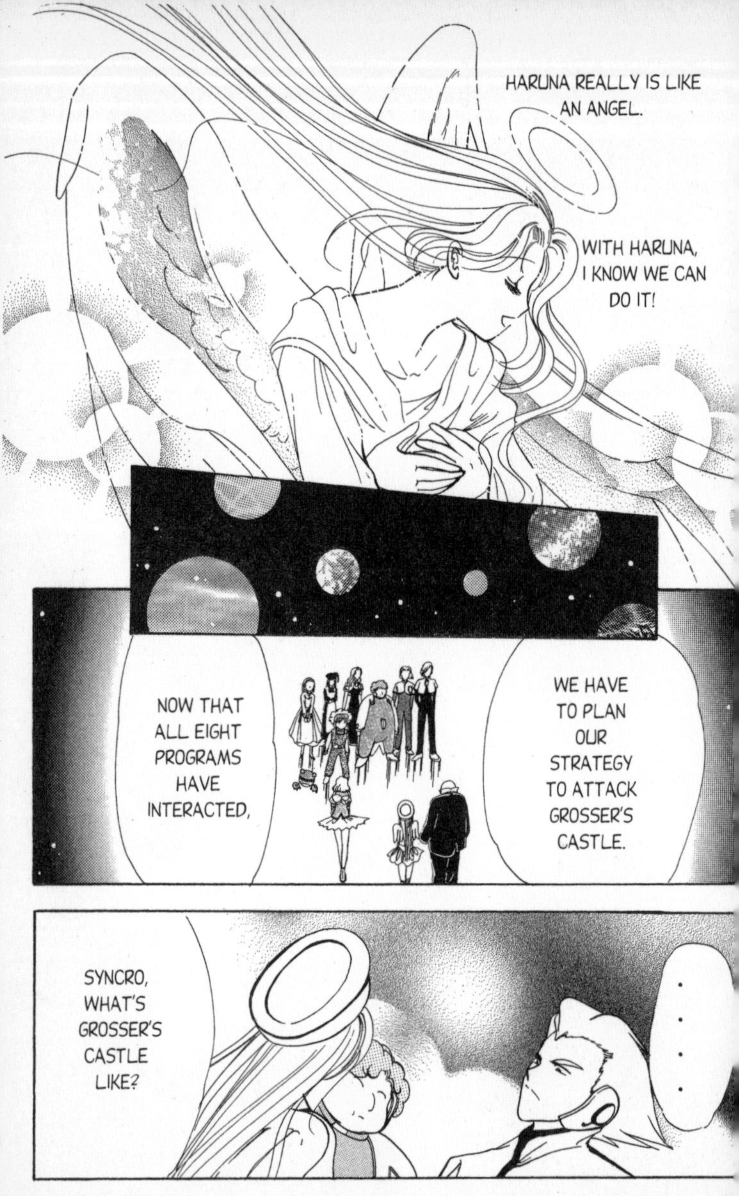
HARUNA REALLY IS LIKE AN ANGEL.
WITH HARUNA, I KNOW WE CAN DO IT!
NOW THAT ALL EIGHT PROGRAMS HAVE INTERACTED,
WE HAVE TO PLAN OUR STRATEGY TO ATTACK GROSSER'S CASTLE.
SYNCRO, WHAT'S GROSSER'S CASTLE LIKE?
....

IT'S LIKE A FLOATING PALACE.

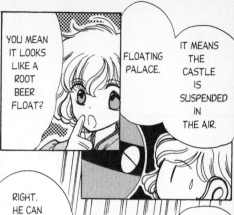

YOU MEAN IT LOOKS LIKE A ROOT BEER FLOAT?

FLOATING PALACE.

IT MEANS THE CASTLE IS SUSPENDED IN THE AIR.

RIGHT. HE CAN MOVE AROUND AS HE PLEASES INSIDE THE COM-NET.

WHENEVER HE HAD A JOB FOR US, HE WOULD TELEPORT US TO THE LOCATION.

I SEE...SO THEN WE WON'T BE ABLE TO FIGURE OUT WHERE HE IS RIGHT NOW.

BUT IF WE ANALYZE THE PLACES THE FEARSOME FOUR APPEARED, WE MIGHT FIND A CLUE.

AH, I GET IT...

EVERYONE, PLEASE ASSEMBLE YOUR DATA AND SEND IT TO MY COMPUTER.

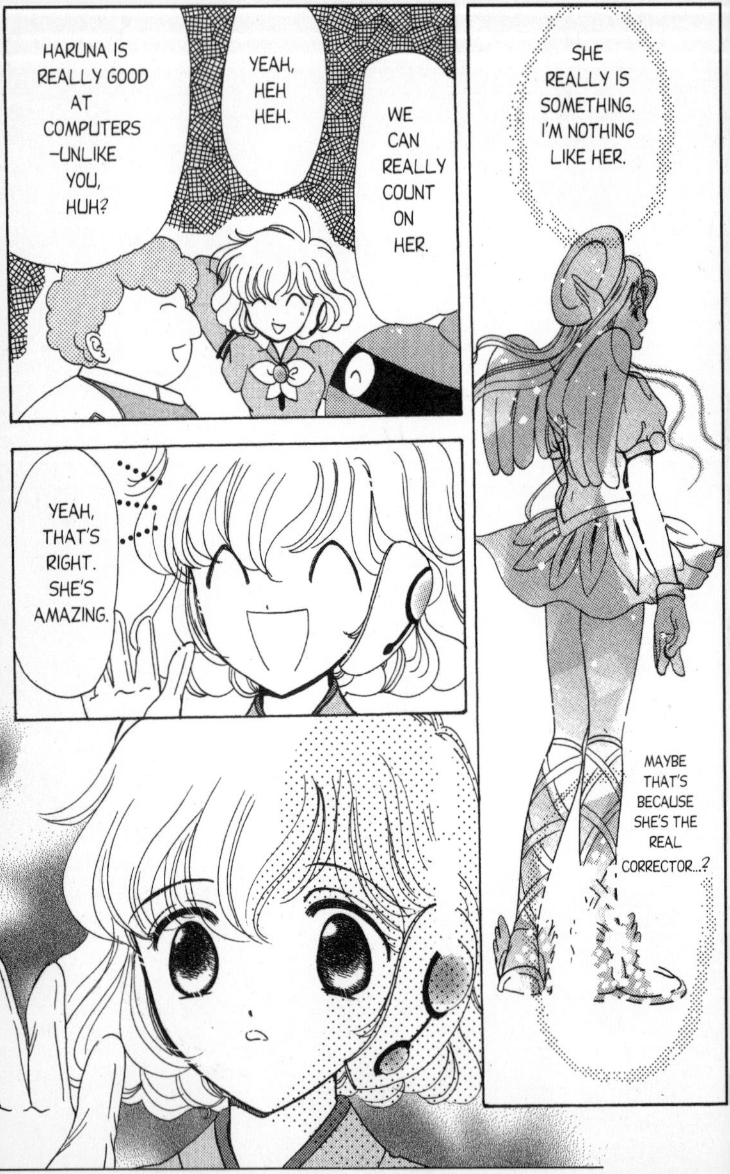
HARUNA IS REALLY GOOD AT COMPUTERS—UNLIKE YOU, HUH?
YEAH, HEH HEH.
WE CAN REALLY COUNT ON HER.
YEAH, THAT'S RIGHT. SHE'S AMAZING.
SHE REALLY IS SOMETHING. I'M NOTHING LIKE HER.
MAYBE THAT'S BECAUSE SHE'S THE REAL CORRECTOR...?

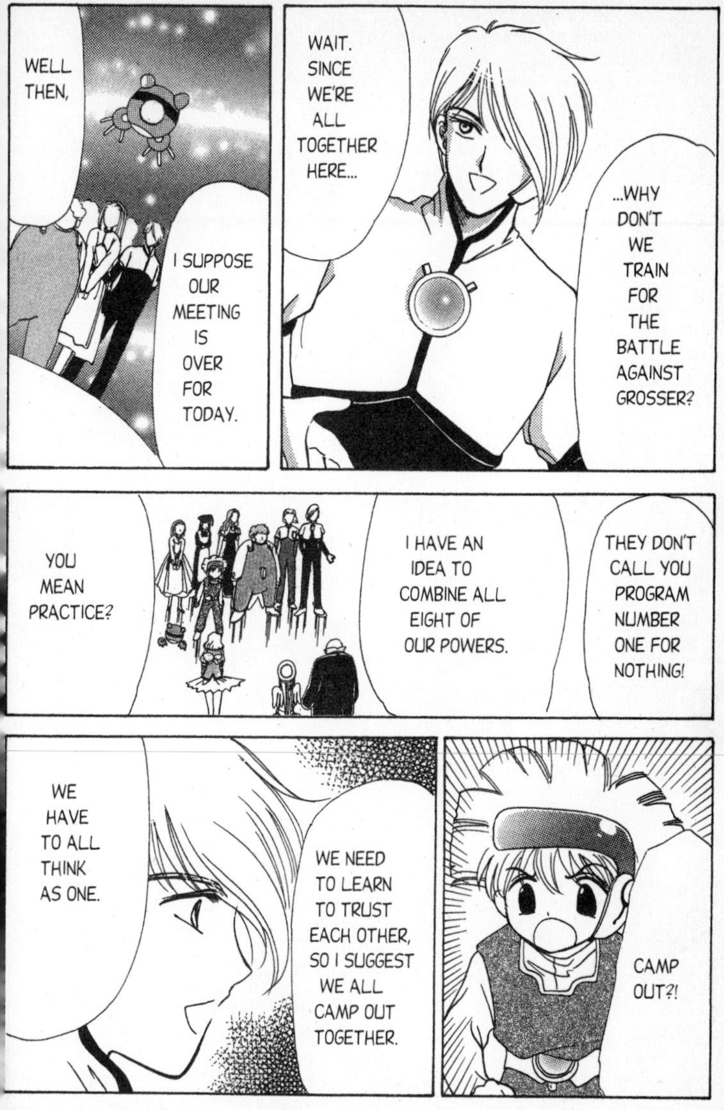
WELL THEN,
I SUPPOSE OUR MEETING IS OVER FOR TODAY.
WAIT. SINCE WE'RE ALL TOGETHER HERE...
...WHY DON'T WE TRAIN FOR THE BATTLE AGAINST GROSSER?
YOU MEAN PRACTICE?
I HAVE AN IDEA TO COMBINE ALL EIGHT OF OUR POWERS.
THEY DON'T CALL YOU PROGRAM NUMBER ONE FOR NOTHING!
WE HAVE TO ALL THINK AS ONE.
WE NEED TO LEARN TO TRUST EACH OTHER, SO I SUGGEST WE ALL CAMP OUT TOGETHER.
CAMP OUT?!

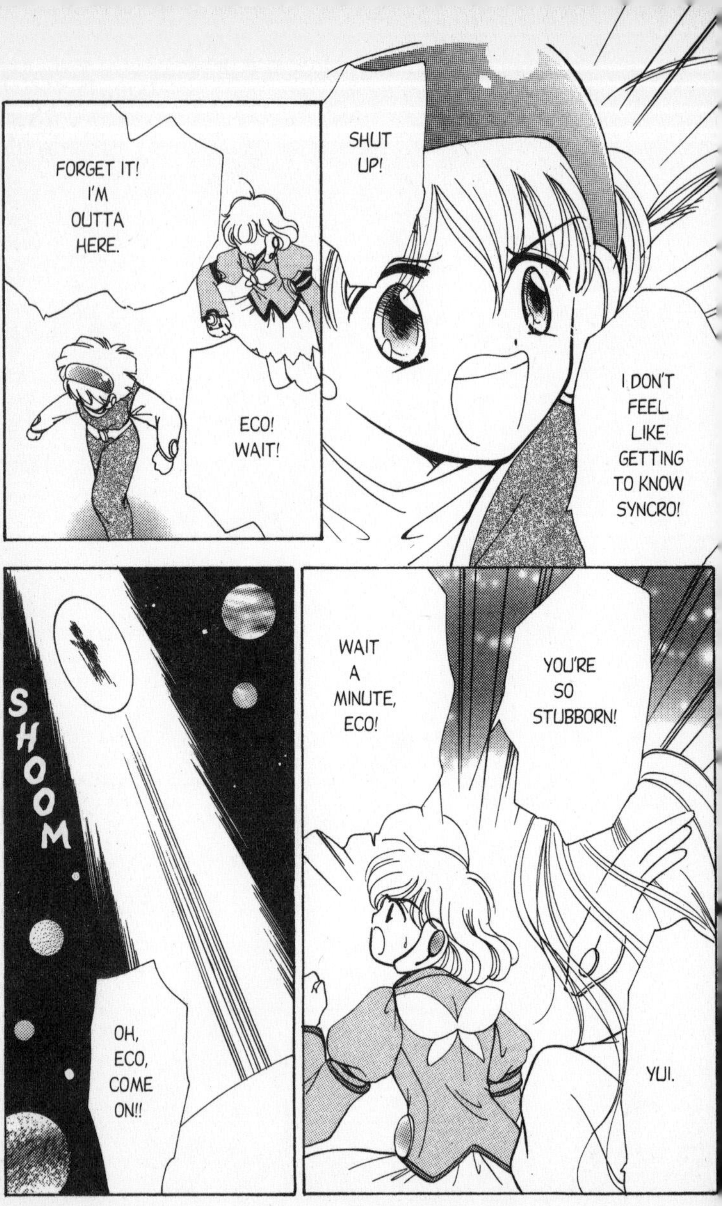
SHUT UP!
I DON'T FEEL LIKE GETTING TO KNOW SYNCRO!
FORGET IT! I'M OUTTA HERE.
ECO! WAIT!
YOU'RE SO STUBBORN!
WAIT A MINUTE, ECO!
YUI.
SHOOM
OH, ECO, COME ON!!

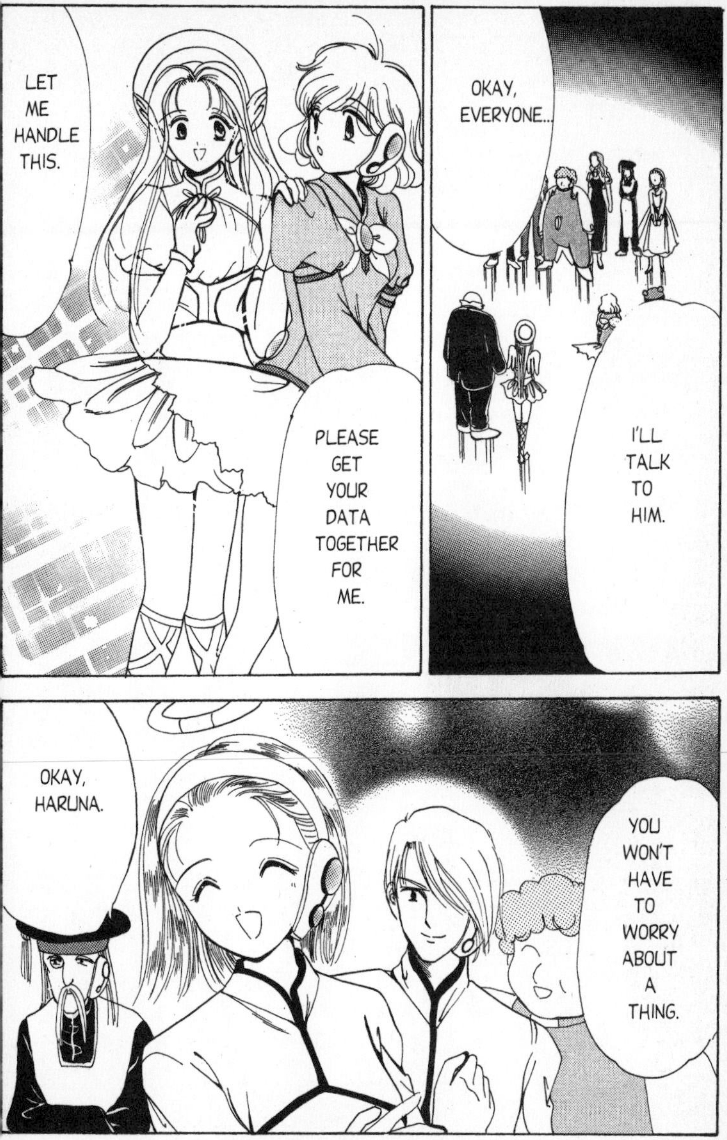
I'LL TALK TO HIM.
OKAY, EVERYONE...
PLEASE GET YOUR DATA TOGETHER FOR ME.
LET ME HANDLE THIS.
YOU WON'T HAVE TO WORRY ABOUT A THING.
OKAY, HARUNA.

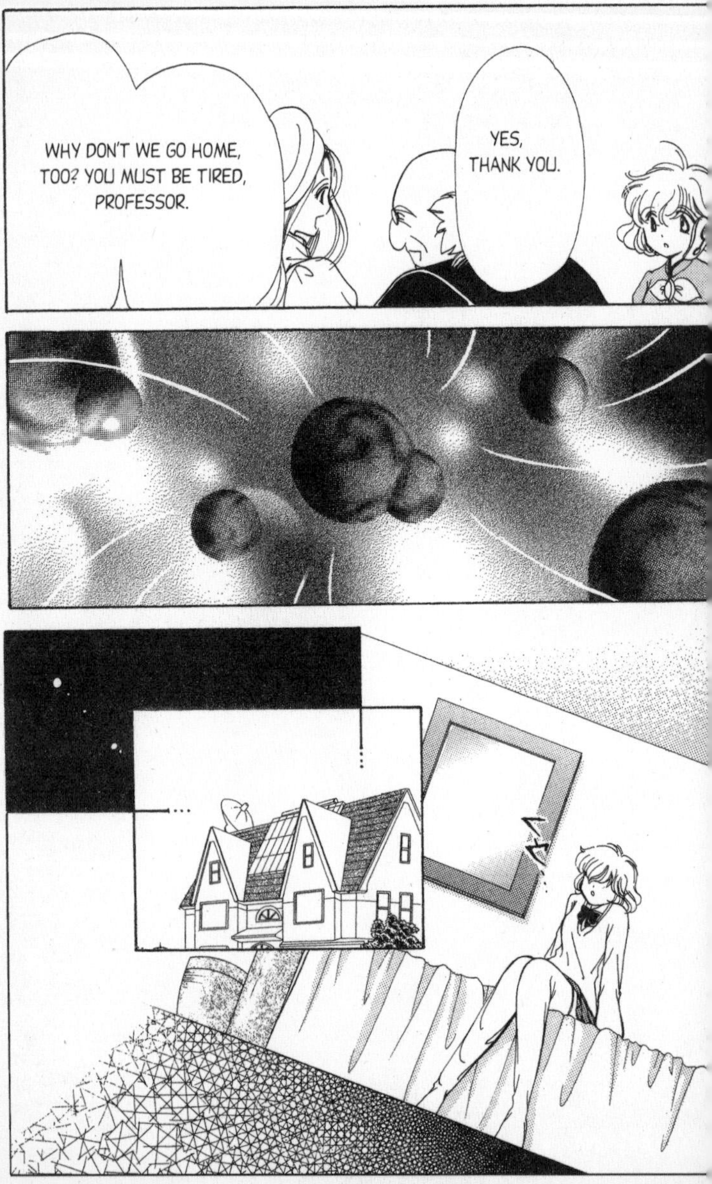
YES, THANK YOU.
WHY DON'T WE GO HOME, TOO? YOU MUST BE TIRED, PROFESSOR.
...
...

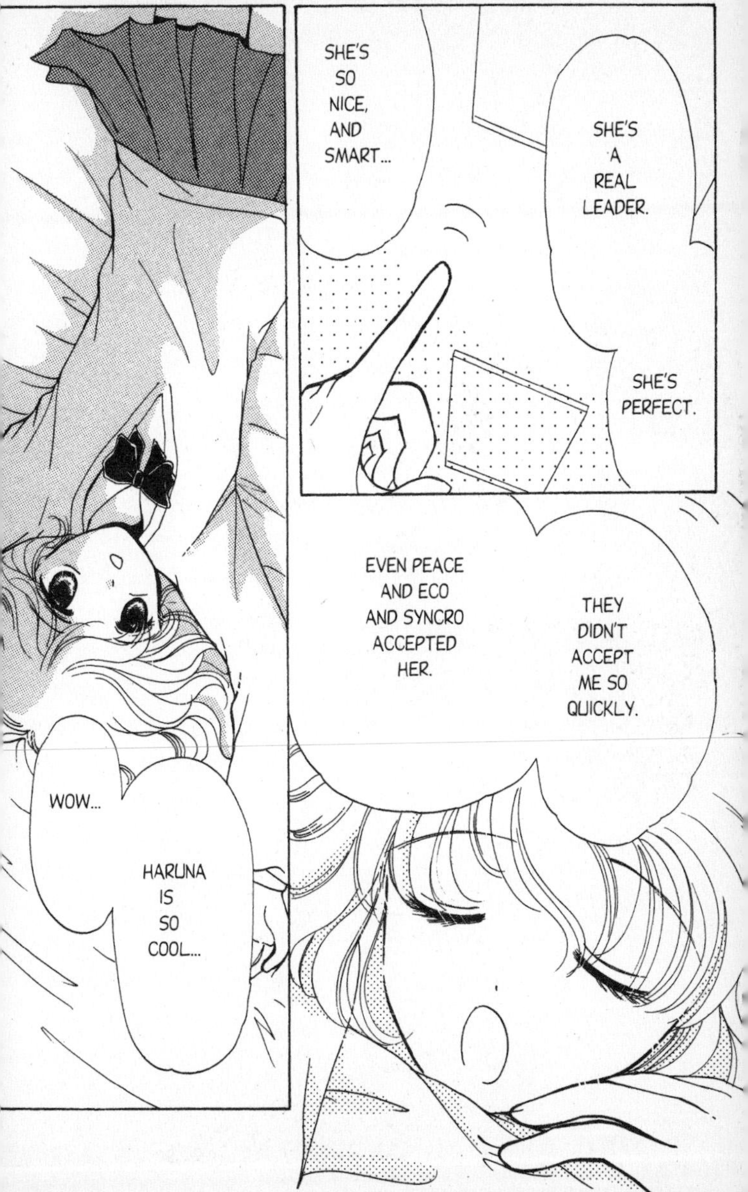
SHE'S SO NICE, AND SMART...
SHE'S A REAL LEADER.
SHE'S PERFECT.
EVEN PEACE AND ECO AND SYNCRO ACCEPTED HER.
THEY DIDN'T ACCEPT ME SO QUICKLY.
WOW...
HARUNA IS SO COOL...

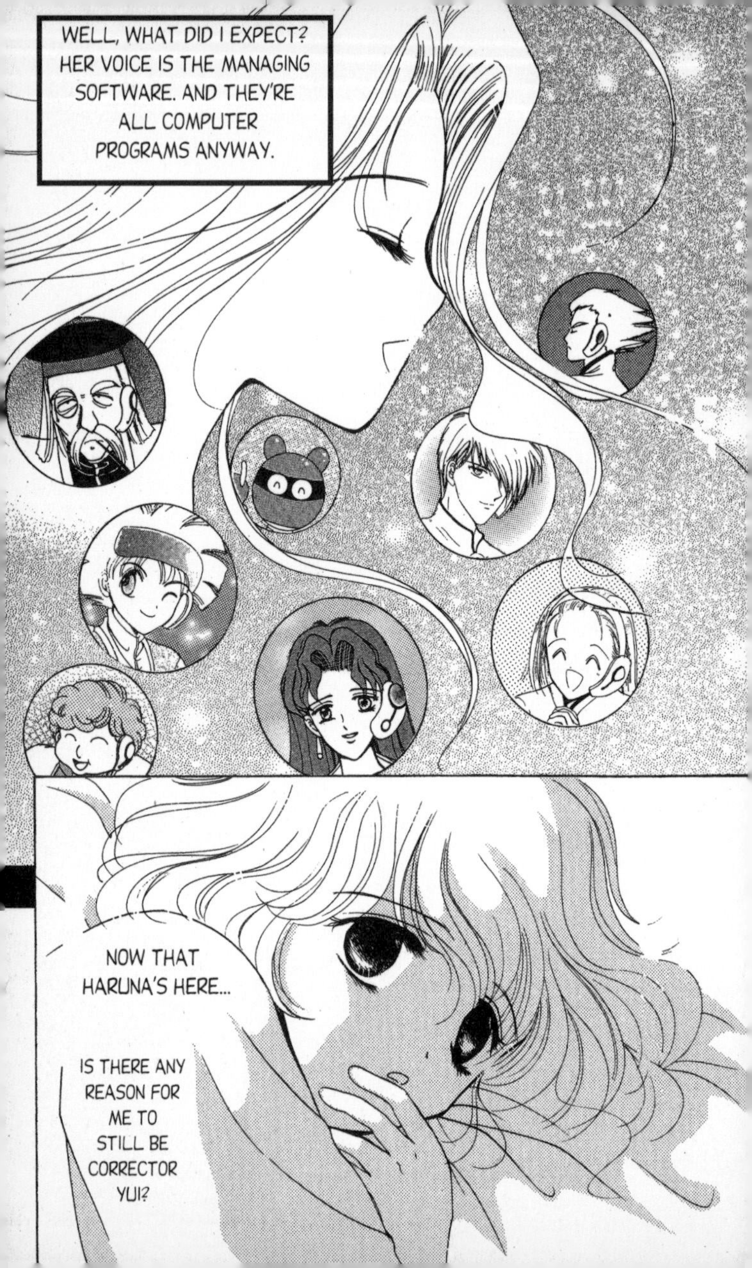
WELL, WHAT DID I EXPECT? HER VOICE IS THE MANAGING SOFTWARE. AND THEY'RE ALL COMPUTER PROGRAMS ANYWAY.
NOW THAT HARUNA'S HERE...
IS THERE ANY REASON FOR ME TO STILL BE CORRECTOR YUI?

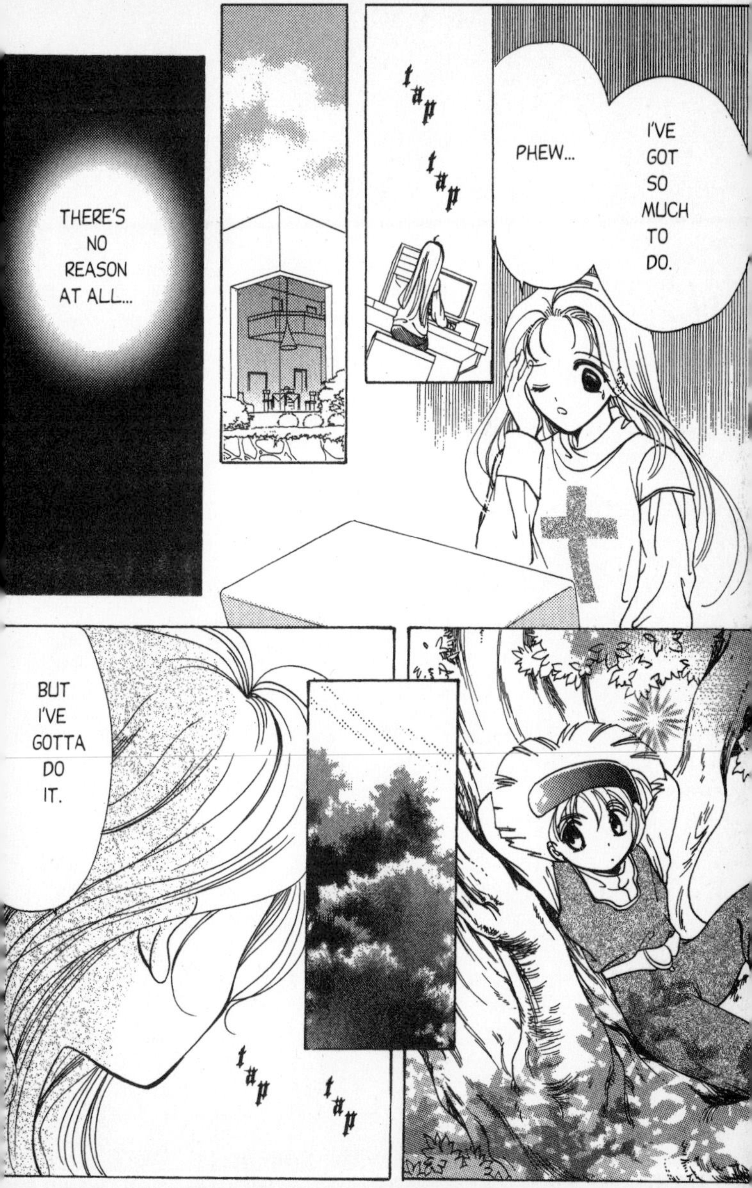
PHEW...
I'VE GOT SO MUCH TO DO.
tap tap
THERE'S NO REASON AT ALL...
tap tap
BUT I'VE GOTTA DO IT.

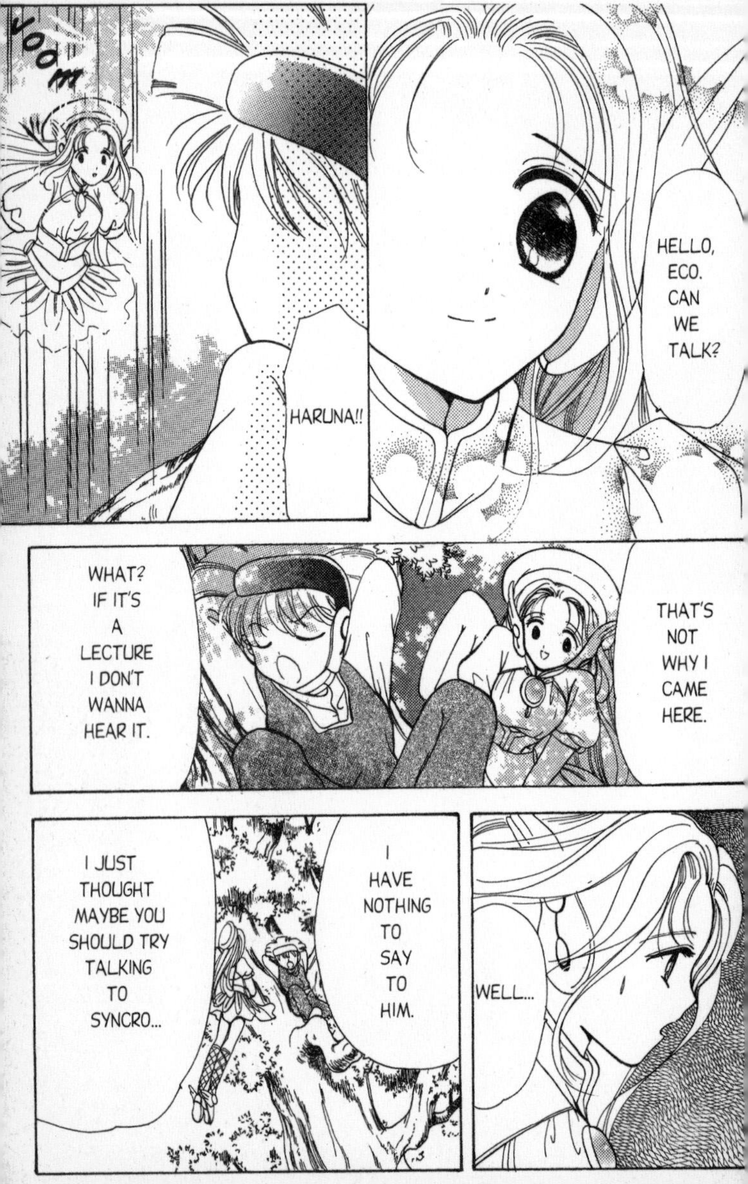
VOOM
HARUNA!!
HELLO, ECO. CAN WE TALK?
WHAT? IF IT'S A LECTURE I DON'T WANNA HEAR IT.
THAT'S NOT WHY I CAME HERE.
I JUST THOUGHT MAYBE YOU SHOULD TRY TALKING TO SYNCRO...
I HAVE NOTHING TO SAY TO HIM.
WELL...

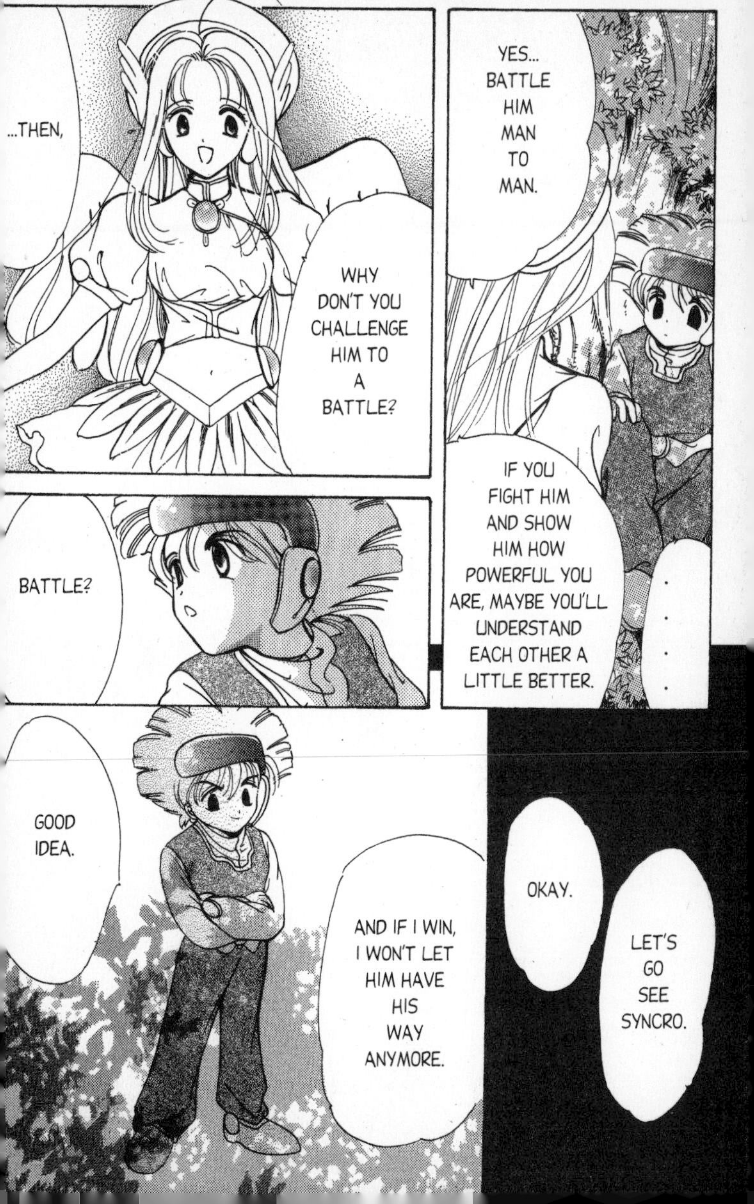
...THEN,
WHY DON'T YOU CHALLENGE HIM TO A BATTLE?
BATTLE?
YES... BATTLE HIM MAN TO MAN.
IF YOU FIGHT HIM AND SHOW HIM HOW POWERFUL YOU ARE, MAYBE YOU'LL UNDERSTAND EACH OTHER A LITTLE BETTER.
....
GOOD IDEA.
AND IF I WIN, I WON'T LET HIM HAVE HIS WAY ANYMORE.
OKAY.
LET'S GO SEE SYNCRO.

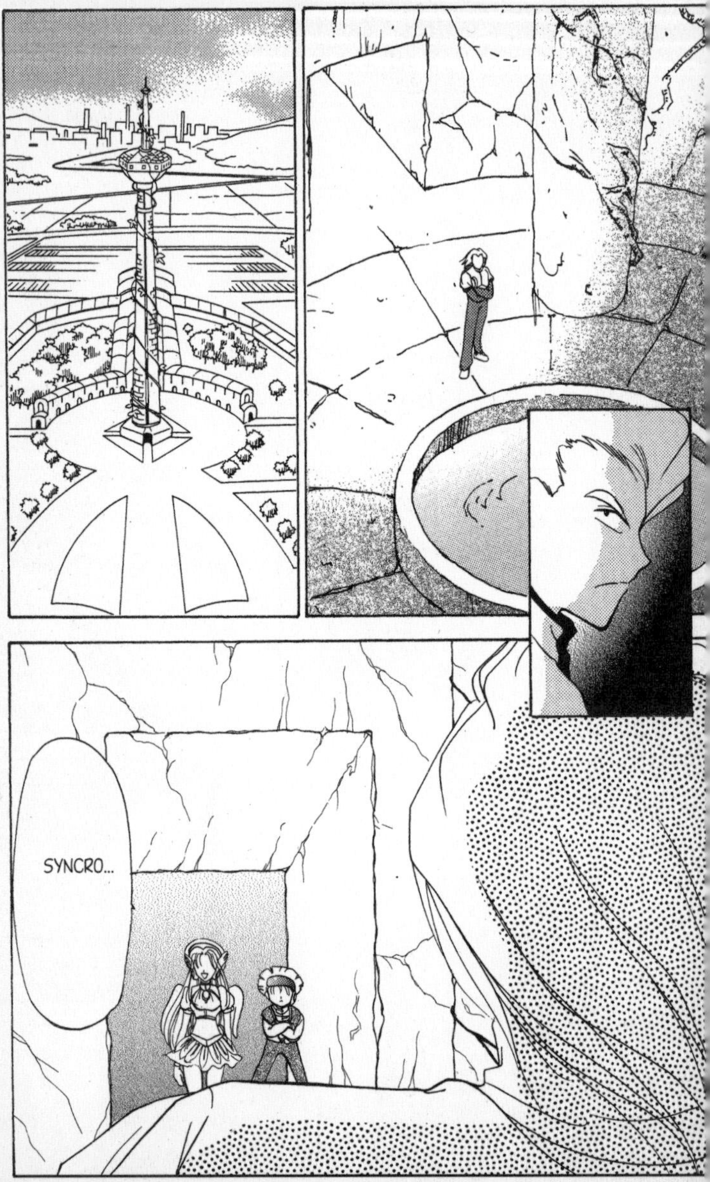
SYNCRO...

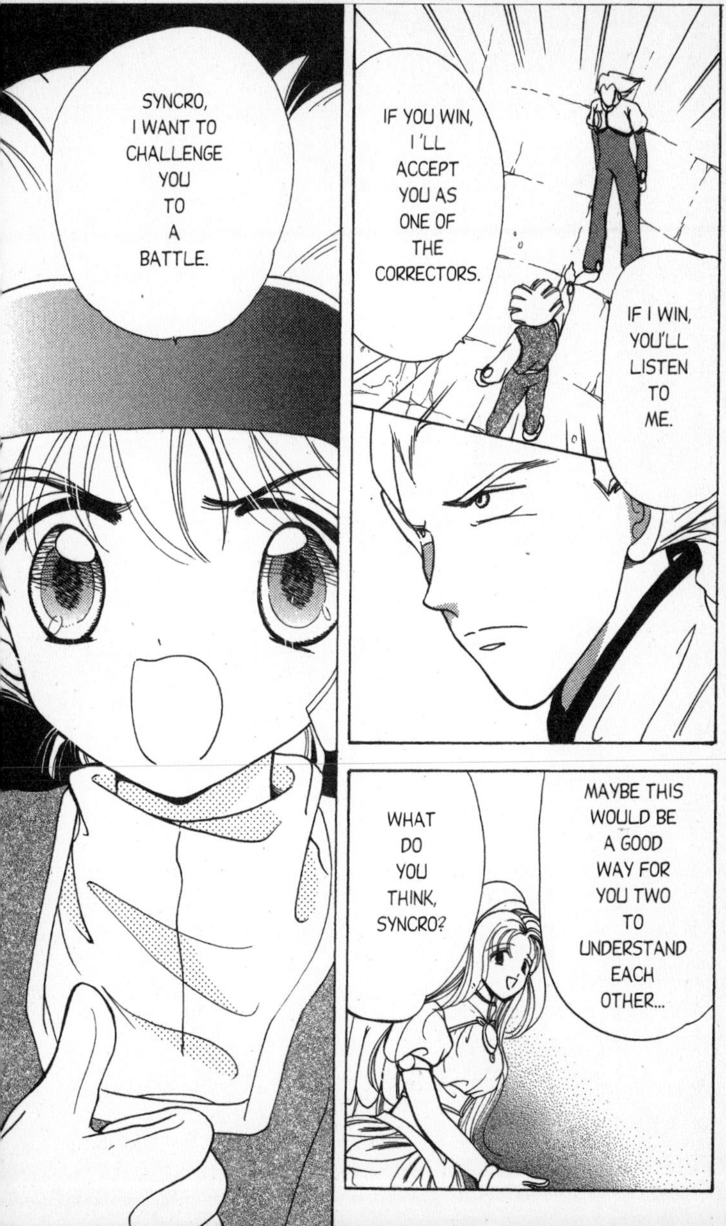
SYNCRO, I WANT TO CHALLENGE YOU TO A BATTLE.
IF YOU WIN, I'LL ACCEPT YOU AS ONE OF THE CORRECTORS.
IF I WIN, YOU'LL LISTEN TO ME.
MAYBE THIS WOULD BE A GOOD WAY FOR YOU TWO TO UNDERSTAND EACH OTHER...
WHAT DO YOU THINK, SYNCRO?

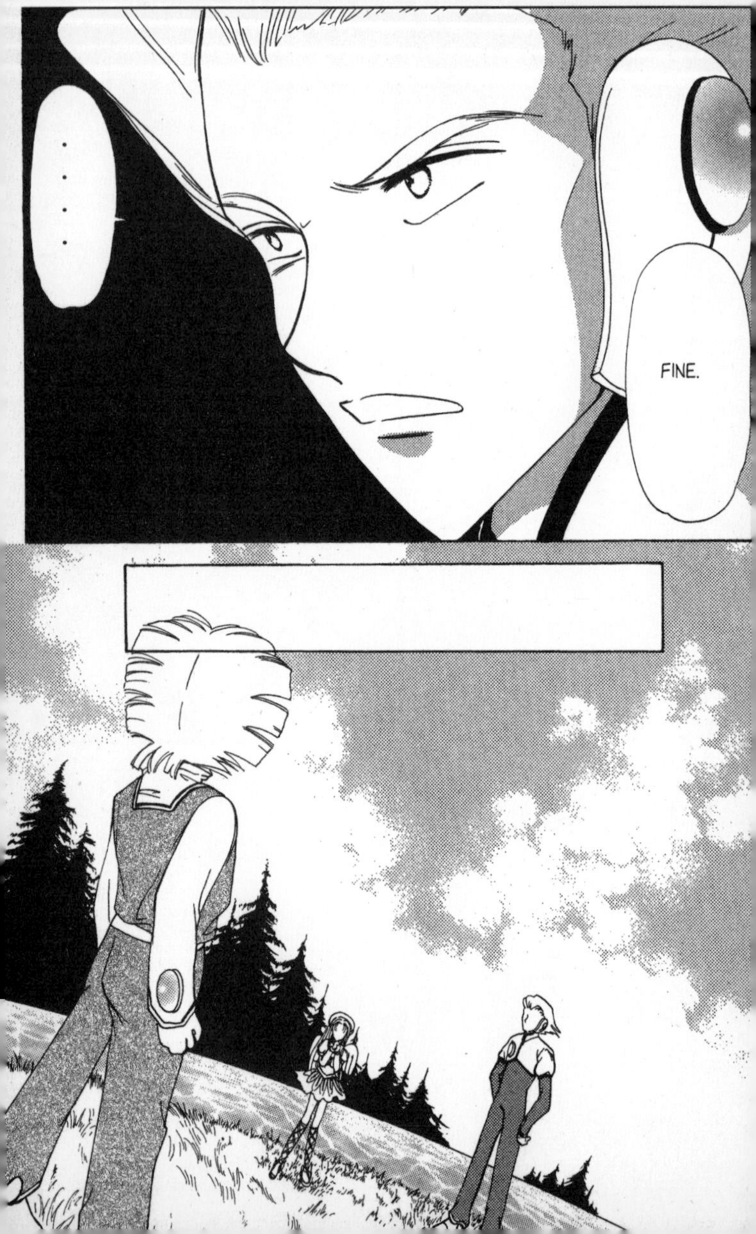
FINE.
....

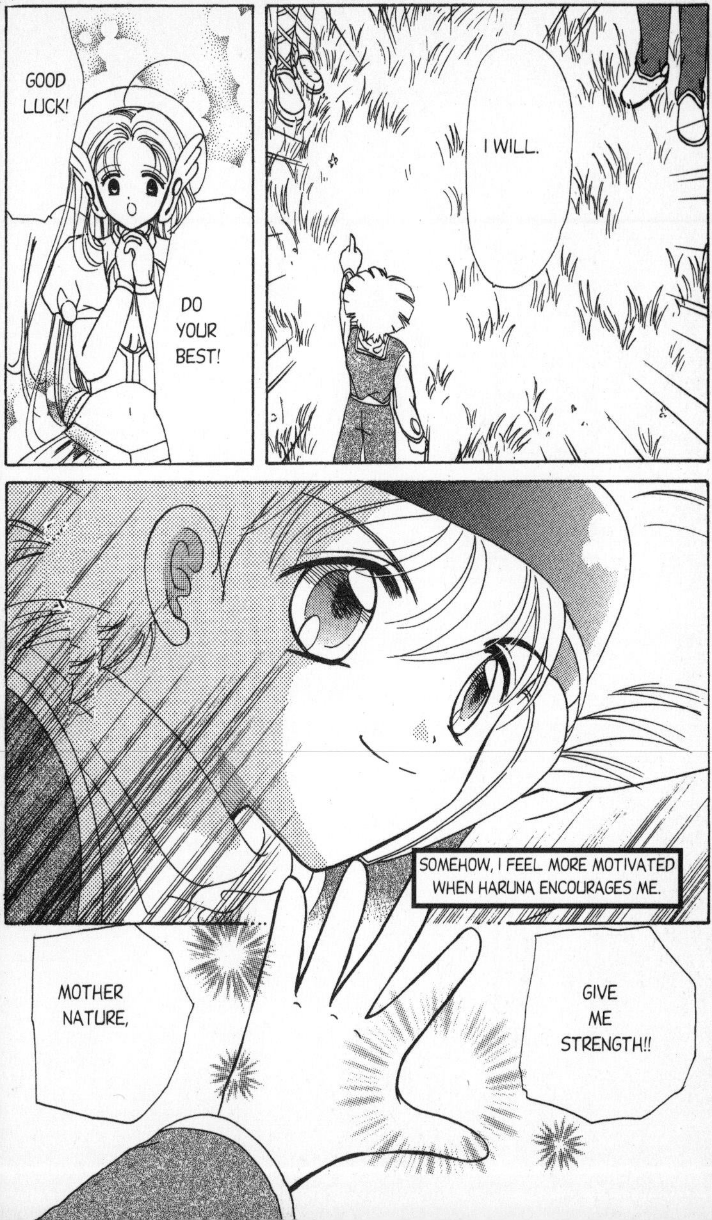
GOOD LUCK!
DO YOUR BEST!
I WILL.
SOMEHOW, I FEEL MORE MOTIVATED WHEN HARUNA ENCOURAGES ME.
MOTHER NATURE,
GIVE ME STRENGTH!!

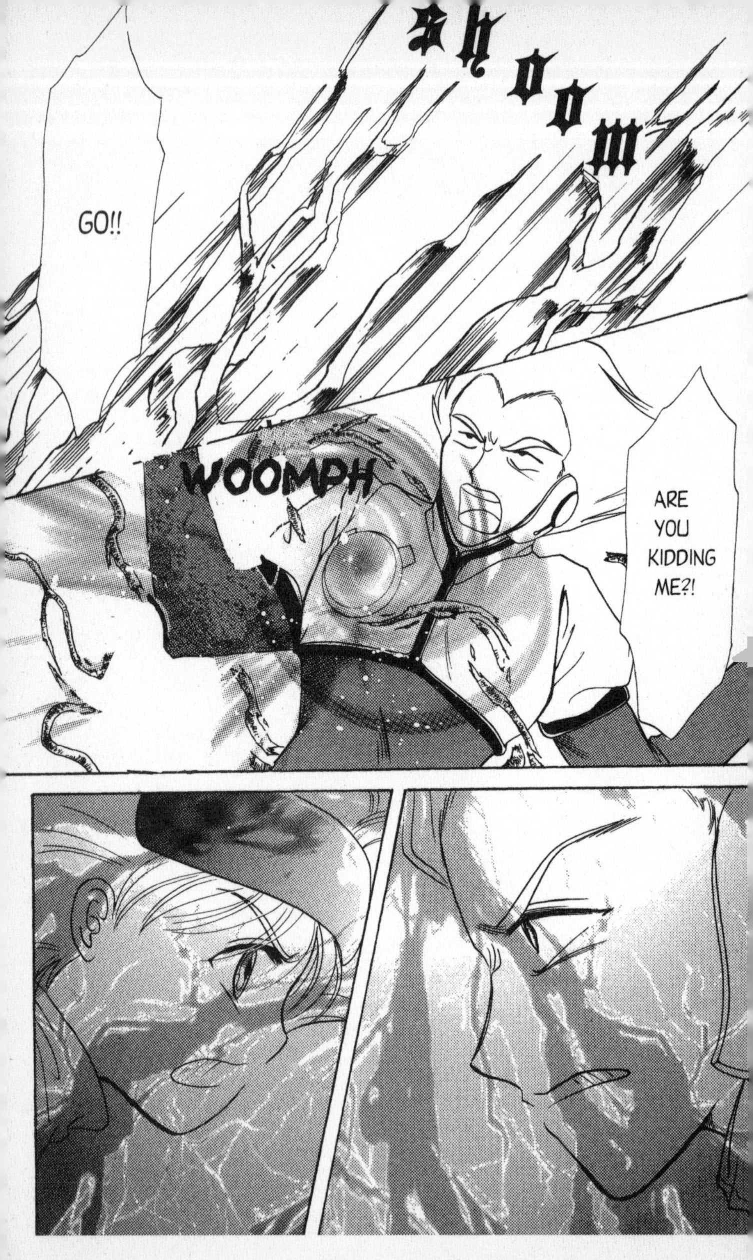
shoom
GO!!
ARE YOU KIDDING ME?!
WOOMPH

FIGHT YOUR HARDEST!

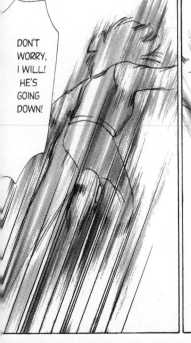

DON'T WORRY, I WILL! HE'S GOING DOWN!

IN YOUR DREAMS!

WHAAMMM
WHAT'S GOING ON?!
I'M GETTING VERY STRONG SIGNALS!
BEEP BEEP BEEP

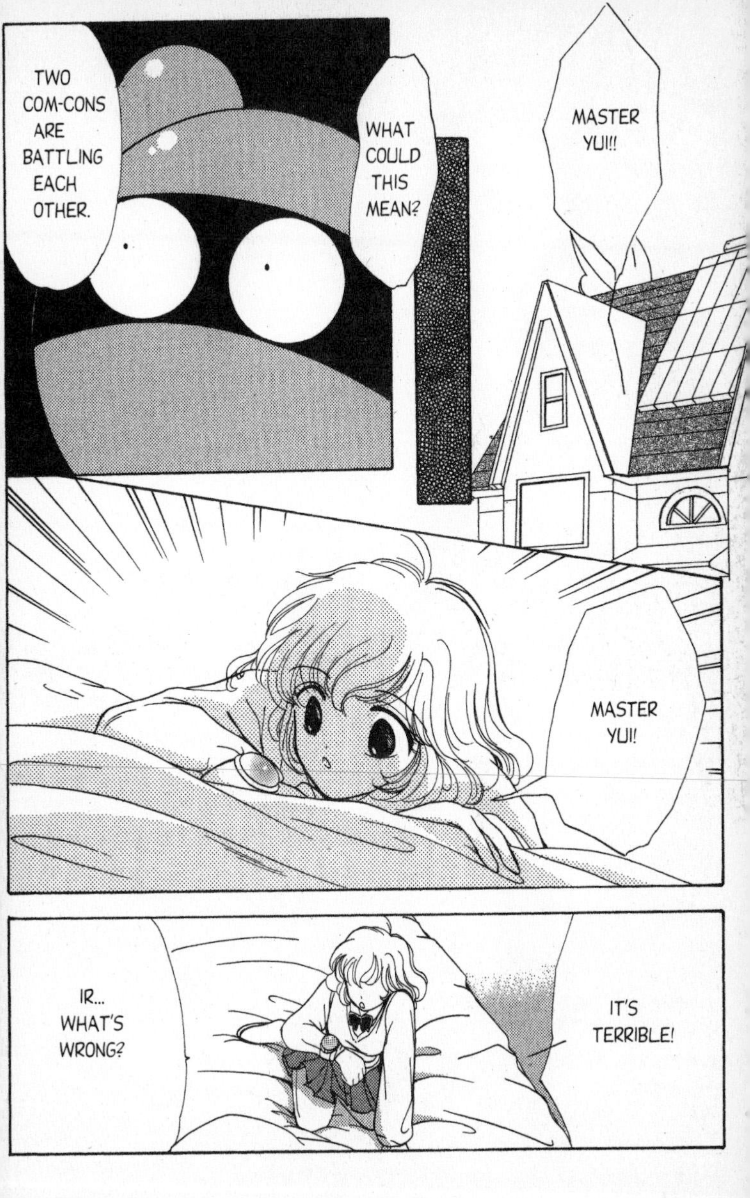
MASTER YUI!!
TWO COM-CONS ARE BATTLING EACH OTHER.
WHAT COULD THIS MEAN?
MASTER YUI!
IT'S TERRIBLE!
IR... WHAT'S WRONG?

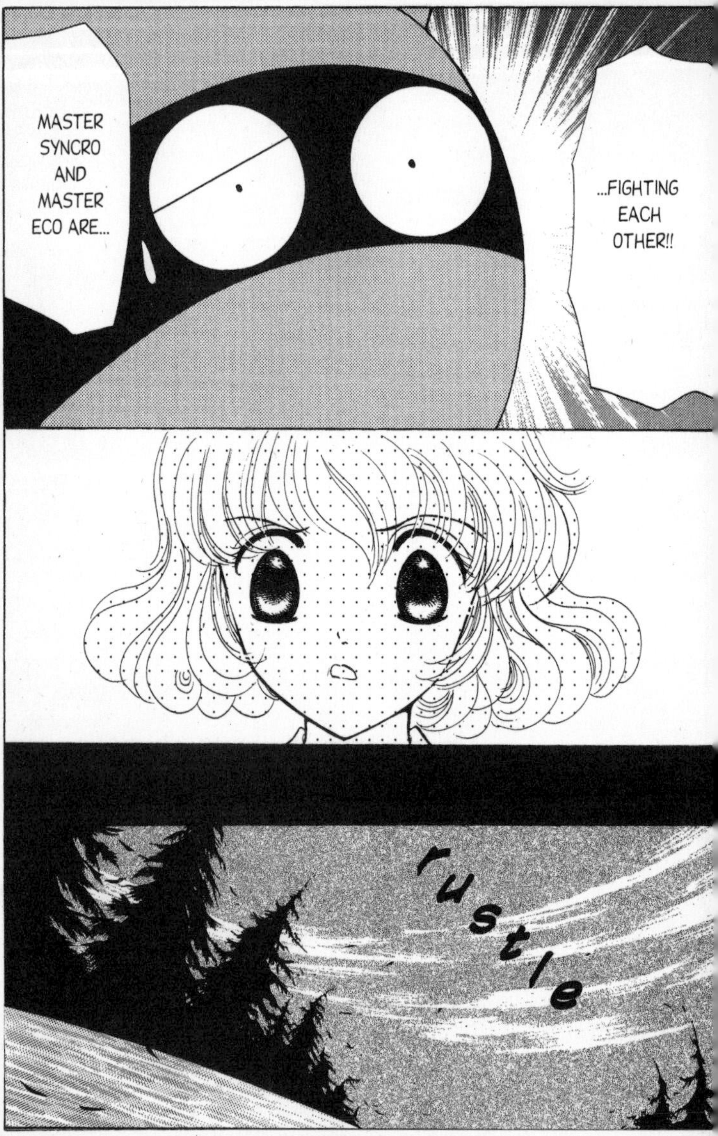
MASTER SYNCRO AND MASTER ECO ARE...
...FIGHTING EACH OTHER!!
rustle

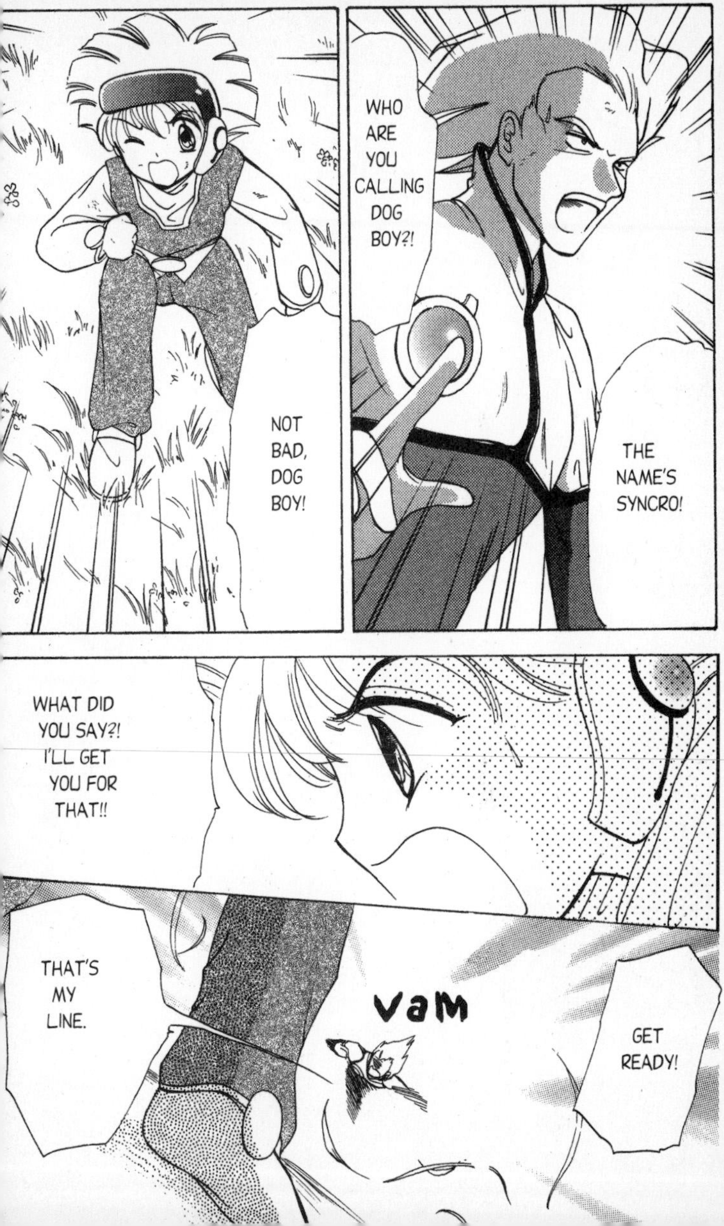
NOT BAD, DOG BOY!
WHO ARE YOU CALLING DOG BOY?!
THE NAME'S SYNCRO!
WHAT DID YOU SAY?! I'LL GET YOU FOR THAT!!
THAT'S MY LINE.
vaM
GET READY!

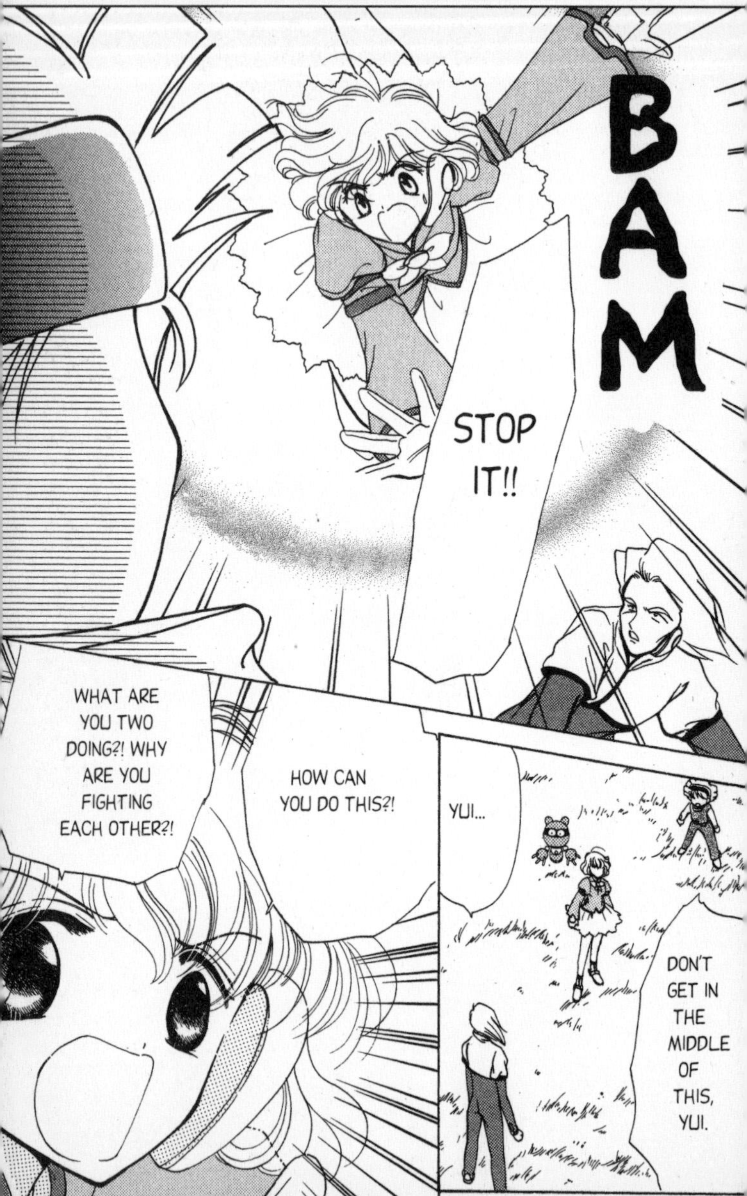
BAM
STOP IT!!
YUI...
DON'T GET IN THE MIDDLE OF THIS, YUI.
HOW CAN YOU DO THIS?!
WHAT ARE YOU TWO DOING?! WHY ARE YOU FIGHTING EACH OTHER?!

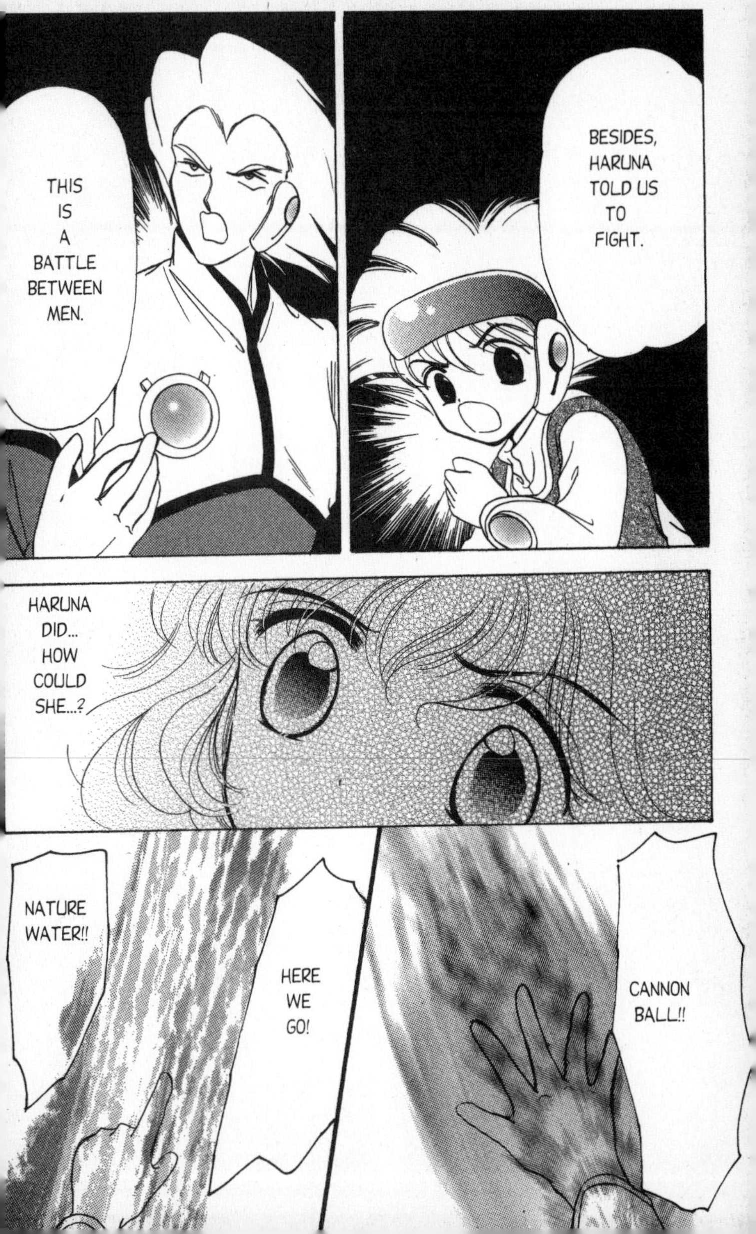
BESIDES, HARUNA TOLD US TO FIGHT.
THIS IS A BATTLE BETWEEN MEN.
HARUNA DID... HOW COULD SHE...?
CANNON BALL!!
HERE WE GO!
NATURE WATER!!

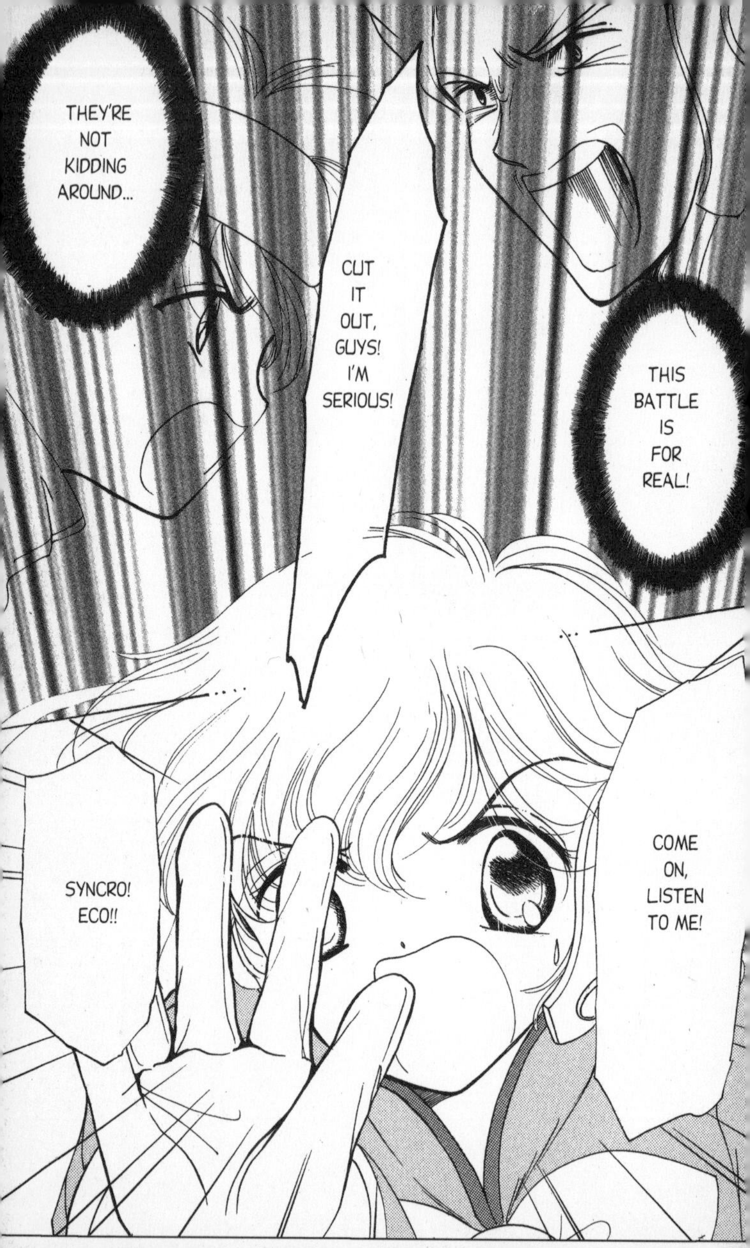
CUT IT OUT, GUYS! I'M SERIOUS!
THEY'RE NOT KIDDING AROUND...
THIS BATTLE IS FOR REAL!
COME ON, LISTEN TO ME!
SYNCRO! ECO!!

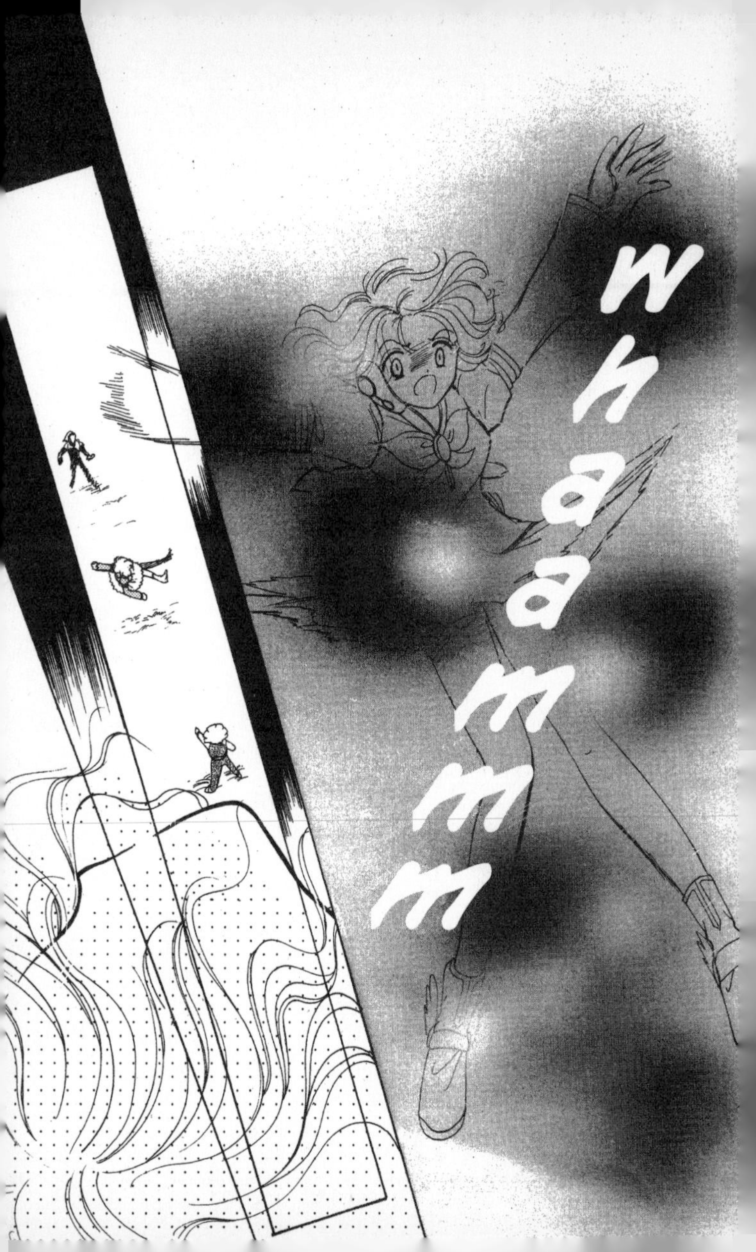
Whhaammmm

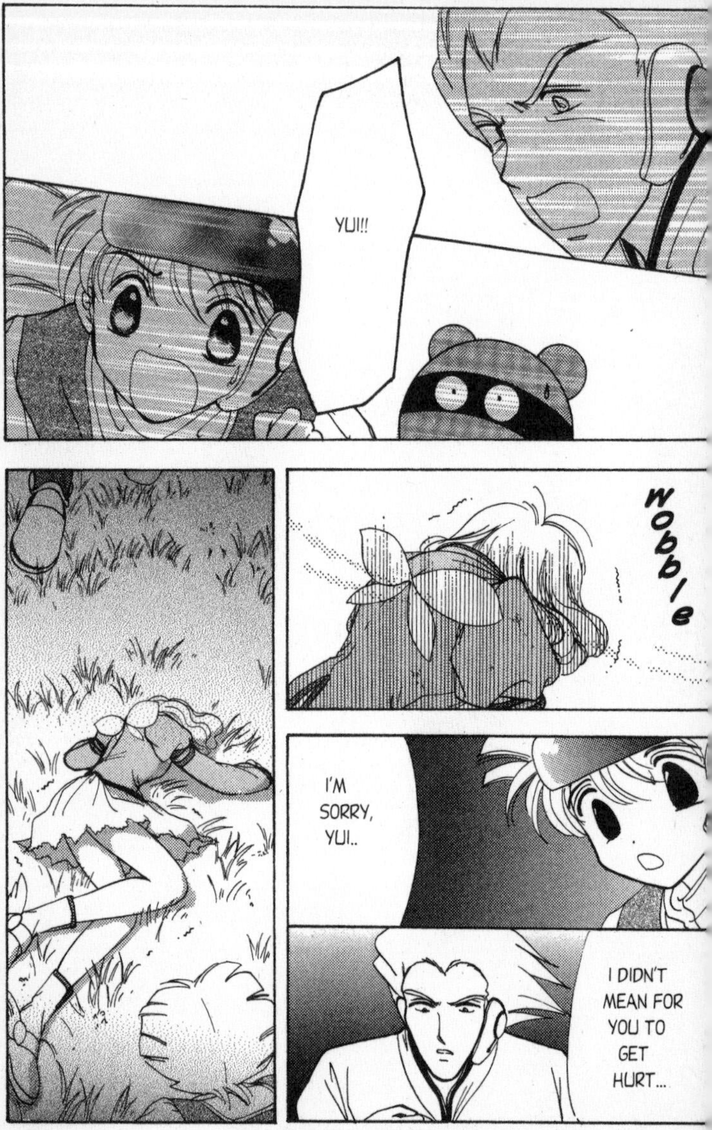
YUI!!
WOBBLE
I'M SORRY, YUI..
I DIDN'T MEAN FOR YOU TO GET HURT...

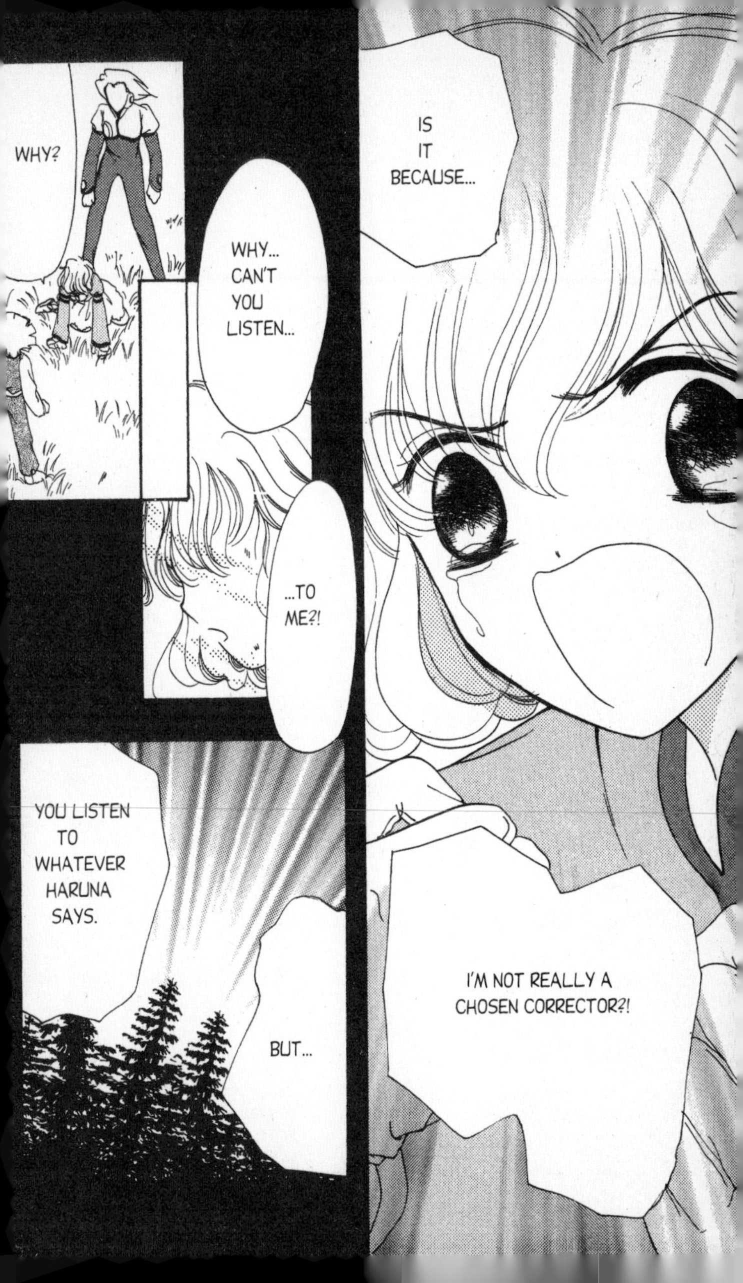
WHY?
WHY... CAN'T YOU LISTEN...
...TO ME?!
YOU LISTEN TO WHATEVER HARUNA SAYS.
BUT...
IS IT BECAUSE...
I'M NOT REALLY A CHOSEN CORRECTOR?!

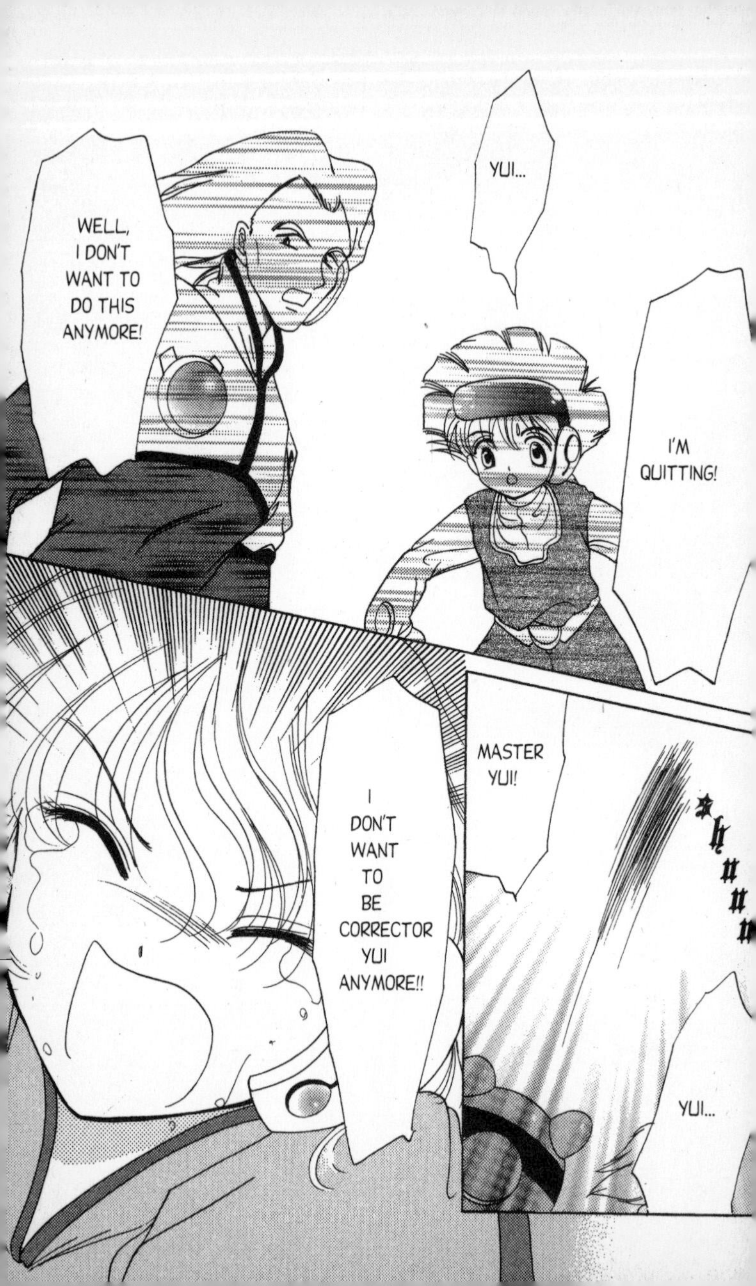
YUI...
WELL, I DON'T WANT TO DO THIS ANYMORE!
I'M QUITTING!
MASTER YUI!
YUI...
I DON'T WANT TO BE CORRECTOR YUI ANYMORE!!

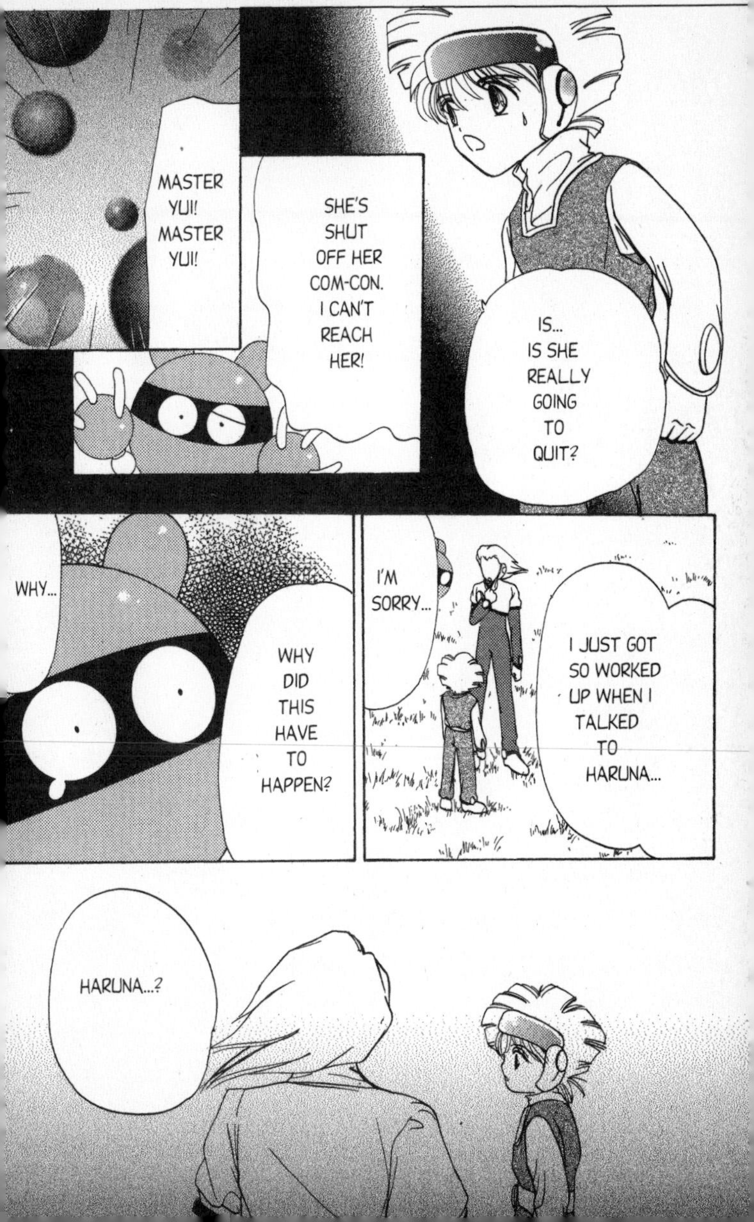
IS... IS SHE REALLY GOING TO QUIT?
MASTER YUI! MASTER YUI!
SHE'S SHUT OFF HER COM-CON. I CAN'T REACH HER!
I'M SORRY...
I JUST GOT SO WORKED UP WHEN I TALKED TO HARUNA...
WHY...
WHY DID THIS HAVE TO HAPPEN?
HARUNA...?

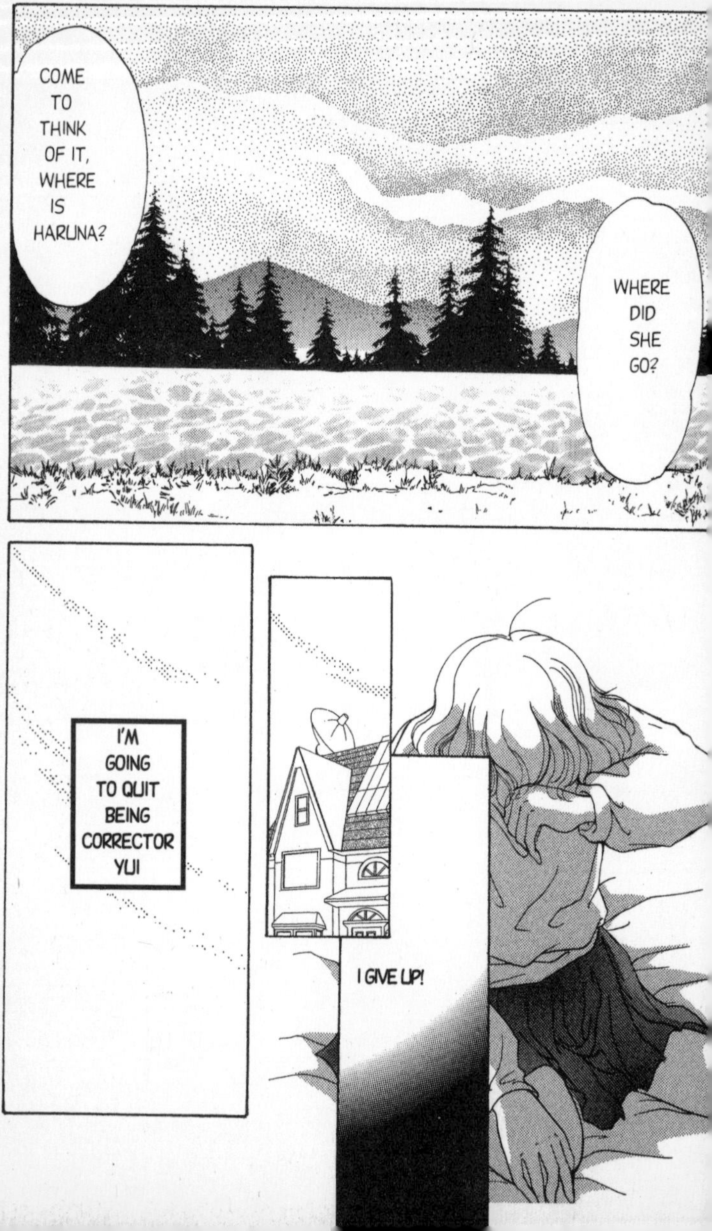
WHERE DID SHE GO?
COME TO THINK OF IT, WHERE IS HARUNA?
I GIVE UP!
I'M GOING TO QUIT BEING CORRECTOR YUI

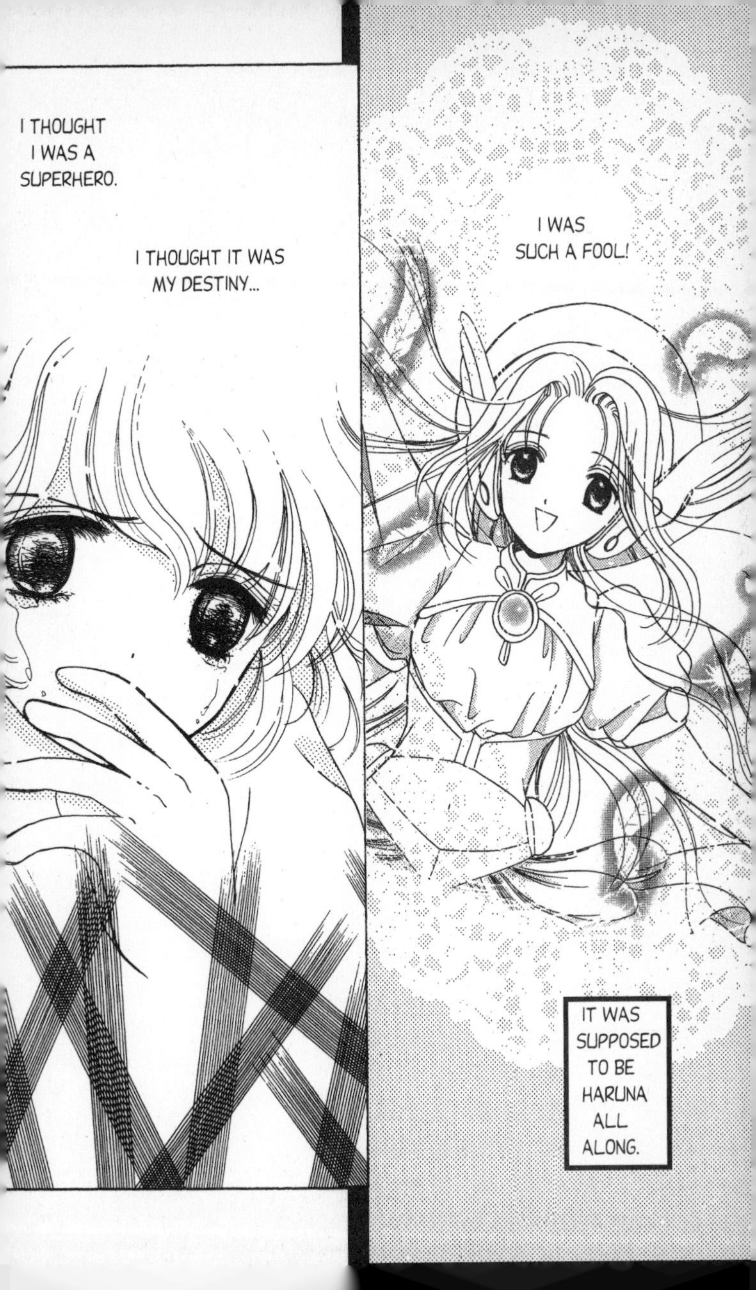
I WAS SUCH A FOOL!
IT WAS SUPPOSED TO BE HARUNA ALL ALONG.
I THOUGHT I WAS A SUPERHERO.
I THOUGHT IT WAS MY DESTINY...

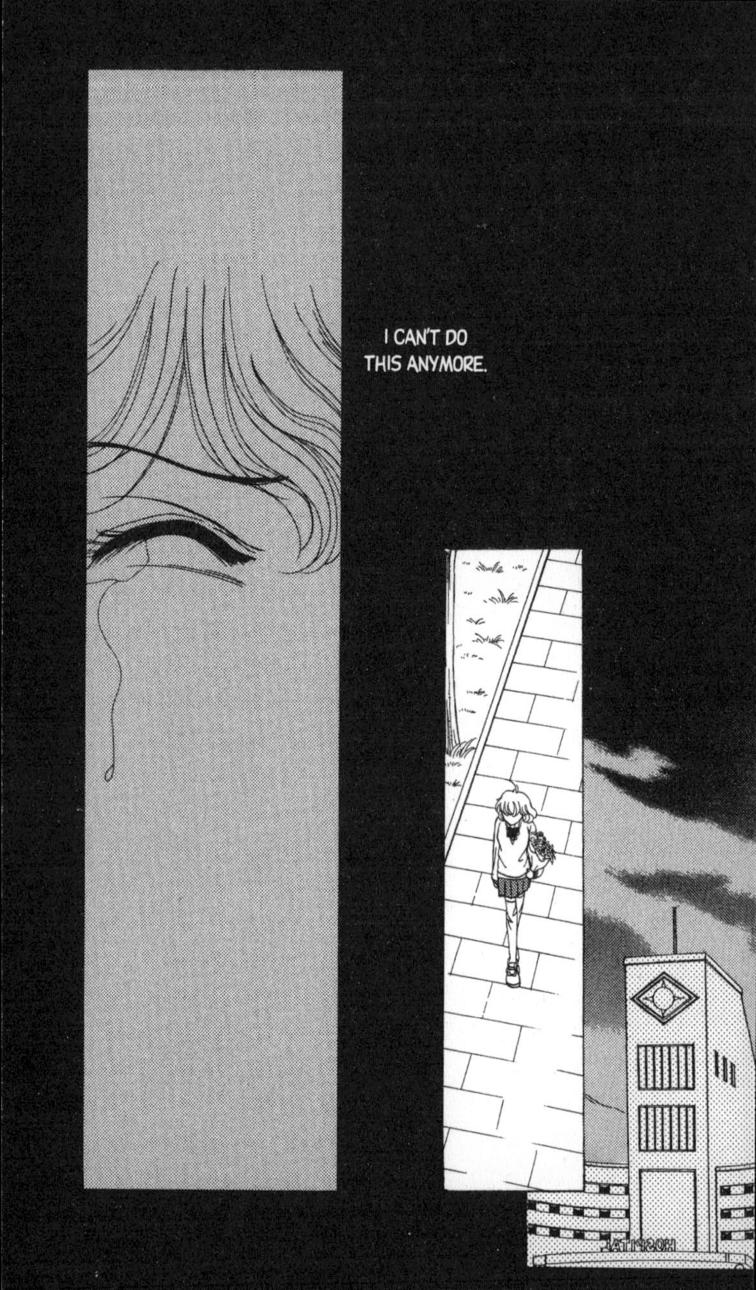
I CAN'T DO
THIS ANYMORE.

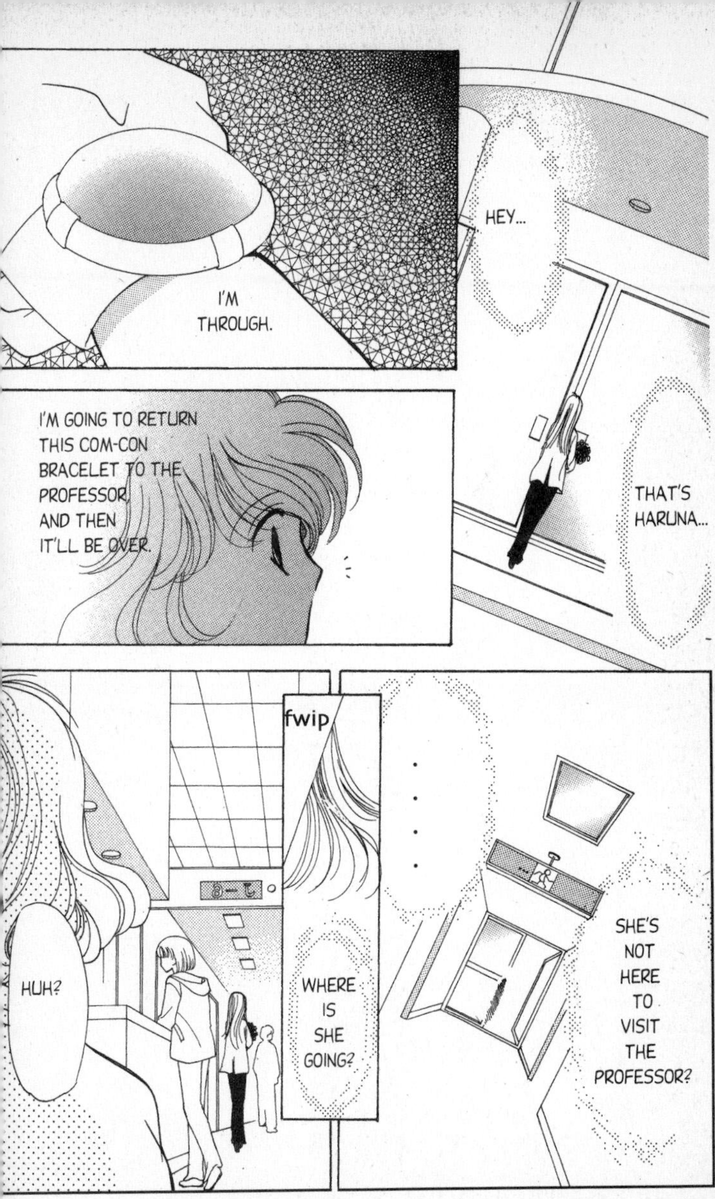
HEY...
THAT'S HARUNA...
I'M THROUGH.
I'M GOING TO RETURN THIS COM-CON BRACELET TO THE PROFESSOR AND THEN IT'LL BE OVER.
. . . .
SHE'S NOT HERE TO VISIT THE PROFESSOR?
fwip
WHERE IS SHE GOING?
HUH?

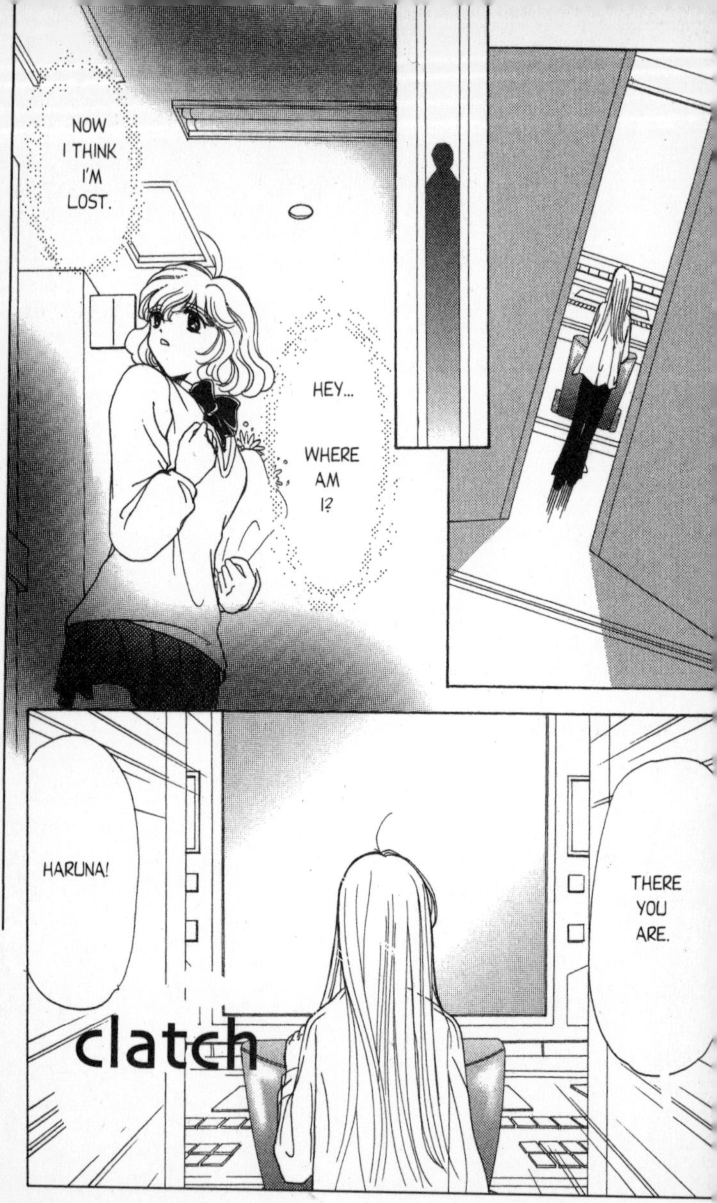
HEY... WHERE AM I?
NOW I THINK I'M LOST.
THERE YOU ARE.
HARUNA!
clatch

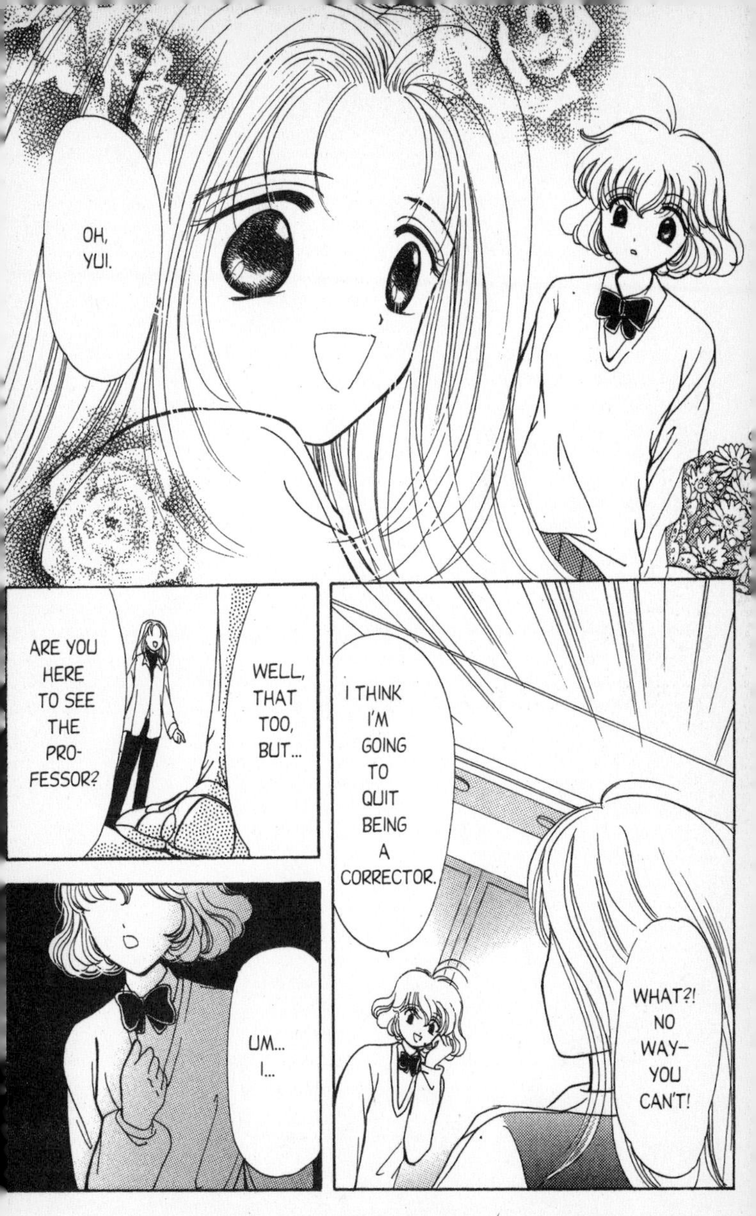
OH, YUI.
ARE YOU HERE TO SEE THE PRO- FESSOR?
WELL, THAT TOO, BUT...
UM... I...
I THINK I'M GOING TO QUIT BEING A CORRECTOR.
WHAT?! NO WAY– YOU CAN'T!

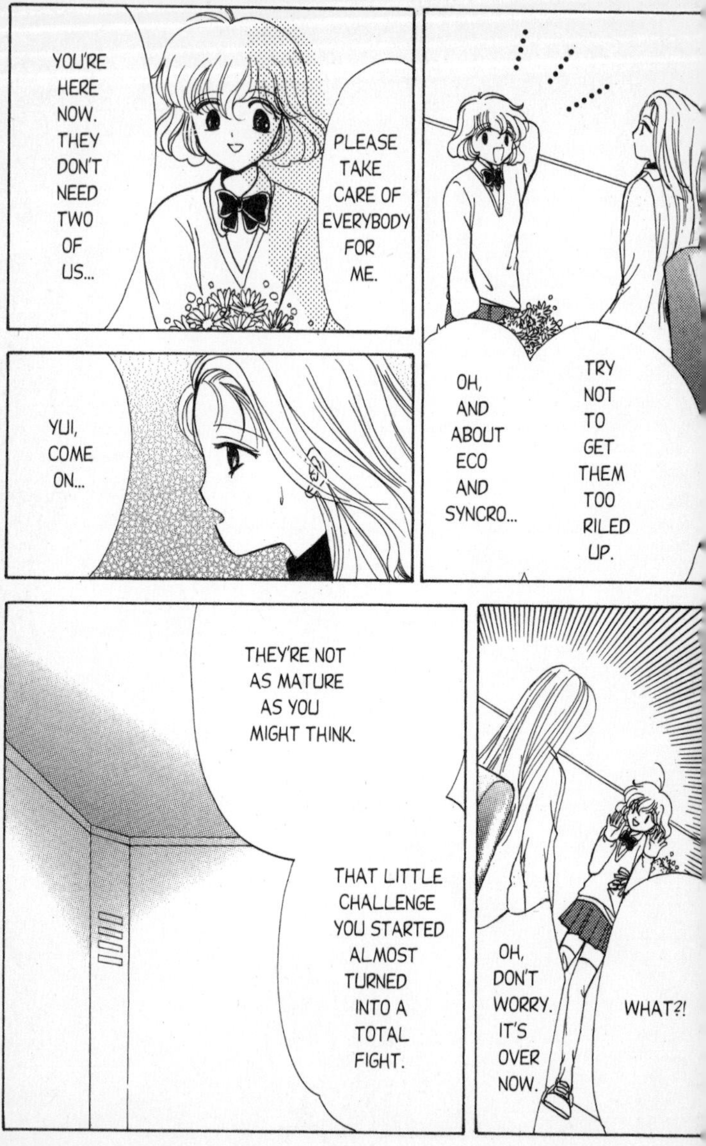
PLEASE TAKE CARE OF EVERYBODY FOR ME.
YOU'RE HERE NOW. THEY DON'T NEED TWO OF US...
YUI, COME ON...
OH, AND ABOUT ECO AND SYNCRO...
TRY NOT TO GET THEM TOO RILED UP.
WHAT?!
OH, DON'T WORRY. IT'S OVER NOW.
THEY'RE NOT AS MATURE AS YOU MIGHT THINK.
THAT LITTLE CHALLENGE YOU STARTED ALMOST TURNED INTO A TOTAL FIGHT.

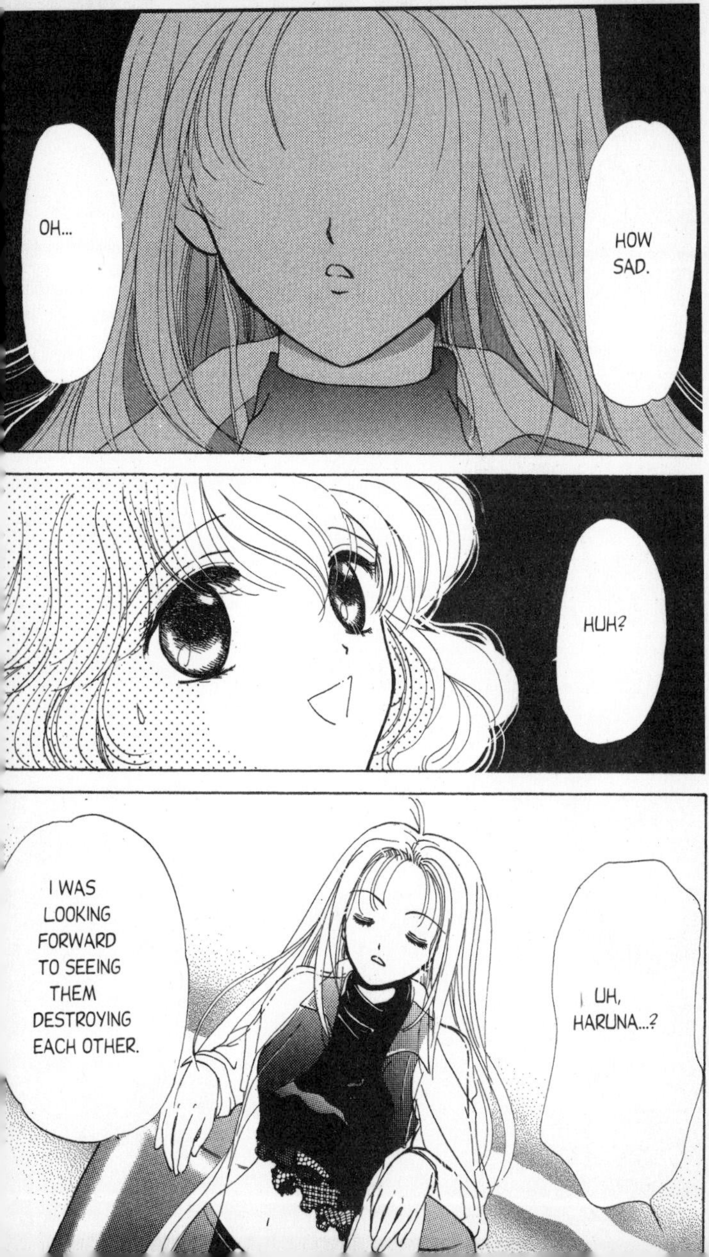
HOW SAD.
OH...
HUH?
UH, HARUNA...?
I WAS LOOKING FORWARD TO SEEING THEM DESTROYING EACH OTHER.

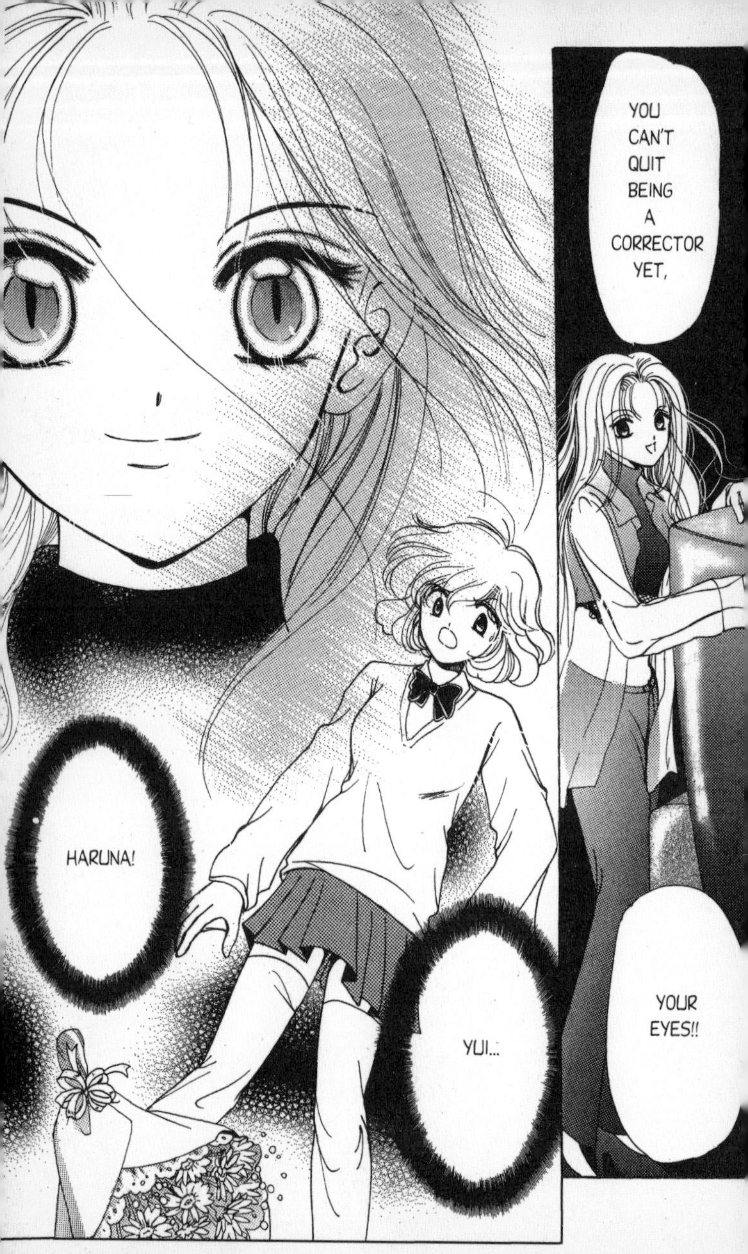
YOU CAN'T QUIT BEING A CORRECTOR YET,
YOUR EYES!!
HARUNA!
YUI...

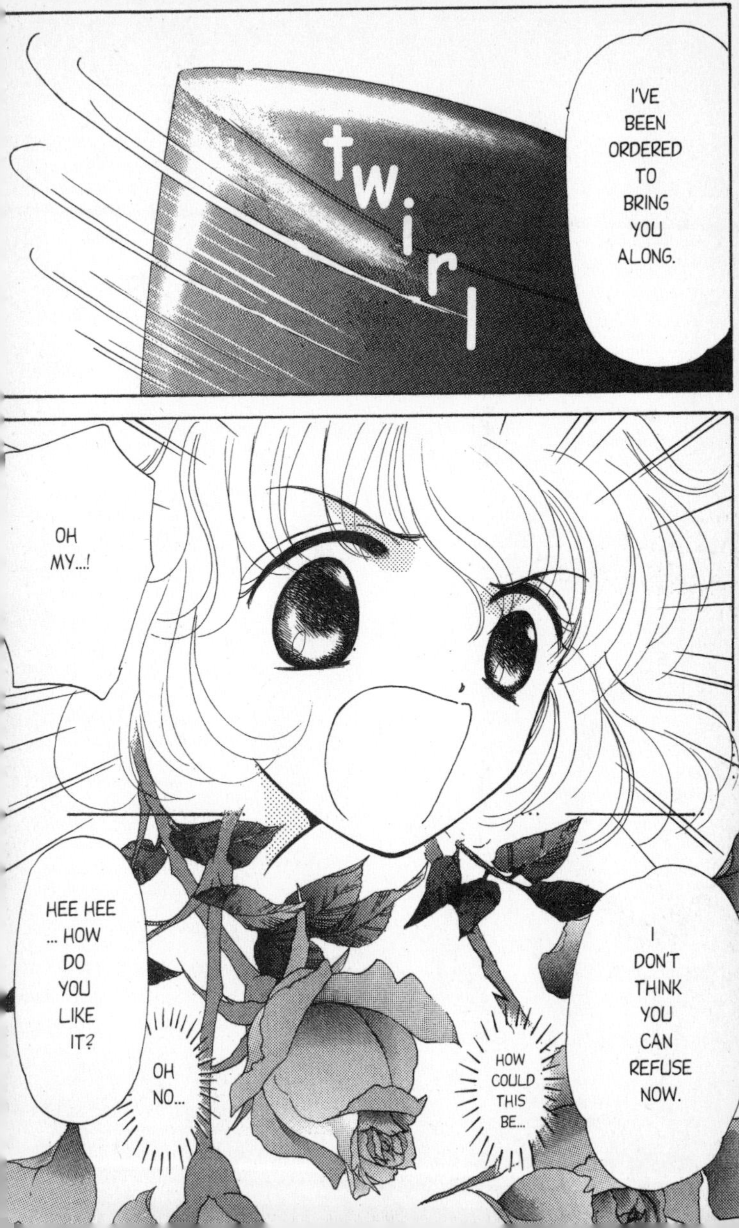
I'VE BEEN ORDERED TO BRING YOU ALONG.
twirl
OH MY...!
I DON'T THINK YOU CAN REFUSE NOW.
HOW COULD THIS BE...
OH NO...
HEE HEE ... HOW DO YOU LIKE IT?

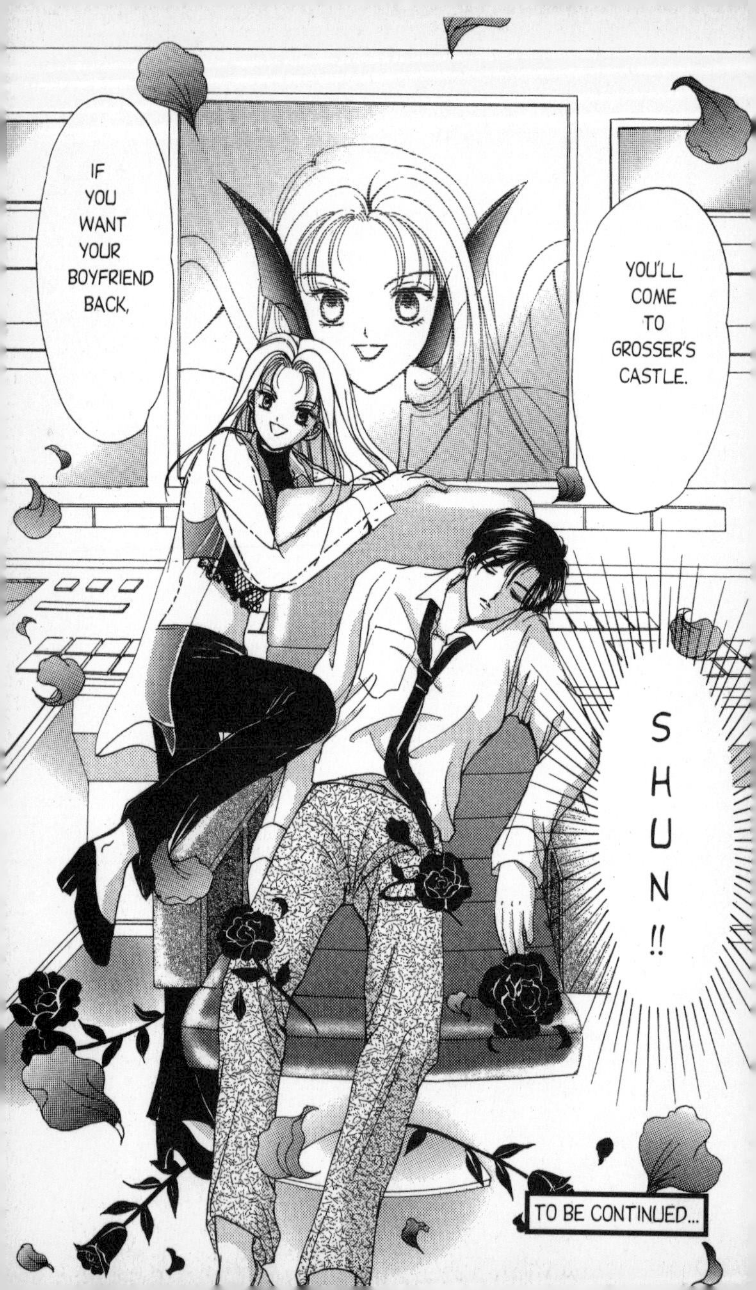
IF YOU WANT YOUR BOYFRIEND BACK,
YOU'LL COME TO GROSSER'S CASTLE.
SHUN!!
TO BE CONTINUED...

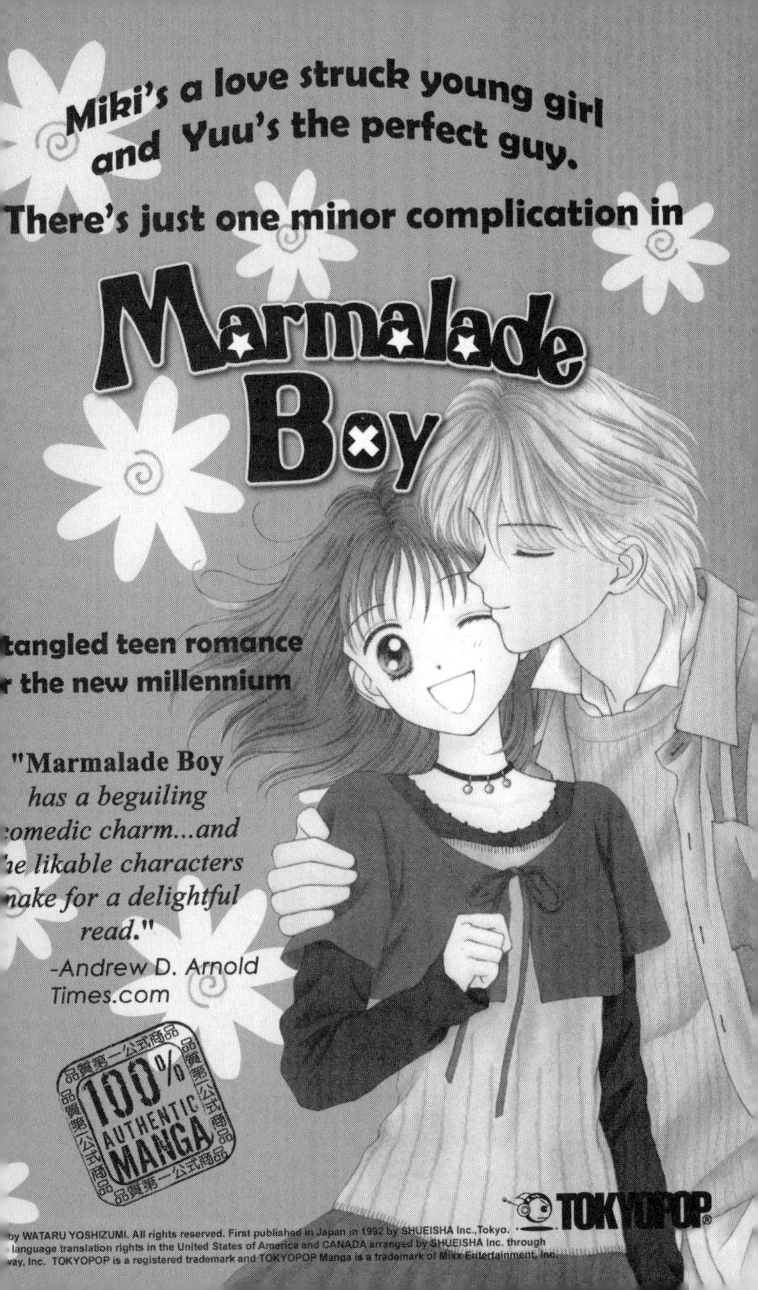
Miki's a love struck young girl
and Yuu's the perfect guy.
There's just one minor complication in
Marmalade Boy
tangled teen romance
r the new millennium
"Marmalade Boy
has a beguiling
comedic charm...and
he likable characters
make for a delightful
read."
-Andrew D. Arnold
Times.com
100% AUTHENTIC MANGA
品質第一公式商品
TOKYOPOP®
by WATARU YOSHIZUMI. All rights reserved. First published in Japan in 1992 by SHUEISHA Inc.,Tokyo.
language translation rights in the United States of America and CANADA arranged by SHUEISHA Inc. through
vay, Inc. TOKYOPOP is a registered trademark and TOKYOPOP Manga is a trademark of Mixx Entertainment, Inc.

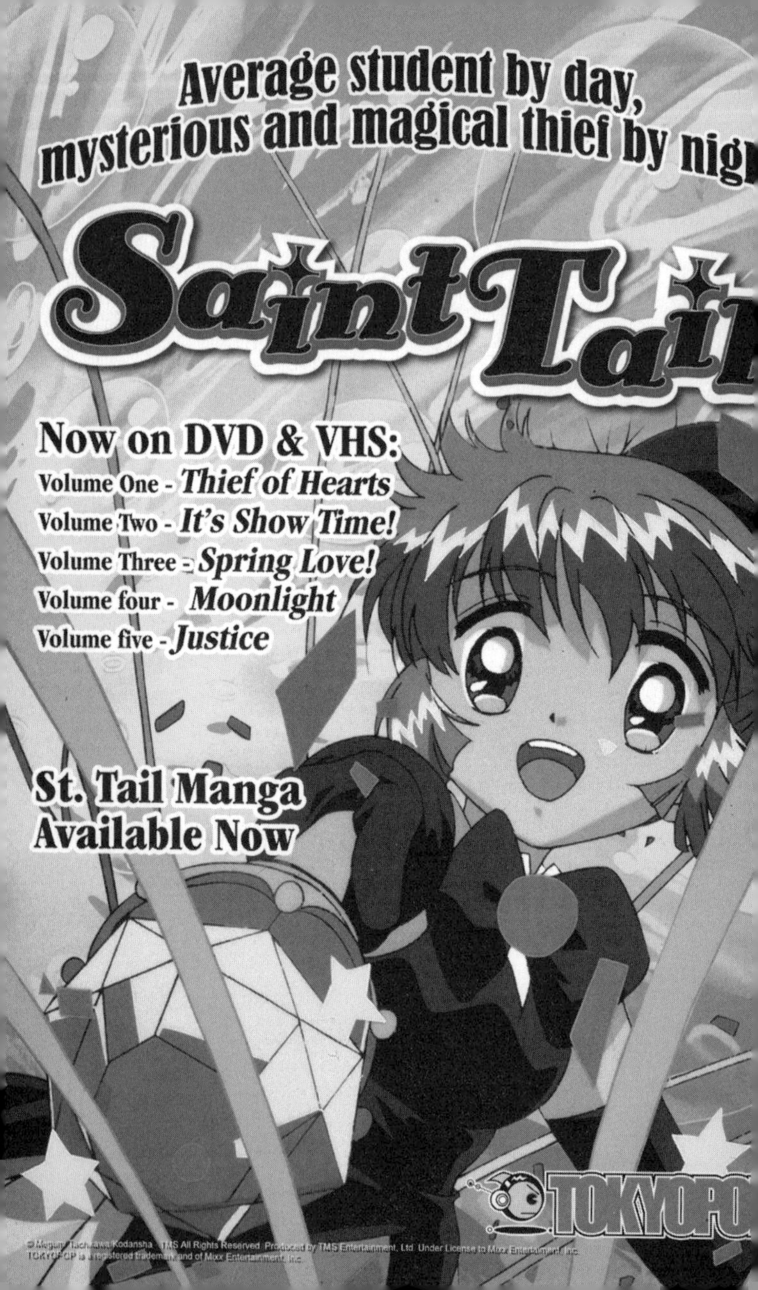
Average student by day,
mysterious and magical thief by nig
Saint Tai
Now on DVD & VHS:
Volume One - Thief of Hearts
Volume Two - It's Show Time!
Volume Three - Spring Love!
Volume four - Moonlight
Volume five - Justice
St. Tail Manga
Available Now
TOKYOPO
© Megumi Tachikawa/Kodansha · TMS All Rights Reserved. Produced by TMS Entertainment, Ltd. Under License to Mixx Entertainment, Inc.
TOKYOPOP is a registered trademark and of Mixx Entertainment, Inc.

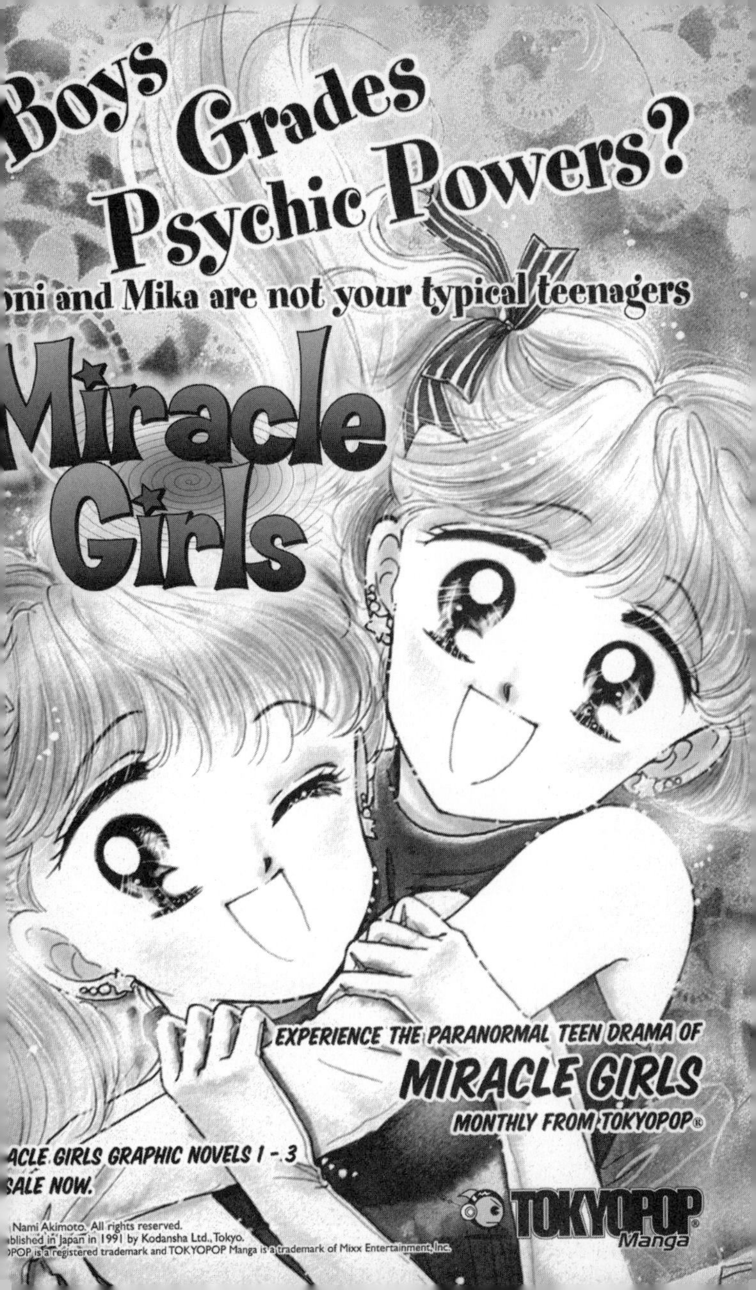

Boys
Grades
Psychic Powers?
oni and Mika are not your typical teenagers
Miracle Girls
EXPERIENCE THE PARANORMAL TEEN DRAMA OF
MIRACLE GIRLS
MONTHLY FROM TOKYOPOP®
ACLE GIRLS GRAPHIC NOVELS 1 - 3
SALE NOW.
Nami Akimoto. All rights reserved.
blished in Japan in 1991 by Kodansha Ltd., Tokyo.
OPOP is a registered trademark and TOKYOPOP Manga is a trademark of Mixx Entertainment, Inc.
TOKYOPOP® Manga

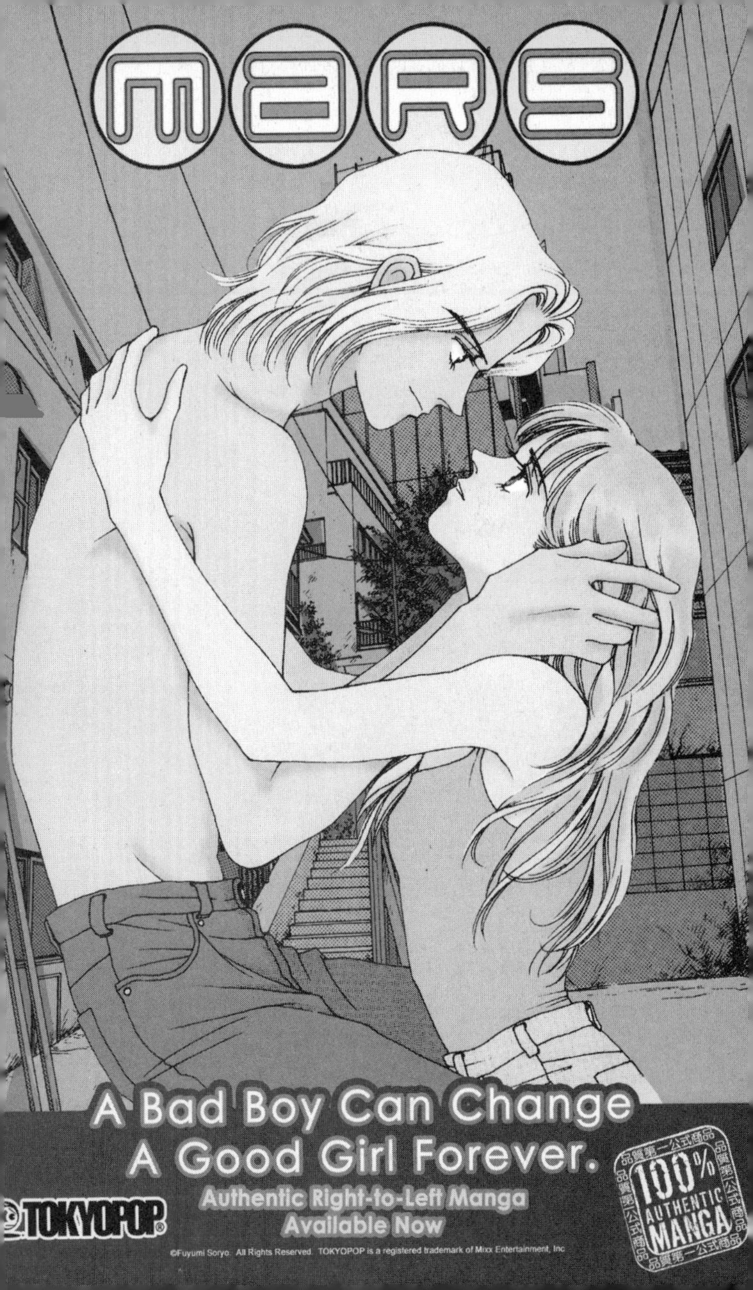
MARS
A Bad Boy Can Change
A Good Girl Forever.
Authentic Right-to-Left Manga
Available Now
TOKYOPOP®
100% AUTHENTIC MANGA
©Fuyumi Soryo. All Rights Reserved. TOKYOPOP is a registered trademark of Mixx Entertainment, Inc.